Investment Cycles in Capitalist Economies

NEW DIRECTIONS IN MODERN ECONOMICS

General Editor: Malcolm C. Sawyer,
Professor of Economics, University of Leeds

New Directions in Modern Economics presents a challenge to orthodox economic thinking. It focuses on new ideas emanating from radical traditions including post-Keynesian, Kaleckian, neo-Ricardian and Marxian. The books in the series do not adhere rigidly to any single school of thought but attempt to present a positive alternative to the conventional wisdom.

A list of published titles in this series is printed at the end of this volume.

Investment Cycles in Capitalist Economies

A Kaleckian Behavioural Contribution

Jerry Courvisanos
University of Tasmania

New Directions in Modern Economics series

Edward Elgar
Cheltenham, UK • Brookfield, US

Published by
Edward Elgar Publishing Limited
8 Lansdown Place
Cheltenham
Glos GL50 2HU
UK

Edward Elgar Publishing Company
Old Post Road
Brookfield
Vermont 05036
US

A catalogue record for this book
is available from the British Library

Library of Congress Cataloguing in Publication Data
Courvisanos, Jerry, 1949–
    Investment cycles in capitalist economies: a Kaleckian
behavioural contribution / Jerry Courvisanos.
    (New directions in modern economics)
    Includes bibliographical references and index.
    1. Kalecki, Michal. 2. Business cycles. 3. Capital investments.
I. Series.
HB3720.C68   1996   96-14167
332.6—dc20   CIP

ISBN 1 85898 410 6

Printed and bound in Great Britain by
Hartnolls Limited, Bodmin, Cornwall

Contents

Figures and Tables

FIGURES

TABLES

Preface

In June 1979, the Alcoa company announced that one of the world's largest aluminium smelters would be built in Portland, Australia. Observing the project as it unfolded was to experience a gyrating ride; through suspensions, search for equity partners, forced state utility power cost reductions, modifications and scrapping of later stages. Private business investment, in this case, did not seem to be a smooth process from planning to realised capital goods, as most economics tends to assume. Instead, investment seemed to be a highly unstable process with strong susceptibility to change.

In 1983, I began to research this idea of instability rooted in some cycle of susceptibility with specific reference to the Portland smelter. Later I extended this research to other aluminium companies, and then to other industries. In my Ph.D. studies I broadened my theoretical understanding of investment decision-making behaviour and found more general empirical applications of the susceptibility cycle concept. These studies have forced me to alter and adapt the concept. After ten years of research, this is my progress report. It is based on my 1994 thesis, but with many refinements suggested by the examiners of the thesis and other colleagues.

This book extends investment cycle analysis developed by Michal Kalecki, with support from behavioural and evolutionary views, to a more formal assessment of how levels of confidence experienced by entrepreneurs affect their decisions to invest. The confidence of investment decision-makers is known to be fragile due to the long-term, expensive and uncertain nature of the projects to be undertaken. This leads to such confidence being, to varying degrees, susceptible to a wide range of factors. This concept of susceptibility provides the foundation for an improved understanding of the empirically observed cyclical instability of capital accumulation.

Historically based empirical patterns of cyclical investment show how the nature of susceptibility alters over time to create different structures of investment profiles in an economy at different periods in its economic development. Implications are drawn from this susceptibility cycle model for improving the capacity of corporate and government strategic planners to design policies mitigating the degree of instability that investment exhibits. The result could be to diminish the aggravating effect that investment instability has on business cycles and employment as a whole that are so pervasive in capitalist economies.

With such a long period of research, there are many people who influenced my thoughts in the development of the susceptibility cycle concept. Also, many people and organisations greatly assisted me in my regular immersions into the very murky and secret world of private business investment decision-making, which was essential in my attempts to develop a strong historical perspective on the topic. None of these people are responsible for any of the views expressed here, nor the particular interpretations of historical data, nor any remaining errors in this book. However, I owe a great debt of gratitude to all those who patiently offered their assistance in my attempts to produce this work, whether or not they agree with the final product. Here is the list of names and organisations that I must thank.

My thesis supervisor Allen Oakley has been influential and inspiring in his comments on numerous drafts of this large research project. His detailed and creative advice generated many critical refinements. Bruce McFarlane was helpful with the final stages of putting the thesis together.

In respect to the theoretical analysis, I especially have the following intellectual debts. Phil Hellier encouraged and supported my initial very novice efforts at this theory. My stay in North America resulted in immense insights from the lectures of and discussions with four gifted economists, the late Tom Asimakopulos, the late Jack Weldon, and the still very active David Levine and Tracy Mott. More recently, on my visit to Trieste and Rome, I was privileged to obtain excellent advice on my more advanced model from the late Josef Steindl, Paolo Sylos Labini and Bart Verspagen.

My detailed empirical analysis requires primarily the acknowledgments of Peter Southwell who helped in organising the historical data and conceiving many suggestions on how to relate these data to the theory. Harry Bloch and James Guthrie gave their very diverse expertise on industry analysis in response to my many requests.

Peter Earl, Claudio Sardoni and Peter Kriesler read and made many helpful comments on the very much larger thesis from which this book derives. I appreciate their efforts at what was a daunting task. Their encouragement to distil the work has produced this much slimmer volume. Harry Bloch provided much advice on most of the chapters when they were produced as conference or discussion papers. He always responded quickly with succinct and powerful arguments and suggestions. Whilst writing this book I was employed by the University of Western Sydney, Macarthur. I would like to acknowledge its support, both financially and academically. Colm Kearney, as my department head, continually encouraged me and provided assistance on interpreting empirical patterns. The other staff colleagues who helped with intellectual advice and computer support were Neil Hart, Sean Toohey and Martin Tolar.

A non-English speaking 'mother tongue' has created problems in communicating many of my thoughts on paper. Peter Lewis Young spent many hours and issued many edicts in his scholarly and editorial efforts to make this book more readable. Carmel Hurley was ever present to correct my English in the final version with a skilful eye for detail. As a Luddite I needed much computer assistance. Olga Underwood and Jacquie Spencer provided this over the last few years. Debbie Plumb spent many hours on the computer getting this large project into a presentable form and solving all my computer crises, often at very inconvenient times. As a first-time author, I am very grateful for the support of Edward Elgar and his editorial staff. Hopefully the results are comprehensible.

Madeline Courvisanos and Carmel Hurley are the personal joys in my life who, with great patience, have put up with this major obsession in my life. I thank them.

To the memory of my parents,

Areti and Spiros

Little moon shining above
Light my way
To go to school
To learn letters
Important letters
God's great gift.

Traditional Greek
children's poem

1. Introduction: The Need for a Theory of Investment Cycles

the determination of investment decisions by, broadly speaking, the
level and the rate of change of economic activity . . . remains the
central *pièce de résistance* of economics. (Kalecki, 1968, p. 263)

1.1 A LACUNA IN ECONOMICS

The purpose of this book is to examine the cyclical (or wave-like)
nature of investment decisions of the entrepreneur. The theoretical and
empirical foundations of this study are the works of Polish economist
Michal Kalecki (1899–1970), which analyse investment
fundamentally as a temporal activity with lags, irreversibility,
modification and postponement of plans. All such short-term temporal
decisions involve innovation and the role of the state in Kalecki's
analysis, with significant effect on the growth and structure of the
economy. This is in contrast to conventional neoclassical analysis of
investment that begins on the basis of optimal choice profit-
maximising decision-making, with only limited extensions to
incorporate temporal conditions, innovation and the state (Nickell,
1978, pp. 225–9).

The opening quotation establishes Kalecki's own view of the need
for a theory of investment cycles. His review of *The General Theory*
(Keynes, 1936), published in Polish 32 years earlier expresses the
same view: that Keynes's analysis 'does not say anything about the
sphere of investment *decisions* of the entrepreneur' (Kalecki, 1982, p.
251, original emphasis). This continues to be a lacuna in economics.
Nearly 20 years after the opening quotation, Goodwin (1987, p. 63)
observes that '[i]nvestment, because current decisions depend on an

unknown future, has tended to be something of a black hole in economic theory'. Attempting to develop this area further has led to analysis of investment confidence (e.g. Boyd and Blatt, 1988) and its impact on business cycles as 'an endogenous generator of irregularity' (Goodwin, 1987, p. 125). It is to the level of confidence of agents who make the investment decisions that this study is drawn, in the process developing an endogenous model of investment cycles. Concern here is with understanding investment instability at the firm and industry level and how that instability varies over different periods of economic history.

Investment, in this study, is defined as the time rate of change in a stock of private sector durable assets used for the production of manufactured goods. The investment focus is on the variability of capital expenditure within manufacturing industry. This is consistent with Kalecki's own focus on manufacturing investment. Investment decisions are commitments of funds by decision-makers (or entrepreneurs) to investment orders. It is for both short- and long-term influences 'that in reality the individuals who are typically concerned with such [investment] decisions more or less make up the ruling class, whatever the socio-economic structure of the society concerned' (Nickell, 1978, p. 3, fn. 1). This is the capitalist class, and it holds monopoly power over the means of production (MOP) that come out of investment decisions made by entrepreneurs.

The investment cycle pattern is irregular but recurrent, creating wave-like effects which do not exhibit any regular magnitude or frequency, but 'vary from more than one year to ten or twelve years'. (Mitchell, 1951, p. 6). The short term in this study refers to the analysis of such fluctuations, whereas the long term is related to growth trends in these aggregate measures. This study starts from the endogenous mechanical approach to investment cycles with regular periodicity developed by Kalecki, but then proceeds schematically to incorporate the endogenous generator of irregularity known as uncertainty. In the context of this analysis the periodicity of investment cycles is of less concern than the actual attempt at understanding instability.

1.2 ECONOMIC FLUCTUATIONS AND INVESTMENT

In the first half of the twentieth century, both neoclassical and Marxian analyses were used to identify investment as the most unstable component of the national income, and thus the chief factor in the explanation of short-term business cycle activity (Hansen, 1964, p. 122). However, it was not until the work of Keynes (from the neoclassical tradition) and Kalecki (from the Marxian tradition) in the early 1930s that the self-generating business cycle was specified, with investment as the central endogenous factor in their theoretical models (McFarlane, 1982, pp. 69–71). Both analyses established, in aggregate, the impact on effective demand generated by unstable investment activity. This impact would then generate short-term business cycles without the need for any exogenous shocks to the economy. To understand investment instability, this study reverses this procedure of theory construction by assuming the existence of the business cycle and then specifying a typical temporal investment process (see Kalecki, 1950, p. 57).

Kalecki (1954, p. 101) discerns no appreciable time lag in the cyclical pattern of 'actual investment' and private sector gross product for the US in the period 1929–40. In this data, 'actual investment' relates not to capital expenditure, but to shipments of equipment and to 'value put in place' for construction (ibid, p. 109). The lag patterns are more clearly delineated in Zarnowitz (1985, p. 531) who notes that 'production of business equipment' coincides with, while 'business expenditures for new plant and equipment' lags, general economic activity. The former lag pattern is in concurrence with the one identified by Kalecki. The latter pattern shows capital expenditure lagging business cycles (see also Hall, 1990, p. 61).

Based on long-run US data, Hall (1990, pp. 15–17) concludes that percentage changes in business investment (together with residential construction and inventories) are from two to four times the amplitude of percentage changes in output. This greater variability in investment, 'even adjusted for the smaller dollar magnitude of investment compared to consumption, [still makes it] . . . the greatest procyclical spending variability over business cycles' (ibid, p. 18). Investment spending's role as the major source of economic instability in capitalist economies is the *raison d'être* for attempting to get behind these aggregate figures and improve understanding of unstable business investment behaviour.

The nature of investment instability and its effect on major business cycles can best be seen by studying heavy manufacturing industries, with their strong linkages to the rest of manufacturing and the economy generally. No expansion of goods or services can go on without the demand for durable MOP, which require basic goods like steel and aluminium to help produce the needed fixed plant and equipment. Other heavy industries, like motor vehicles, are the core of the consumer goods sector. These heavy goods industries are 'peculiarly susceptible to violent cyclical fluctuations'. (Hansen, 1964, p. 21).

Temporal assumptions in Kalecki (1950, p. 57) indicate an average of no more than one year for the lag between investment decisions and expenditure. This is about half the time lag between start and completion of investment plans (Kalecki, 1954, p. 109). Such time lags in the investment process have been supported by widely cited independent studies. Almon (1968, p. 204) reports a median lag between appropriations (when decisions are operationalised) and investment expenditures (actual spending on production of investment goods) of nine months to a year, depending on the degree of pressure in the market for investment goods. Mayer (1958, p. 364) finds a 21–month average lag between final decision and completion of building new industrial plants in the US, and a four- to five-month average lag between ordering and delivery of new equipment. These lags are further supported by more recent studies (Zarnowitz, 1973, pp. 505–19; Hall, 1977).

In the long term, gross investment above the level of actual depreciation (net investment > 0) allows MOP to increase the capacity of production. This has the potential of increasing the growth rate in real output, which is realised if aggregate demand also increases to take up this new capacity. This provides another clue to investment instability. The spending on MOP in the short term stimulates output, but it also sets up a longer-term negative feedback where the accumulating capital stock lowers the profit rate as the rate of aggregate demand slows. Investment then collapses, leaving large excess capacity as the durable MOP depreciate very slowly. Thus, 'growth generates cycles and . . . cycles interrupt growth. Such was the view of Marx, a view that was absorbed and elaborated by Schumpeter, but has remained peripheral to mainstream economics' (Goodwin, 1987, p. 106).

The growth cycle concept aids in recognising this excess-capacity-based instability arising from the interdependence between investment demand and capacity of MOP. Fluctuations of growth cycles are sharply different from fluctuations of major business cycles. The former cycles are more frequent and more symmetrical as they only measure fluctuations of the growth rate from a rising trend. The instability shown in growth cycles is based on Karl Marx's 'general law of capitalist accumulation' (Marx, 1954, p. 574), which 'provided inspiration to contemporary writers, in particular Kalecki and Goodwin' (Medio, 1987, p. 667). The more rigorous analyses of the latter two writers on growth and cycles will act as the institutional framework for this firm and industry investigation of investment instability.

A severe recession needs to be distinguished from periods of low but positive growth for policy action. For this reason, the major business cycle is still of more importance than the growth cycle. The experience of the early 1990s recession supports this. As noted in a recent study of business cycles, 'since economies still experience recessions, our main focus is on cycles in the level of economic activity' (Hall, 1990, p. 9). The present study of investment cycles is conducted with the major business cycle as the crucial macroeconomic assumption.

Schumpeter's work on the innovation process provides the other link between cycles and growth. Under the impulse of a 'bunch' or 'cluster' of entrepreneurial innovation activity, expansion of investment and the business cycle occurs. This eventually results in an end to the boom as adaptation to innovation weakens investment (Schumpeter, 1939, pp. 100–2). The 'bunching' effect has inspired the evolutionary school to examine economic growth as an evolutionary process, where emergence of new technological systems retard older systems. 'Out-of-equilibrium dynamics and bounded rational behaviour are key concepts in this literature' (Verspagen, 1992, p. 14). These two concepts link work of the evolutionary school to the Kaleckian microanalysis of investment behaviour.

1.3 NATURE OF MACROECONOMIC INVESTMENT ANALYSIS

Investment analysis at the macroeconomic level has been very extensive, ever since Keynes (1936) placed the investment function at centre stage when analysing why a market capitalist economy does not necessarily achieve a full employment equilibrium. In doing so, Keynes took the neoclassical (Marshallian) theory of the firm as the micro-foundations for his downward-sloping marginal efficiency of capital (MEC) concept, the essential determinant for an underemployment equilibrium position (Sardoni, 1987, p. 111). Then, through Chapter 22 of *The General Theory*, Keynes (1936) was able to link his analysis to the previous business cycle theorists who pointed to investment as the key variable in the instability of the economy.

Two paths have been followed in the macro-investment analysis since Keynes. The conventional neoclassical path is to adapt the MEC concept by incorporating into Keynes's present value a maximisation objective. This objective is subject to a production function where the flow of output is a function of the cost of both labour and capital services relative to output price. It specifically centres firms' investment demand in optimising micro-firm behaviour within an explicit perfectly competitive fully employed economy. Investment by businesses ought to result in a stable function as the calculations are based on accurate long-term future rates of return. For this reason, the observable cyclical nature of investment can only be due to external shocks. As noted in a classic first year textbook, '[p]rimary causes of these capricious and volatile investment fluctuations are found in such external factors as (1) technological innovation, (2) dynamic growth of population and of territory, and even in some economists' view, (3) fluctuations in business confidence and "animal spirits" ' (Samuelson, 1980, p. 246).

The alternative path is to accept cyclical fluctuations as inherent in market economies, and establish how the MEC can be affected by effective demand and planned capacity of MOP, which then produce unstable investment. This specifically centres firms' investment demand in an oligopolistic competitive structure, where time lags and irreversibility force firms to use their market power to overcome the uncertainties of unstable demand and inflexible capital stock quantities. Investment by businesses results in an unstable function as calculations are based on a climate of confidence, in terms of the potential benefits of new MOP, which varies according to demand factors and the related use of the capital stock in existence. Flexible accelerator-type models (based on output or profit) with cash-flow financing constraints epitomise this path. The present study follows this path, using Kalecki's work as its foundation.

The neoclassical investment analysis path, based on firm profit optimisation, has been dominant in economics. There are two major variants of this approach. One is the user cost of capital model, pioneered by Jorgenson (1963). This model concentrates on the average long-term behaviour of investment 'as determined by the requirements that the expected returns over the life of a project exceed its cost' (Zarnowitz, 1985, p. 536). Such an approach cannot capture the short-term effects of supply price rises emphasised by Keynes (1936, pp. 122–5) nor the expectational effects 'which are not distinguishable from the gestation periods or delivery lags' (Zarnowitz, 1985, p. 536). Then, this model aggregates the micro-investment function with a distributed lag stock-adjustment hypothesis which is *ad hoc* and inconsistent with the neoclassical assumptions of perfect knowledge and, thus, no adjustment costs (Junankar, 1972, p. 60).

Empirical studies have generally shown the cost of capital model to have little correlation with the actual investment patterns of economies (Dornbusch and Fischer, 1984, p. 222; Sawyer, 1982, p. 156). Clark (1979, p. 104) argues that aggregation problems and slow adjustment of the capital stock, and not defects in the theory, account for the poor overall performance of the neoclassical model. Yet these very same problems are what the theory itself cannot handle as it proceeds from the firm to the macro level.

The other variant of the optimising approach is the q theory pioneered by Tobin (1969). It provides a strong theoretical challenge because of its attempt to incorporate Keynes's own analysis of share (stock) price instability (1936, pp. 147–64) into fixed investment volatility and its relatively simple use of observable aggregate variables (Hall, 1990, p. 52). Zarnowitz (1985, p. 536) gives a substantial list of research to support the view that this 'hypothesis has not fared well in empirical tests'.

An attempt by McKibbin and Siegloff (1988, p. 214) to use q theory to explain aggregate investment explains only 10 per cent of the predicted investment by q theory. The other 90 per cent is explained by an *ad hoc* incorporation of the profits theory in non-optimising behaviour. This latter addition is inconsistent with the optimising assumption of q theory.

One strength of the neoclassical approach, both cost of capital and q theories, is the rigorous microeconomic investment function which it develops. It is favoured for textbook and classroom expositions since both theories can be grounded more formally into an overall economic model of the economy than the alternative approach (Poterba, 1988, p. 200). What is lacking from the alternative path, as Kalecki makes clear in the opening quotation of this chapter, is a microeconomic theory of investment behaviour which is based on the cyclical nature of aggregate investment and business cycles. A rigorous construction at the firm and industry level can supplement all the rigorous work done at the macroeconomic level to provide aggregate investment functions which are consistent with the empirical evidence noted above. This is particularly the case where the Kaleckian macro-investment analysis has reaped impressive results in the 1980s (see section 2.7).

When linking macro-cyclical activity with micro-firm behaviour it is critical to eschew any backsliding towards exogenous explanations. In the Samuelson quotation above listing the 'external factors', one of them should be internalised into firm behaviour – 'animal spirits', while another has crucial internal firm dynamics – 'technological innovation'. Samuelson, two paragraphs later, states that bringing inventions into the production process 'will most certainly depend on business conditions' (1980, p. 246). Keynes (1936) and Schumpeter (1939) in their respective views of 'animal spirits' and 'innovation' thought them to be internal. Both fell back to some exogenous initiating force in order to preserve their endogenous equilibrium models (on Keynes, see Levine, 1984; on Schumpeter, see Sylos Labini, 1984b). The Kaleckian micro-foundations are based on monopoly power and not perfect competition, allowing internal instability to be generated without worrying about inherent stable equilibrium.

1.4 THEORY OF INVESTMENT DECISIONS

The need to restore profitability of investment is crucial in any revival from Marx's 'crisis in capitalist economies'. Such restoration depends on individual entrepreneurs and their investment decisions. Entrepreneurs have monopoly over the MOP and they alone can determine the timing and speed of revival. At the micro-level, entrepreneurs' positive long-term expectations create the tendency to push production and investment to the highest possible level. At the macro-level, constrained purchasing power creates realisation failure and depressed short-term expectations for the same entrepreneurs (Sardoni, 1987, p. 48). These Marxian contradictions are the basis for investment instability, but Marx does not provide a formal model linking firms' investment decisions to the realisation crisis. The macro-level 'possibility of crisis' and the role of entrepreneurs in making decisions on investment based on profitability (accumulation and devalorisation of MOP) form the basic framework of Kalecki's own work on investment and consequently of this study as well.

There has been some important work in the 1980s on linking Marx's crisis model and Keynes's underemployment equilibrium model (Kenway, 1980; Sardoni, 1987; Burkett and Wohar, 1987). All the authors agree that at the macro-level Keynes also had a possibility of crisis analysis based on insufficient aggregate demand, with investment instability at its centre. This then emphasises firms' investment decisions; a situation recognised by Keynes as one where the 'entrepreneur is interested, not in the amount of product, but in the amount of money which will fall to his share' (Keynes, 1979, p. 82).

Thus, the concept of 'the entrepreneur economy' put forward by Keynes in his rough draft of *The General Theory* can be understood.

Keynes has two models of investment decision-making in *The General Theory*. The first one is the MEC analysis in Chapter 11, which is a formal equilibrium model of investment that aims to show the possibility of crisis due to the breakdown of Say's Law, when the objective MEC calculations make investment unattractive and hoarding occurs. Neoclassical economics has taken this model and incorporated it into its mechanistic econometric view of investment, which makes the investment function internally stable and dependent on exogenous factors for its instability, as outlined in the previous section.

The second model of investment by Keynes is in Chapter 12 of *The General Theory*. The concern here is to account for the observed instability in investment. The 'entrepreneur economy' developed in Keynes's early draft surfaces in this informal analysis when a particular group within society takes on investment as a 'way of life' (1936, p. 150). Based on this strong classical perspective, Keynes argues that a speculative MEC emerges from the introduction of financial markets. The speculative MEC, reflecting 'a prediction of short-run majority opinion in the [financial] market place', diverges from the objective MEC 'in the latter stages of a boom and during the contraction phase of the trade cycle'. (Burkett and Wohar, 1987, p. 41). Thus, short-term expectations undermine fundamental (objective) long-term expectations that go into investment strategies. This model received strong impetus a year later in the opening remarks of Keynes (1937) about uncertainty inherent in investment decisions which lead to variations in aggregate expenditures.

The strength of Kalecki's analysis is the ability to take 'the entrepreneur economy' from a Marxian base and apply it to an oligopolistic competitive market (Sardoni, 1987, p. 133). The result is a 'possibility of crisis' premise, which is given a deterministic outcome of economic fluctuations because of the formal theory of unstable (cyclical) investment decisions – which is not in the works of either Marx or Keynes. As Kalecki's opening quotation implies, his own formal firm investment decision models are inadequate. Kaleckian analysis that followed has generally become too mechanical (see Chapter 2), losing Kalecki's own feel for entrepreneurs' behaviour and the investment decision.

1.5 FOCUS OF THIS STUDY

This study traces backwards from the Kaleckian investment analysis to the Keynes-inspired behavioural theories and the evolutionary school. The aim is to develop an analysis of investment behaviour by agents of firms which is inherently unstable. Such a behavioural analysis would need to have the Kaleckian elements of investment decision-making as the measurable, and thus visible, manifestations of a much deeper behavioural pattern within firms and industries in 'the entrepreneur economy'. In attempting this backwards movement from Kaleckian to behavioural, an integration ensues of 'two distinct strands of thought' on investment analysis within radical political economy tradition (Sawyer, 1989, p. 382).

This explanation of investment cycles does not rely on external shocks to stimulate fluctuations. New classical rational expectations models that centre on external shocks to cycle activity have been unsatisfactory in both theoretical and practical terms (Zarnowitz, 1985, pp. 569–71). Instead, the explanation is based on building up tensions within entrepreneurs in investment decisions. Entrepreneurs are increasingly susceptible to reducing the level of capital expenditure as more investment orders build in further tension. Eventually the productive relations (represented by the Kaleckian elements of investment) reach an unsustainable level of tension. A structural break eventuates with an abrupt downturn of investment orders and a slow alleviation of tension. At much lower tension levels entrepreneurs feel more resilient and inclined towards investment in innovations and a related upturn in investment orders. This forms the basis of the notion of the susceptibility cycle, and provides a rigorous understanding of the idea that investment is susceptible to booms and busts.

This approach helps to understand what lies behind investment functions of Kaleckian elements that have gained strong empirical support. The decisions which lead to the increase in investment orders build up tension. Relief of such tension comes through altering and reneging on previous committed decisions, as well as from decommissioning old capital stock. This understanding of the behavioural forces behind econometric investment equations enables the development of more sensitive methods for entrepreneurs and public policy-makers to anticipate and ameliorate the investment instability inherent within capitalism.

A self-replicating susceptibility cycle which explains instability of investment decisions emerges out of this theoretical enquiry. This is followed by an examination of some important exogenous factors that can shift the susceptibility cycle. An inspection of long-run empirical patterns of cyclical investment in the penultimate chapter reveals that capitalist economies conform to the notions of susceptibility in investment decision-making.

From long-run historical patterns, an empirically based explanatory hypothesis emerges which places the notion of a susceptibility cycle within the structure of specific capitalist economies. It involves carrying over as much of the theoretical analysis as seems necessary to produce a suggestive historical correlation. This allows for the appreciation of how confidence in investment decision-making is influenced by the socio-cultural dimensions in each economy. A secular framework within which the susceptibility cycle operates provides an empirical application of the theoretical analysis, while adding a long-run pattern to short-term investment cycles.

The empirical analysis 'is in no sense meant as a test of the theory' (Salter, 1960, p. 9). This study concurs with Salter that a weaker form of statistical analysis is appropriate given 'the gap between the empirical and theoretical approaches'. (ibid). Behavioural economists who are interested in explaining economic behaviour, support this view of the role for empirics (Earl, 1983, p. 105).

Kalecki's essays include empirical studies to accompany theoretical expositions. Like Salter, Kalecki's work observes the more circumspect approach to data, so that 'the purpose of the statistical analysis here is to show the *plausibility* of the relations between economic variables arrived at theoretically rather than to obtain the most likely coefficients of these relations' (Kalecki, 1954, p. 5, added emphasis). Long-run empirical patterns, using both quantitative and qualitative data, produce a plausible story of specific firm and industry investment behaviour that is not theoretically inconsistent with the susceptibility cycle model developed.

Conclusions are set out in Chapter 8. This chapter has a final iterative statement of the susceptibility cycle in the context of long-term historical change of investment behaviour. This is followed by some notional policy implications drawn from the dual theoretical-empirical analysis of the book. The research could enable entrepreneurs to plan their investment strategies and commitments so as to reduce susceptibility and stabilise their investment cycles at a high growth trend. Public policy-makers could also develop controls which appreciate better the motivational patterns of firms' investment orders. The chapter ends by illustrating the type of further research required to make these policy implications explicit. Primarily this requires a goal-specific research strategy along lines proposed in

Adolph Lowe's instrumental analysis (Lowe, 1965, p. 143). Such a strategy aims to develop a path towards a more stable, yet still a dynamic and creative economic system with investment planning that is responsive to the needs of both the physical and social environments. The investment analysis presented here is an attempt to set up the prerequisites for such a policy-oriented research programme.

2. Kaleckian Analysis of Investment

2.1 INTRODUCTION

This chapter reviews Kaleckian analysis of investment, from Kalecki's own work to the current Kaleckian scholars who have revised and extended Kalecki's treatment of investment. The chapter first examines the role of investment in the three versions of Kalecki's business cycle theory (Steindl, 1981b). In each version, Kalecki develops important firm-based decision elements which are identified as crucial to the susceptibility cycle model. Weaknesses of Kalecki's investment analysis, from a firm's perspective, are also noted. Kaleckian scholars' attempts to overcome these weaknesses in the three crucial decision elements of Kalecki's original investment cycle formulation – excess capacity, profits and financial constraints – are outlined in the following section. The chapter then examines the institutional framework and structural aspects within which the investment decisions are made. Kalecki highlights the importance of specifying the institutional framework as basic to economic dynamics – notably investment.[1] Kalecki's framework of markets, agents and the role of the state is critically reviewed, together with Kaleckian adaptations.

The chapter then examines how the role of investment is structurally affected by the economic power of the state and the results of innovation. Both these factors are seen by Kalecki as distinct from the cyclical forces on investment which lead to the business cycle theory. However, both these factors have the ability to exacerbate or ameliorate investment cycles already apparent. They also add a long-term development implication to the investment analysis. The last structural aspect outlined in the chapter is Kalecki's time pattern of investment between the investment decision and the resulting change in the MOP. This time lag in investment allows for changes in entrepreneurial reactions on the demand side of investment and also for supply problems in investment goods-producing industries. The final section is a brief survey of recent complete Kaleckian investment models – their theoretical basis and their empirical support.

2.2 ROLE OF INVESTMENT IN KALECKI'S BUSINESS CYCLE THEORIES

The investment process has been the central concern of all Kalecki's business cycle analyses. Steindl (1981b, p. 125) identifies in Kalecki's writings three versions of the business cycle, and states that '[t]he difference between these versions concerns almost entirely the investment function'. Version I dates from an original Polish monograph (Kalecki, 1933) with two abbreviated English journal articles (Kalecki, 1935; 1937b). This version has an undamped endogenous business cycle, criticised mathematically by Frisch and Holme (1935). Version II dates from Kalecki (1943b) and was revised in 1954. This version maintains a linear equation. It has a damped business cycle which eventually requires a random shock to oscillate the business cycle again in the manner of a pendulum (Goodwin, 1964, p. 421). Version III from Kalecki (1968) also has a linear damped business cycle, but allows for greater fluctuations as it concentrates on the profitability of new capital stock. In this way, it incorporates technical progress with a trend above cyclical oscillations.

In version I, the cyclical nature of investment is due to the time lag (θ) between investment orders (I) and deliveries of means of production (D).[2] The lag θ is the average gestation period of all means of production (MOP), due to production and delivery delays. Kalecki identifies gross accumulation (A) as the level of all production of MOP between I and D, assuming the spread of investment orders is even over time. At any point in time (t) this accumulation is 'approximately equal to the investment orders at the time t–1/2θ.' (Kalecki, 1971, p. 4). Thus, A_t can be represented as a moving average of investment orders I_t over the gestation period:

$$A_t = \frac{1}{\theta} \int_{t-\theta}^{t} I_\tau d\tau \tag{2.1}$$

Differentiating equation (2.1):

$$A = 1/\theta(I_t - I_{t-\theta})$$
(2.2)

From equation (2.2), accumulation rises if what goes in I_t is greater than what comes out of the previous investment orders $[I_{t-\theta}]$.

This analysis is all conducted on an aggregate basis for the oligopolistic manufacturing sector as a representation of a closed economy. The investment system established is closed by identifying aggregate investment orders as a function of both anticipated gross profitability and interest rates.

Kalecki then makes two assumptions. The first is to drop the negatively related interest rate variable on the basis that it varies pro-cyclically with economic activity, but not sufficient to outweigh the positively related effects of expected profits to economic activity. The second is to use actual profit level (P) as a proxy for the incalculable expected profit level. Thus, the rate of investment orders in relation to the volume of capital stock (K) is given by the linear function:

$$I_t/K_t = mP_t/K_t - n$$
(2.3)

where P/K is the average profit rate.

At a macro-level, when workers do not save, actual profits derive from the capitalists' own consumption (B) and gross accumulation. Replacing P with (B + A), and dividing by K:

$$I_t = m(B + A_t) - nK_t$$
(2.4)

Differentiating equation (2.4) with respect to time to obtain the rate of change in investment orders:

$$\dot{I}_t = m\dot{A}_t - n\dot{K}_t$$
(2.5)

The analysis of investment lags provides an understanding of the rate of change in gross accumulation, as noted in equation (2.2). The other variable in equation (2.5) is the rate of change in capital stock, which is determined by the difference between MOP deliveries (D) and replacement requirements per unit of time (U). Kalecki assumes the latter is constant over the life of the business cycle. Since the delivery lag is defined as $D_t = I_{t-\theta}$, the rate of capital stock change is:

$$K_r = D_r - U = I_{r-A} - U \qquad (2.6)$$

Equations (2.2) and (2.6) can be substituted into equation (2.5) to explain investment orders at an aggregate level:

$$I_r = m/\theta \; I_r - (m/\theta + n)I_{r-A} + nU \qquad (2.7)$$

The mixed difference-differential equation (2.7) gives a cycle of investment orders with turning points occurring 'because the accumulating (or shrinking) capital stock reacts back on the rate of profit' (Steindl, 1981b, p. 126). An increase in the investment orders, as a result of an upward variation in the actual profit level (see equation (2.4)), increases gross accumulation and (with a lag) deliveries of MOP (D). When D becomes greater than U, the capital stock (K) starts to rise. Equation (2.5) shows the rise in K puts a drag on the upward moving I, slowing down the rate of increase in I and A. Eventually, I ceases to increase while K is still rising due to the lag. This reduces the average profit rate (see equation (2.3)) which leads to decisions by manufacturers to reduce I, setting off a downward spiral in the investment orders cycle. A cumulative contraction in I occurs until the negative feedback effect of a rise in the average profit rate sends the investment orders cycle back into expansion. Equation (2.7) shows a trendless cycle with no accumulation of MOP over the whole cycle.

There are three essential aspects of this version I investment cycle which lay the foundations for the model developed in later chapters. First is the crucial distinction between investment orders and deliveries of MOP, with the production of MOP being a flow between the two stock concepts. Second is the positive effect of variations in the profit level on investment orders. Third is the negative effect on investment orders of changes in capacity of MOP as a result of accumulating or shrinking capital stock.

Version II does not distinguish between A and D in the investment process. Kalecki instead follows what he now calls investment decisions with the θ lag, which 'includes the delayed reaction of entrepreneurs to factors determining investment decisions' (Kalecki, 1954, p. 109). This lag conflates the distinction by relating A as a stock concept at the time of completion of MOP, at the same time as D. The change is in line with altering the investment cycle equation to one of discrete time finite differences only and omitting any continuous time dynamics implied in the flow concept of gross accumulation (A).[3] This allows for a damped cycle solution, with numerous random shocks to maintain a cyclical pattern over the long term (Goodwin, 1989, p. 250).

The 'profit rate as the unique determinant of investment decisions' in version I is replaced in version II 'by two separate sets of determinants: financial resources available to the firm on the one hand, and its marketing prospects on the other' (Steindl, 1981b, p. 126). Kalecki develops these sets of determinants from an analysis of the behaviour of a single firm in a manufacturing oligopolistic environment. This is in contrast to the broad macro-assumptions used in version I.

Financial resources are the first set of determinants, represented by current saving out of profits by the firm. In contrast to version I, the re-investment from profits is considered in general not to be complete, based on the macro view that complete re-investment would ensure investment stability (Sawyer, 1985, pp. 49–50). This neglects the crucial role in investment instability of the negative feedback of gross accumulation in version I (Steindl, 1981b, p. 127).

Marketing prospects are the second set of determinants, represented by two effects; variations in profit levels and changes in the capital stock of the industry. The first effect reflects changes in sales over the current period. An increase in profits or sales (positive $\Delta P/\Delta t$) has the mathematical look of an accelerator with ΔP rather than ΔY (change in output). Kalecki gives the term a microeconomic interpretation from the firm's perspective: 'the increase in profits (or sales) makes it possible to overcome the barriers of imperfect competition and thus makes room for new investment' (Steindl, 1981b, p. 127). The second effect reflects the adverse (or favourable) effect that an increase (decrease) in capital stock has on the firm, by increasing (decreasing) the level of competition. This effect 'is most easily seen in the case where new enterprises enter the field and thereby render investment plans of the established firms less attractive' (Kalecki, 1954, p. 98).

Kalecki, after identifying the three investment decision determinants, places them in an equation for all firms in the economy. He assumes that gross savings of firms is total gross private savings (S), which is also total savings in a closed economy with no government and where workers do not save. A finite difference equation emerges:

$$I_t = aS_t + b\Delta P/\Delta t - c\Delta K_t/\Delta t + d \qquad (2.8)$$

where a < 1 (incomplete re-investment), and d is a constant subject to long-term changes (especially technical change).

With respect to the investment cycle model generated in this book, the important concept from version II is 'increasing risk'. The firm's propensity to risk increases as the gearing ratio rises in order to fund further investment in MOP. Only greater internal savings (profits) can alleviate this risk and allow investment in MOP to continue. Having already embraced variations in profits from version I, it is the risk concept which acts as a negative influence on the investment decisions of firms. The marketing prospects set have already been embraced from version I, despite the downgrading in version II of the 'negative feedback from capital accumulation acting back on profit rate and investment decisions' (Steindl, 1981b, p. 127).

There is an important difference between the two versions of the investment cycle. Kalecki tries to disguise the difference between the two versions by claiming that version I 'appears to be a special case of the present [version II] one' (Kalecki, 1954, p. 102). As Steindl (1981b, p. 129) states: 'The claim that version I is a special case of version II must, however, not be taken literally.' Incomplete re-investment of profits in version II, Steindl (1981b, p. 129) argues, makes it quite different to the complete re-investment in version I.

Also, there is a difference between the time patterns of investment of the two versions. Version I is based on a backward approach to analysing the investment process, where current investment orders are assumed to depend on all orders undertaken in a period of the past of a length equal to θ, the gestation period. The forward approach of version II shows current investment decisions are dependent on recent changes in the explanatory variables in equation (2.8) and result in deliveries of MOP after a gestation period of θ. Steindl (1981b, p. 131) argues that directly incorporating the degree of capacity utilization into the investment decision function can overcome the problem in the 'forward approach' of relying on the weak cyclical effect of the acceleration principle. At the same time, it is crucial to incorporate in the investment decision function the 'financial resources' strength of version II.

In version II, Kalecki includes the constant d in equation (2.8) to denote '"development factors" – such as innovations which prevent the system from settling to a static position and which engender a long-run upward trend' (1954, p. 151). Kalecki identifies innovation as the crucial development factor in a purely exogenous manner divorced of the cycle.[4] Kalecki specifically tackles the integration between trend and cycle in version III. The result is an investment decision equation 'essentially of the same form as in version II' (Steindl, 1981b, p. 128). The difference is the route to get to an equation similar to equation (2.8). This route also provides the novel part of version III. It incorporates technical change by isolating the increment in profits from newly installed MOP, which are more efficient than old capital stock, endogenising the innovation effect as a factor which adds power to the investment cycle turning points. Kalecki's explanation of the innovation behaviour that determines this technical change is examined in section 2.5.

The innovation effect introduces efficiency, which forces the increment in profit from newly installed capital stock to increase at the expense of profit increments on old capital stock. The marginal profit rate ($\Delta P/\Delta K$) replaces the average profit rate (P/K) of version I as the expectations guide to further investment orders. Kalecki assumes that the size of the productivity advantage which new MOP has over old MOP is constant over the course of the business cycle. Through this approach, Kalecki 'demonstrates that the greater part of the change in profitability in the course of the cycle is thrown on the new investment' (Steindl, 1981b, p. 128). As the rate of investment orders slows down towards the top of the boom, the marginal profit rate declines more sharply than the average profit rate, developing negative expectations and the eventual reduction in investment orders. In this way the negative feedback of capital accumulation, downgraded in version II, is reinstated to overcome the problem of weak investment cycles out of the accelerator with only incomplete re-investment as support (Steindl, 1981b, pp. 127–8).

In section 5.4.1, version III marginal profit rate is used to develop the investment cycle analysis. This provides a strong basis for understanding the turning points, for it is the impact of investment order levels on the marginal rate of profit (with technical progress) which reacts on future investment decisions.[5] Kalecki's analysis is taken further into the realm of tensions that investment orders develop and the expectations guide which follows such tensions. The lower turning point is given special attention, for this is where the strength of Kalecki's endogenised innovation can help to explain an area of weakness in all investment cycle analyses.

Kalecki's investment cycle analyses raises problems which have been just as much an inspiration to model construction as the various elements of the investment decision which he identifies. The most serious problem, in the context of the aim of this study, is an inadequate perspective of firms' investment decision-making processes. Kalecki slips from the more precise 'investment orders' in his earliest writings to 'investment decisions' without any explanation. In version I he uses the terms interchangeably, not recognizing the administration lag between the two and the possibility of varying the decisions before contracts are signed. Both these terms are used by

Kalecki to set up plausible assumptions about the nature of single firm investment behaviour. The 'increasing risk' analysis is the only specific discussion of micro-investment behaviour. The equations that he then sets up are in aggregate terms, in order to fit into a macro-model of business cycles.

Sordi (1989, pp. 263–4) notes that there are estimation problems as a consequence of moving from firm behaviour to empirical macro-model equations. For this study, the problem is more substantial. There are two missing logical steps in Kalecki's work. First is the need to develop a clear model of investment behaviour at the micro-level that operationalises the elements in Kalecki's investment cycles. Second is the need to trace the path of accumulation from investment decisions through to when the new MOP are fully operational. The time pattern involved is affected by supply constraints in the capital-producing industries. Kalecki separated consumer goods and capital goods industries in his micro-institutional framework for capitalism, and he also identified the supply constraints in investment for socialist economies, but he never put these two strands together in capitalist investment analysis (see section 2.6). These two logical steps form the basis of the susceptibility cycle model in Chapter 5.

2.3 KALECKIAN ELEMENTS OF THE INVESTMENT CYCLE

From Kalecki's business cycle theories, an investment cycle emerges with three endogenous elements. This section examines Kaleckian writings on each of these elements to see what they have to offer for the development of an industry-based investment cycle model. A review of this literature reveals weaknesses which demand the more thoroughgoing analysis conducted in later chapters. Although many modern Kaleckian scholars have developed Kalecki's work in a variety of areas – particularly in the econometric specificity of Kalecki's macro-model and in the substantiation of Kalecki's micro-analysis – very little has directly addressed Kalecki's underlying assumptions and structural contingencies of investment behaviour.

2.3.1　Excess capacity and accumulation

Josef Steindl is the most important Kaleckian writer on excess capacity and accumulation.[6] The previous section notes the passive way in which Kalecki includes the capacity utilisation concept in version I of his investment cycle, neglects it in version II and then in a circuitous way introduces it again in version III. Steindl (1981b, pp. 130–2) shows that by replacing the acceleration principle with capacity utilisation in Kalecki's version II (equation (2.8)), demand can be more directly introduced and the negative feedback of accumulation can again contribute strong backward linkage to past investment decisions. Kalecki 'explicitly rejected the capacity concept (Kalecki, 1968), because it was doubtful whether obsolete equipment should be counted as capacity or not' (Steindl, 1981b, p. 132). To overcome such an objection, Steindl develops three definitions of capacity utilisation: unplanned, planned, and actual.

Kalecki's institutional framework of oligopolistic industries ensures that excess capacity, which is unplanned, exists over the whole (or majority) of the business cycle. When new entrants come into an industry, this adds unplanned capacity utilisation to the industry as the stock of MOP rises; it also acts as a disincentive to entrepreneurs in carrying out their investment plans. Rowthorn (1981, p. 174) explains that this disincentive acts in Kalecki's work through reductions in the industry average profit rate (P/K). The coefficient of capacity utilisation in relation to investment is zero, which means that any changes in utilisation have a zero direct effect on investment. Unplanned capacity utilization is the concept that Kalecki implicitly uses in his investment cycles.

Most writers who followed Kalecki's approach to oligopolistic competition made capacity utilisation a direct variable affecting investment, such that the coefficient of utilisation is greater than zero. This is done by the concept of planned capacity utilization, first introduced in Steindl (1952).

Steindl (1976) notes that 'firms wish to establish a planned degree of utilisation over a number of years (boom and slump)', in order to take advantage of future expected and unexpected increases in quantity demanded.[7] 'They will push out competitors to obtain this result if the process is not too costly.' From this planned (or desired) level, the negative feedback of accumulation comes into operation: 'If utilization is below the desired level, this acts as a deterrent to investment' (Steindl, 1976, p. xiv). Thus, when *actual* excess capacity is *below* the planned level in an industry, attempts are made by the large firms to remove the uncompetitive fringe of smaller firms in order to get back to the planned level. If *actual* excess capacity is *above* the planned level in the industry, firms postpone investment commitments in order not to exacerbate this situation. 'It may be noted that the planned excess capacity, in terms of this mechanism, will be approximately realised only for an industry as a whole, not necessarily for individual firms' (Steindl, 1952, p. 12). This is in contrast with Andrews (1949), who focuses on the need for excess capacity at the individual firm level so as to cater for new customers without disappointing regular customers.

Steindl recognizes that when actual reduction of investment commitments are needed to restore a desired level in the industry, this action in itself reduces demand in the economy. If enough industries react in the same way, the reduction in aggregate demand reacts back on these industries as further excess capacity. This time the excess capacity is unplanned (or undesired), which creates a fear of overcapacity in 'imperfect' markets where profit margins hold up as large firms continue to maintain high levels of planned excess capacity. Investment planning needs to take account of the possibility that individual firms' planned excess capacity may become so large in terms of the whole industry that the overcapacity could be undesirable. The fear of excess capacity increases as an industry becomes more oligopolistic (with each firm having higher desired excess capacity), to the point where 'investment will be reduced without any *actual* decline in utilisation' (Steindl, 1952, p. 132, original emphasis).

From Steindl's analysis, there is no general criterion for distinguishing between planned and unplanned excess capacity (Steindl, 1952, p. 12). The only way is by observing firms' reactions to their degree of utilisation in their industry. By Steindl introducing entrepreneurs' sensitivity to unused capacity in terms of 'safety' (planned) and 'fear' (unplanned), the investment process begins to take on a strong behavioural posture which is only implicit in Kalecki's work, but is the explicit foundation of this study's analysis. Qualitative historical patterns identified in Chapter 7 provide support to these behavioural reactions of entrepreneurs.

Steindl (1952) concentrates on the long-term stagnation implications of growing excess capacity as industries become increasingly concentrated, threatening the investment process. He also recognises the dynamic instability that the discrepancy between planned and actual excess capacity creates. This is shown in Steindl (1981b, p. 131), where he reinterprets Kalecki's aggregate investment function set out in equation (2.8), in terms of this discrepancy, rather than the accelerator. The resulting equation is:

$$D_t/Z_t = aS_t/Z_t + b(Y_t/Z_t - u_o) \qquad (2.9)$$

where Y is gross product, Z is capacity (replacing Kalecki's K), and u_o is desired capacity utilisation (replacing Kalecki's P/K).[8] This means that Y/Z is actual utilisation [u].[9] Steindl goes on to show that by reintroducing the θ production lag, equation (2.9) can become essentially the version I investment cycle equation (2.7). The micro-investment cycle model in Chapter 5 is based on this dynamic instability in capacity utilisation, with the trend of long-term investment reflecting the resolution of the excess capacity dilemmas.

Modest fluctuations over the course of the business cycle in both Kalecki's capital stock (K) and Steindl's capacity (Z) variables are of concern for they look to be weak generators of instability. Steindl (1979) resolves the problem by noting entrepreneurs' reactions to the difference between the depreciation rate (d') and the drop-out rate of MOP (d_r), both as ratios of gross capital. A high growth rate of MOP in a given period t, with high capacity utilisation 'will tend to retard withdrawal of equipment, thus lengthening actual lifetime' (Steindl, 1979, p. 6). This can be seen by a fall in d_r, while d' is assumed constant. A rise in the differential term $d'-d_r$ above its long term average results, leading to the first signs of fear of overcapacity. This situation makes the investment boom prone to a downturn, which becomes more evident as utilisation falls with large MOP installation. During a recession the low growth rate of MOP, with low capacity utilisation 'will lead to some premature withdrawal of equipment, and therefore to a decrease of $d'-d_r$ below its long-term average' (Steindl, 1979, p. 6). This reduces overcapacity fears and allows the opportunity for investment to make a resurgence.

The stock adjustment approach of equation (2.9) has an inherent result of greater change in net investment, compared with the relatively small excess capacity adjustment to desired level, that is needed to bring capacity back to desired level (Steindl, 1981b, pp. 131–2). This factor, together with the differential term $d'-d_r$, shows how modest capacity utilisation fluctuations over the business cycle can generate much larger investment cycles.

Spence (1977) discusses the use of planned excess capacity as a deliberate barrier to entry. Rather than reducing price to deter potential entry, an entrepreneur who has a substantial share of the market can create a degree of excess capacity utilisation which acts as deterrent to any potential entrants and present competitors who want to increase their market share. With the mark-up pricing approach in Kaleckian literature being related to long-term profit maximisation (see section 2.3.2), the Spence thesis could be effectively incorporated into this system. Cowling (1982, pp. 17–19) is the most elaborate incorporation of the Spence thesis into a Kaleckian microeconomic analysis. For Cowling, planned excess capacity is a deterrent because of the entrepreneur's ability to increase output quickly and substantially as well as temporarily price-cutting the margin until the uncompetitive fringe is removed (no short term profit maximization).[10] This aspect of capacity utilisation is incorporated into the Kalecki–Steindl framework of reasonable mark-up stability and resulting growth of excess capacity that shuts off further investment plans (see section 5.4.3).[11]

Excess capacity arising from innovation also leads to problems of overproduction. Discussion of this relationship is left until section 2.5 on innovation as the initiating factor. Taking the innovation factor into account as well, the conclusion from the literature briefly surveyed above is that excess capacity is 'perhaps the most important factor determining investment in the short run [over the business cycle]' (Foster, 1986, p. 20).

2.3.2 Role of Profits and the Mark-up in Investment Decision-making

Basic to a Kaleckian approach is to recognise the role profits play in providing both (a) an ability to finance investment, and (b) an inducement to invest. In the context of the ability to finance investment, Kalecki (1937a) sees the importance to firms of internal finance as the cheapest source of finance available, and for providing favourable access and terms in the credit market. This Kalecki incorporates into version II of his investment cycle.

Steindl (1952), Sylos Labini (1967) and Wood (1975) go on to identify the importance of 'internal accumulation' and how the actual current level of profits affects the ability to obtain retained earnings and depreciation provisions for investment. Wood (1975, p. 17) measures this proportion between internal finance (retained earnings and depreciation provisions) and level of profits as the 'gross retention ratio'. At a macro-level, the current level of profits acts as a positive influence on current investment orders, materialising as the next period's investment activity (A).

Keynes (1936) identifies expectation of profits as the inducement to invest. Kalecki (1933) is the first to trace this expectational inducement back to the behaviour of the actual profit rate as a guide to future profitability from capital stock (see section 2.2). Kalecki uses the current average profit rate (P/K) as a guide to expectations. Modern Kaleckian analyses use instead the rate of change of actual profit from last period to the current period as 'the profit rate' on the basis that 'valuation of capital stocks involves numerous practical difficulties' (Wood, 1975, p. 3). The actual increment in profit realised this period over last period acts as 'a positive feedback on investment decisions' (Bhaduri, 1986, p. 177). At a macro-level, investment deliveries (D) in the past confer the basis for profits earned, thus, the incremental increase in profit levels stimulates further investment orders (I), leading to future increases in investment activity (A).

The two roles of profit in investment are the basis of a macro-functional investment equation developed in Bhaduri (1986, pp. 169–81). The equation is:

$$I_{t+1} = f(P_t, P_t - P_{t-1}) = f(P_t, \Delta P) \qquad (2.10)$$

where, I_{t+1} is the level of aggregate investment orders in the forthcoming period; P_t is the current level of profits; and P_{t-1} is the past period level of profits.

Bhaduri's function is a development of Kalecki's linear investment analysis by incorporating 'systematic contradictory pulls' between P_t and ΔP in real time. 'This gives rise to various types of *non-linear accelerators*, or more generally, *non-linear feedback* mechanisms from profit (or income) to investment' (Bhaduri, 1986, p. 179, original emphasis). For internal financing the level of P_t is important, however, new investment orders are guided by the actual increment in profit (ΔP) during the current period, which acts as the expectational factor. This places expectations into a mechanism which creates a contradictory pull if P_t is high but ΔP is decreasing, resulting in an upper turning point in investment orders. The lower turning point occurs with P_t at a low level, but ΔP is increasing. Bhaduri (1976, p. 179) argues that this occurs 'because continued negative *net* investment over time as well as run-down stocks of inventories create opportunities for new investment through replenishing stocks and replacing worn-out capital equipment' (original emphasis).

The self-generating investment cycle that results from equation (2.10) is based on Goodwin (1951), and forms the macro-environment for the micro-investment analysis of Chapter 5. Although Bhaduri goes one step closer to explaining investment cycles by explicitly incorporating the two roles of profit, the macro-level Goodwin approach yields too mechanical an endogenous mechanism. The 'own seeds of destruction' view of the upper turning point lacks (like Kalecki) a micro-level motivation that generates such destruction. The 'recreation of investment opportunities' view of the lower turning point revival of investment, even more significantly, lacks an awareness of the risks and uncertainty involved in revitalising investment when excess capacity is considerable. All investment cycle theories lack an adequate explanation of the motivations for an investment upturn. Nevertheless, Bhaudri's systematic contradictory pulls can be applied at the micro-level, enabling an endogenous motivational investment cycle to emerge.

The *microfoundations* to the two roles of profit in investment outlined above, have been developed by Kaleckian and related post-Keynesian authors. In Kalecki's work, the mark-up provides the profitability for investment. Kalecki's mark-up hypothesis is determined by the degree of monopoly (ϕ) under oligopoly conditions. This mark-up behaviour relates to investment only indirectly via the mark-up's macroeconomic effect on income distribution and capitalist consumption (Kalecki, 1954, pp. 59–63). Kalecki's 'integration of mark-up pricing and accumulation is nonexistent' (Goldstein, 1982, p. 56). The only specific micro-investment analysis by Kalecki is his recognition of the financial constraints on investment.[12]

Kaleckian mark-up pricing models have refined Kalecki's micro-model, but at the cost of some distortions of Kalecki's own work. Cowling (1982) develops a precise relationship between the mark-up (μ) and the three factors that affect it: price elasticity of demand (η); Herfindahl's index of industrial concentration (H); and reaction to rivals' response on the firm's mark-up decision (γ). These factors specify Cowling's ϕ, yet his model assumes each firm pursues Cournot assumptions of 'independent profit maximisation but taking account of the expected reactions of its rivals' (Reynolds, 1987, p. 59).

Kalecki (1954, pp. 12–19) is clear that the firm's μ is dependent on four major influences on ϕ. These influences make the cost-determined μ subject to intraindustry competition over market share, such that the mark-up price depends on the weighted average price of all firms in the industry ($\bar{p}$). Goldstein (1982, p. 15) recognises the behaviour of $\bar{p}$ as a demand (or competitive) constraint on the cost-determined mark-up price. 'This implies that the mark-up may be squeezed or forced to decline if the behavior of $\bar{p}$ limits the response of p (price) to a rising u (prime costs) experienced by the firm' (Goldstein, 1982, pp. 15–16). With the Cowling-type pricing model excluding any consideration of the effect of $\bar{p}$ on mark-up behaviour, it leaves the cost-dominated μ to act through profits only as an expectational factor on investment at the macro-level. There is no microfoundation to investment behaviour in this type of Kaleckian pricing model.

The alternative Kaleckian pricing model in Asimakopulos (1975) has the degree of monopoly reflecting expected target rates of return on investment in a non-profit-maximising environment. A microeconomic link between the pricing and the investment decision is established, with an implied long-term growth rate for the firm. This model converges to the post-Keynesian growth-maximisation pricing model. Eichner (1976, 1987) furnishes the two most exhaustive microeconomic accounts of this post-Keynesian model. In Eichner's model the mark-up price is determined by the target rate of return in the oligopolistic sector which would 'enable the firms in that sector to finance the level of investment necessary to maximise – or at least move further towards maximising – their long-run growth' (Eichner, 1976, pp. 2–3). The mark-up in both Asimakopulos's and Eichner's models is set by the industry leader (with tacit acquiescence of the other firms) based on its own standard capacity utilisation rate. These mark-up models are known as standard volume target return pricing (SVTRP). This approach directly tackles the role of profit for internal financing of investment at the micro-level.

Consistent with Kalecki's non-profit-maximising approach, the SVTRP models are inconsistent with Kalecki's view that the capitalist system's price mechanism cannot provide balanced growth (Kalecki, 1954, pp. 62–3). Eichner argues that his pricing model allows for the success of investment plans tailored to maximum long-term growth of the firm. Goldstein (1982, pp. 51–5) develops a critique of SVTRP models which points out that they lack any effective competitive (demand) constraints on price. Although SVTRP models have a microfoundation in the ability-to-invest factor, the assurance of balanced investment growth means that investment instability only becomes evident at the macro-level without any microfoundation. Also, these models only relate to the marginal investment decision, leaving replacement investment undetermined.

Harcourt and Kenyon (1976) describe a short-term SVTRP model which internally generates a demand-for-investment schedule, based on the comparison of price and expected marginal costs for new and existing plants of different vintages. This advances the microfoundations by extending the technical progress analysis in Salter (1960) into an oligopoly structure. However, the model still ignores the competitive constraints on the mark-up, leaving investment instability with no microfoundations.

Wood (1975), in his long-term SVTRP model, identifies three specific financial ratios which clarify the required profits in relation to planned investment. This enables firms to maximise growth of sales revenue subject to these financing constraints. These long-term outcomes that the model generates do not allow for short-term adjustments in investment, the central aspect of this present study. Nevertheless, both the Harcourt–Kenyon and Wood analyses contribute micro-investment perspectives which are useful in developing the modified Kaleckian institutional framework in section 4.2.

The recent development of a dynamic theory of pricing over the product life-cycle does take competitive constraints into account. Based on Steindl (1952) and Levine (1981), which examine the price dynamics in new industries (see section 2.5), Shapiro (1981) sees the stagnation in demand for mature industries affecting the SVTRP approach to adequately fund investment. She goes on to show how this stagnation is avoided by large oligopoly firms through product development and diversification into new products. In this way, the firm can overcome competitive constraints in an effort to maintain balanced growth. Ong (1981) analyses the impact of the firm's SVTRP pricing decision on its long-term competitive standing. Goldstein (1985b, p. 122, fn. 2) notes that Ong allows the firm to alter its financial ratios, without any optimal determination, in order to manoeuvre around the competitive constraints. This leads to μ being unrestrained, which leaves investment instability unexplained at the micro-level. Still, life-cycle analysis can add another micro-investment perspective within an investment instability model which recognises profit squeeze at the micro-level. This is attempted in Chapter 5.

Eichner (1987) maintains the SVTRP model, but modifies it in relation to a full analysis of the firm's investment decisions. It is a very comprehensive discussion of the micro-investment decision, incorporating Kalecki's gestation time period and Levine's life-cycle development to recognise the problem of investment instability. What is missing is a causal linkage over time between these important elements of the investment decision and an endogenously generated industry investment cycle (i.e. microdynamics). As the term 'macrodynamics' in the title suggests, it is only at the macro-level that a specified dynamic linkage to cycles is established. By developing a more flexible mark-up approach than the SVTRP model, such microdynamics are possible.

Flexibility of the mark-up and the resulting profit squeeze should yield a strong theoretical integration of Kaleckian micro-investment behaviour and macro-based profit squeeze of the type in equation (2.10). It is upon Kaleckian literature on profit squeeze that the 'monopoly capitalism' institutional framework of section 4.2 is partly based.

The concept of 'strategic price', introduced by Sylos Labini (1962), derives its genesis from the SVTRP approach. It enables investment through internal finance and is set by the large firm(s) with oligopoly power as a result of a strategic scale of output set by the large firm(s). The strategic price, unlike standard SVTRP mark-up theories, is flexible enough to allow for smaller firms influencing aggregate variations of output, or for short-term alternative strategies being applied by the large firms. Sylos Labini's strategic level of output concept yields mark-up flexibility without losing determinacy in the theory.

In the short term, for extraordinary strategic reasons, the large firm(s) can abandon the long-run target. This can occur if there is a concerted market attack by cheap imports, or an attempt to take over the firm. Such external pressures require short-term action. In the first case, this increases output and lower profits; in the second, it can stall current investment decisions for the use of funds to reduce debt/equity and bolster the stock mark-up price. However, once the threat is over, firms can resume their long term strategy. This provides a definite determination of a 'strategic price', but also variations from it due to (a) short-term actions of the price leaders to overcome some threat or crisis; or (b) small variations (usually for a short time) as a result of output variations of smaller firms (or future competitors). This is a complex price behaviour, but one that stays very close to the heart of Kalecki's mark-up approach, providing a cost-determined market but enough flexibility to account for short-term problems.

Sylos Labini (1979b) finds empirical support for his strategic price hypothesis. This mark-up behaviour is incorporated into the institutional framework of section 4.2 and then is used in Chapter 5 to show the impact of such behaviour on investment decisions over the cyclical short term. Two weaknesses in this hypothesis need to be addressed before it can be incorporated in this manner. First is the sketchy nature of the behavioural motivations, which this hypothesis has in common with all standard Kaleckian analyses. Literature that has attempted to transcend this problem is examined in Chapter 3. Second is the lack of a specific link between firm and industry, as with Kalecki's $\bar{p}$ variable. Sylos Labini (1962) has a theoretical model which is based on the strongest oligopoly structure possible – the homogeneous product (concentrated) industry – and thus makes the firm-to-industry (FI) link of minor concern. Section 4.2 attempts to broaden the oligopoly structure and strengthen the FI link.

Recognising the above-mentioned weaknesses in the literature on profits and accumulation, Goldstein (1982) represents a significant contribution to the treatment of short-period fluctuations. He links Goodwin's self-generating macro-cycle movement to Sylos Labini's variable mark-up price approach, and finds empirical support to investment cycles based on this linkage. Goldstein uses the capital–labour (K–L) struggle over the cycle as the central linkage concept. As Goldstein argues, 'the CPS (cyclical profit squeeze) is the result of an ongoing distributional conflict between capital and labor over the entire cycle during which capital assumes the upper hand in certain periods and labor in others' (Goldstein, 1985a, p. 122). After mid-expansion of the cycle, the defensive reaction of large firms to increased international competition by reducing the profit margin below the strategic price is exacerbated as labour makes wage gains, bringing on the profit squeeze and slowing down accumulation. There is a symmetrical release of the squeeze when profit margins increase at a time of weak competitive and labour pressures, leading to 'the exploitation of the profitable initial stages of the cycle' (Goldstein, 1985a, p. 122).

The dialectics of the class struggle which Goldstein uses are incorporated into the institutional framework of Chapter 4. The mark-up analysis conducted by Goldstein adds to the better understanding of accumulation. However, he does not fully specify the relation between accumulation and fluctuations because his main concern is to specify the mark-up decision. The dialectics of accumulation that Kalecki developed are not delineated. A more complete model of investment needs to take this into account.

The inadequacies of Goldstein's model of investment can be summarised in four major points. First, his treatment of the price leader as the 'representative firm' implies a constant cyclical market share in the domestic economy. This is clear when for empirical reasons he 'abstract[s] from domestic intra-industry competition' (Goldstein, 1985a, p. 125, fn. 16), exclusively focusing on international competitive constraints.[13] Secondly, the cyclical investment analysis is narrowly based in that the traverse, and all that can go wrong due to structural impediments to the investment sequence, are ignored. Thirdly, there is no consideration of the role of uncertainty and expectations, which is the basic Keynesian behavioural element to investment instability. Finally, the cycle-trend puzzle that worried Kalecki is ignored. The long-term implications of accumulation and technological progress have a feedback effect on short-term investment instability which needs to be examined.

2.3.3 Financial Constraints on Investment

The mark-up pricing approach enables internal finance, in the form of retained earnings, to generate the vast majority of net funds for firms in all size categories. In a recent study of US manufacturing firms from 1970 to 1984 by Fazzari *et al.* (1988), this strong historical pattern was reaffirmed, showing retained earnings as 71.1 per cent of all firms' source of funds (excluding new equity issues which are small in the aggregate). The authors go on to state that the 'importance of internal finance would be even greater if we were able to include information on depreciation allowances, a source of internal funds roughly equal to retained earnings' (Fazzari *et al.*, 1988, pp. 146–7). The major financial constraint on investment, accordingly, is the extent of any profit squeeze which would limit internal finance (see pp. 28-9).

The same study, however, does show that firms of all sizes use external sources of funding (borrowing and equity), with smaller firms relying very heavily on bank loans. To explain the relative use of external and internal funds, Fazzari *et al.* (1988, pp. 154–7) present a financial hierarchy where the cost of funds rises in a three-step fashion, starting with internal funds, next debt, and finally equity financing. Due to the lack of internal funds, small and immature firms tend to depend on high-cost external (often bank) funding.

The empirics for this financial hierarchy were first established in the 1950s in relation to transaction costs rising from internal funds, through debt to, finally, equity funds. Kalecki's principle of increasing risk is often quoted in these studies as the theoretical basis of these rising transaction costs (see Meyer and Kuh, 1957, p. 10; Matthews, 1959, p. 147). Modigliani and Miller (1958) reject this hierarchy by demonstrating the irrelevance of financial structures and policies for investment (apart from tax considerations and market 'imperfections'). The perfect capital market allows the returns on all financial assets to become equalised, so that firms' ownership should be unconcerned about debt gearing levels, dividend payouts and internal liquidity. 'Applied to capital investment, this general finding provide[s] a foundation for the neo-classical theory of investment' (Fazzari *et al.*, 1988, p. 144), which isolates investment decisions from purely financial factors.[14]

Kaleckian and SVTRP pricing models from the early 1970s have resurrected the financial hierarchy as a theoretically valid position. These models accept Kalecki's view that '[t]he most important prerequisite for becoming an entrepreneur is the *ownership* of [equity] capital', rejecting the notion of a 'business democracy where anybody endowed with entrepreneurial ability can obtain capital [funds] for starting a business venture' (1954, pp. 94–5, original emphasis).[15] This establishes the Kaleckian view that rentiers' capital (whether in the form of loans or share issues not owned by the entrepreneurs) used to finance new investment is seen as constrained due to 'increasing risk'. Three forms of limitation on external funding identified by Kalecki have been developed further in recent studies.[16] In all three, risk rises with increased rentier capital until the risk is so high that no further funds are available.

The first is entrepreneurs' limited 'capacity to borrow'. For Kalecki, its own 'entrepreneurial [equity] capital' sets the limit, although a higher interest rate paid by the entrepreneur may induce some more (but highly limited) funds. Wood (1975, p. 29) explained this same limitation as 'lender's risk'. This is a risk faced by the lender in the event of bankruptcy by the borrower. The risk is that the lender will not get the full principal back after assets are sold and the receipts from the sale distributed among all the various lenders. Lending limits are based on the gearing ratio (ratio of total outstanding debt to total current value of equity), such that a firm with a high gearing ratio must pay a high interest rate to the lender to cover this lender's high risk. Eventually there is a limit about which Wood echoes Kalecki by stating: 'too high a gearing ratio will lead to outright refusal to lend at any interest rate' (Wood, 1975, p. 29). The only difference is that Kalecki uses entrepreneurial capital instead of total equity as the base for limiting loans (in companies 100 per cent owned by entrepreneurs, there is no distinction).

The second limitation is the firm's own increasing risk as borrowings increase. In a detailed study of Kalecki's increasing risk concept, Mott (1982, p. 1) relates increased borrowings to two types of financial problems. First is the increasing danger to the *wealth* of the entrepreneur in the event of failure (the bankruptcy risk). Second is the greater *illiquidity* which arises as more funds are tied up in specific plant and equipment 'which cannot be immediately reconverted into cash without a loss of value in case there is a sudden need for funds' (the cash flow risk). These two risks are incorporated into what Wood (1975, p. 29) calls 'borrower's risk'. The risk is that the firm may be forced into bankruptcy or loss of effective control to the creditors.[17] To protect against such risk, Wood sees entrepreneurs setting gearing ratio limits to borrowing and also maintaining a cushion of liquidity, which is discussed later in this section.

The third limitation identified by Kalecki relates to the issuing of shares as a form of external funding for investment. The concern is that issuing shares to the public reduces the proportion of the controlling group's ownership (share issue risk). This is not a serious problem if the issue is small and the current entrepreneurial group has the vast majority of shares. However, as more shares are issued to fund investment, the risk increases that control slips from this controlling group. Even before that happens, the controlling group could see increasing risk through their dividends squeezed and the share price fall if the new MOP returns are not as good as the old MOP. This risk will 'exert *some* restraining influence upon issues to the "public"' (Kalecki, 1971, p. 107, original emphasis). The ratio of rentier (both borrowings and 'outside' shares) to entrepreneurial capital is the gearing ratio used by Kalecki to derive a gearing limit of external funding for investment.

Fazzari *et al.* (1988) develop rising informational asymmetries to supplement Kaleckian rising transaction costs in explaining the financial hierarchy evident in the stylised facts. As finance is sought from sources increasingly further away from the inside information of the firm, there are rising cost disadvantages to entrepreneurs and rentiers, due to information becoming more incomplete. In this argument, the equity finance constraint is the strongest as 'new shareholders implicitly demand a premium to purchase the shares of relatively good firms to offset the losses that will arise from funding lemons' (Fazzari *et al.*, 1988, p. 150).

Asymmetric information in markets for debt also cause distortions which lead to credit rationing by lenders. 'Lenders cannot price discriminate between good borrowers and bad in loan contracts' (Fazzari *et al.*, 1988, p. 152). This leads to different classes of borrowers who are granted credit on different terms related to the severity of information problems. The greater these problems, the higher the costs of obtaining debt and the lower amount obtainable. Information costs can be reduced by firms maintaining long-term relationships with lenders while growing larger and more mature.

Eichner (1987) goes one step further back into behavioural analysis. He examines why large, powerful oligopolies (called 'megacorps') which use the SVTRP pricing approach to obtain funds for investment, still need external finance. These firms' relatively lower transaction costs and information costs, compared to smaller and less-mature firms, ensure better success in obtaining external finance.

Eichner (1987, pp. 472–80) outlines two reasons for megacorps needing external funds. One is as a short-term measure to overcome any cash flow problems due to a gap between capital outlays and internal funds being generated. Short-term debt, mainly from financial institutions like banks, fills this gap until sales increase and capital spending decreases. The second reason is for long-term funding. This need arises when a large increase in investment is activated quickly as positive business expectations rise and the firm adjusts to a higher secular investment trend path. Such a higher path shift occurred in the 1980s, when the optimal gearing ratio increased in anticipation of higher returns in the near future. This required external funding until the expected higher profits were (hopefully) realised (Eichner, 1987,

p. 479). In such circumstances the financial constraints become weaker, only to become tighter as the expectations are not realised. In the investment cycle model of Chapter 5, this latter long-term funding issue is of central concern.

In Wood's (1975) SVTRP pricing model, profits generated from the mark-up enables (apart from financing investment) the creation of a 'liquidity cushion'. This 'cushion' is made up of liquid financial asset holdings and short-term lending facilities with financial institutions. The liquid financial asset holdings fluctuate over the business cycle around a long-term target level (Wood, 1975, p. 26), and are maintained to cover 'increasing risk' generated by debt commitments. Contraction of the business cycle creates additional pressure in meeting fixed-cost interest commitments. The cushion of financial assets also provides security for further financial lending when the firm wants to expand its capital stock. The short-term lending facilities act for similar concerns, but relate more to immediate cash flow problems. In the long-term, as a company expands it requires a larger lending facility. This is due to the increasing amount of working capital required, and the larger number of fixed investment projects coming into existence.

This 'liquidity cushion' creates what Sylos Labini (1984a, p. 124) calls a financial barrier to entry into the oligopolistic market structures. Large firms have the ability to develop a large 'cushion' both internally (by retained earnings) and externally (financial arrangements for overdrafts and ease of issuing shares). The need for a liquidity cushion creates a serious difficulty for small firms. Their retained earnings would be relatively lower than those of large firms, they have weak security (or collateral) backing and a low earnings capacity. All of which makes access to the financial market or to bank credit a formidable financial barrier. In fact, 'bank lending to small firms will be limited in general by the value of the owner's assets available as collateral' (Kregel, 1989–90, p. 232). To issue shares requires incorporation, which is also limited by size and ability to set up with the equity necessary to start.[18]

The fragile nature of external finance is a constraint on investment when money capital overextends its capacity to lend. Although hinted at by Keynes and Kalecki, this fragility has become clearer to economists by the works of Douglas Vickers at the individual firm level and Hyman Minsky at the aggregate economy level. Vickers (1987) takes Kalecki's 'increasing risk' one step further, identifying the increase in risk caused by the increase in gearing that arises when investment is financed by *increasing* debt. This he calls 'financial leverage'. During booms, firms develop an over-optimistic assessment of expected future yields and an under-assessment of the risk in financial leverage. With a corresponding rise in stock market prices, an expectation of rising financial capital gains adds further to financial leverage. Financial institutions increase their competition for market share by encouraging larger firms to greater financial leverage.

Kregel (1989–90) develops Vickers's analysis further. Kregel notes that after a certain size, which is difficult to achieve, firms find it relatively easier to increase size. This is based on further borrowings and floating of share issue, especially in a booming financial period of rising capital gains in the share valuation of these larger firms. This enables such firms to refinance indebtedness easily. However, this cannot be sustained as effective demand becomes deficient (Kregel, 1989–90, pp. 231–3).

Such a process leads to Minsky's financial instability. Financing is no longer based on borrowing to meet expected increase in returns, but borrowing simply to meet interest payments created by previous borrowings. Minsky (1982, p. 106) calls this 'Ponzi finance'. At this point, financial institutions may begin to realise the increased risks (or 'fragility') in financial leverage; or, instead, may be forced to do so by financial crashes or financial bunglings by some high-profile entrepreneurs (usually entrepreneur-owners, who have fewer constraints on justifying their borrowings to shareholders).

Once this happens, the end of Ponzi financing leads to many unpaid debts, to bankruptcies and a financial collapse that follows as in a domino effect. A severe financial constraint on investment is brought on by financial institutions. Financial instability is exogenous to the firm, although growing indebtedness which occurs in all booms increases the 'fragility' of the boom and is endogenous to the investment cycle model. Minsky's extensive use of Kalecki's increasing-risk concept has much to say about these changes in the risks that entrepreneurs are prepared to run during the progress of the business cycle, particularly the fragility of a high level of increasing risk. This idea of fragility has permeated the endogenous concept of susceptibility in Chapter 5, while in section 6.4 on exogenous factors, the (macro) financial instability issue is examined for its implications on the (micro) endogenous investment cycle.

2.4 MONOPOLY CAPITALISM AND INVESTMENT

Monopoly capitalism is the term used to describe the specific institutional setting in which the above mark-up pricing, finance and capacity utilisation decisions take place. Early Marxists, like Hilferding and Lenin, take concentration and centralisation of capital outlined by Marx as an indication of the emergence of power relations within capitalism. The emergence of large firms with monopoly power over other capitalists, workers and the state redefines the nature of collusion, class conflict and influence over state policies. Monopoly power's role in the investment behaviour of large firms is of concern here.

Kalecki pioneered the work on monopoly capitalism and his framework is based on the manufacturing sector as the 'engine of growth'.[19] The higher degree of monopoly (ϕ) for this sector in the long-term ensures a greater share of profits out of national income.[20] For Kalecki, this does not lead to a higher volume of profits unless expenditure is also increased (Sawyer, 1985, p. 80). As set out in section 2.2, Kalecki sees the regular inadequacy of investment to maintain boom conditions as preventing such higher profit volumes. Kalecki (1945) specifically explains why investment is usually too low for the long-term maintenance of full employment. Discoveries and new technology can temporarily raise investment levels to provide large short term profit increases.

Kalecki's institutional framework is developed by other monopoly power theorists towards specific models of stagnation in which investment plays a crucial role. Steindl (1952) sees the growth of large firms, with lower unit costs than small firms, as establishing higher profit margins throughout the economy. This shifts distribution of income away from wage earners towards capitalists who have a higher propensity to save. From this perspective, the creation of a monopoly reduces demand for manufactured consumption goods and there emerges a long-term problem of deficient aggregate demand. Also, as noted in section 2.3, monopolies involve a higher planned rate of excess capacity, with smaller firms having a fear of actual excess capacity rising above desired levels as firms cut back production levels due to declining demand. In Steindl (1964) it is also the preference for safety that induces the sacrifice of future profits as firms become larger. These forces reduce investment incentives and produce secular stagnation.

Baran and Sweezy (1968) take Kalecki's model and focus on various means by which sufficient expenditure can be generated to overcome stagnation. The authors express strong doubts about the potential of capitalists themselves to provide the expenditure boost. Limitations in purchasing power by the growing lower income groups and restrictions on conspicuous consumption by the higher income groups make sales promotion self-defeating in the long term. In such circumstances, firms' investment plans are stalled without the necessary incentives. The external forces of state spending (civil and military) and imperialism have the sort of counterproductive effects outlined by Kalecki which limit their ability to furnish the needed long-term expenditure growth. For the purposes of cyclical behaviour, these external forces can act as stimuli to turning back investment cycle contractions upwards.

Cowling (1982) draws on Steindl's work to show that merger booms increase monopoly power and excess capacity, which then depress investment. At the same time, investment incentive is further dampened by growing managerial capitalism that leads to increasing unproductive expenditure and to a 'fall in observed profits' share of private sector value added' (Reynolds, 1987, p. 221). The UK and US post-war experiences are used by Cowling (1982, pp. 151–81) to support his arguments.

Bloch (1990) demonstrates how Kalecki's pricing equation (1954, p. 13) can be depicted as a case of price leadership, with the lowest prime-cost firm becoming the leader. He then argues that the price set by the leader is inversely related to the number of firms in the industry. This fits in with Steindl's analysis of emerging undesired excess capacity due to initially constant prices with high gross profit margins. Such a situation entices higher-cost rivals (small firms) to enter or expand in the industry, reducing ϕ. To Bloch, these small firms are an 'uncompetitive fringe', inducing the leading low-cost firms to reduce prices so that μ falls to a lower level. This forces the high-cost rivals to drop out and ϕ to rise again, thus restoring the desired capacity utilisation in the industry. Bloch (1990, p. 449) sees this aggressive price leadership strategy being weakened in the face of 'rapid demand growth, increased capital intensity, and increased outlays for overhead expenses, interest or dividends' throughout the industry. As an industry matures these factors become impotent, allowing monopoly power to stabilise. Then investment decisions of large firms are no longer influenced by the undesired capacity of the uncompetitive fringe.

The mark-up is subject to intraindustry competition which Kalecki identifies as $\bar{p}$, the weighted average price of all competing firms in the industry.[21] It is weighted due to the different prices arising from product differentiation in the industry.[22] In the Kaleckian literature there is much debate on how to measure $\bar{p}$ and the significance of the related coefficients in Kalecki's price equation (e.g. Reynolds, 1983; Asimakopulos, 1975). Sylos Labini (1962) avoids these problems with a non-differentiated oligopoly model using Kalecki's mark-up approach but without the sales promotion needed to differentiate the product. Here homogeneous oligopoly firms maintain (or increase) their ϕ only through barriers to entry like large excess capacity and introducing process innovation very quickly into the production process, in particular. This means that investment decisions act even more strongly as competitive tools.

The homogeneous industries in Sylos Labini's model have unit prime costs that decrease with plant size due to economies of scale and process innovation. This is not in Kalecki's model. Both models assume constant prime costs with respect to the plant level of capacity utilisation. Lowering prime costs is crucial in homogeneous industries' competition, especially at times when an uncompetitive fringe emerges. In these non-differentiated oligopolies rapid demand growth is rare, and increasing already very high capital intensity is difficult. As well, increasing outlays out of gross profits tend to be limited by managements' tight policy control of these areas, much more than in differentiated oligopolies where sales promotions, executive salaries and dividend returns can be forced up. For these reasons, strong co-operative price leadership is crucial in such homogeneous industries. As a consequence, Sylos Labini (1962, p. 155) argues that homogeneous industries are very highly concentrated oligopolies.

For Sylos Labini (1962, p. 152), small firms tend to exist as a fringe of uncompetitive units in differentiated oligopolies. In the more concentrated and capital intensive homogeneous industries there is less of a fringe. In such analysis of monopoly capitalism, investment decisions are only marginally affected by small firm competition (see Bloch, 1990, and p. 38 above).

Sylos Labini (1984a, pp. 94–5, 1990a) revises his view of small firms and their relationship to monopoly power. Innovation in both differentiated and homogeneous industries has recently yielded a larger and more significant role for small firms. Often this role has been one of symbiotic linkage to large firms, based on quality products and specific scientific services provided. As a result, 'the weight of small firms in the economy, as measured by total employment, is now increasing . . . whereas until – say – two decades ago it was declining in all industrialized countries, at least in relative terms' (Sylos Labini, 1990a, p. 12). This does not alter the strategic monopoly power position of large firms, as oligopoly still remains the dominating market structure. However, their investment decisions now need to take earnest recognition of the capacity utilisation, profits and financial constraints of small firms which are linked to them.

The structural implications of the Kaleckian model of monopoly capitalism is the separation of 'actors' on the economic stage into capitalists and workers. On this stage, the crucial role is played by the capitalists who make the investment decisions that create the possibility for future profits. It is the realisation of such profits that enables further investment. This is Kalecki's crucial feedback effect on investment.

Many times Kalecki uses 'capitalist', 'entrepreneur', 'manager', 'firm' to denote much the same thing. This makes it difficult to ascertain his vision of agents within the modern oligopolistic corporation. Kalecki comes closest to defining agents when outlining his 'principle of increasing risk'. He identifies entrepreneurs as 'a controlling group of big shareholders' (Kalecki, 1954, p. 93) who manage the firm. These entrepreneur-owner types have large ownership stakes and also determine major policy directions.

The next group Kalecki identifies is 'the rest of the shareholders [who] do not differ from holders of bonds with a flexible rate of interest' (Kalecki, 1954, p. 93). These 'outside shareholders' are seen as interested only in financial returns and make up the majority of shareholders. 'Rentier' is the term Kalecki uses to identify all financial agents in companies outside of the 'controlling group'. The 'outside shareholders' are one type of rentier. In this case, such shareholders supply rentier capital funds when buying equities, diluting the entrepreneurial capital funds of entrepreneurs. The other group of rentiers are the financial agents who lend funds on fixed terms to the company.

Relating the above agents to the pricing policy of firms, Kalecki's term 'capitalist' refers to the recipients of income from the gross profit determined by the mark-up. The 'gross profit' is distributed as net profit (to shareholders), overhead salaries (to managers), interest (to lending rentiers) and depreciation (on capital goods).

There are empirical problems in breaking down the capitalist group into entrepreneurs and rentiers. In this study, the term entrepreneur refers to the managerial decision-making process conducted by what Kalecki called the 'controlling group' in the company. In companies where the ownership is highly concentrated, this controlling ownership group also act as managers, or managers who are employed implement the detailed decisions of the owners, including all investment commitments.

There are problems with this breakdown of agents within a firm when more diversely owned companies are examined. In such companies there are members of the board who are only interested in high dividend returns. These members are not interested in the details of managing the company and they tend to follow the advice of senior management. This may make them 'rentiers', yet their board membership can indicate some 'entrepreneurial' input. In these cases there needs to be an arbitrary judgement as to what sort of input into board decisions constitutes an effective managerial function and with it the title of 'entrepreneur'.

The term 'workers' refers to recipients of wages that come direct from the prime costs of the companies. The 'workers' in the manufacturing sector (consumption and investment sectors) are seen by Kalecki as organised into effective trade unions as they operate in economies with western conservative governments. Unions are assumed to be antagonistic to both capitalists and the policies of governments. Thus, there is no corporatist-type union system as there is in Japan (conservative) or even Sweden (liberal). From the earlier discussion on degree of monopoly, unions can have some influence on wages through industrial action – especially during booms. As will be discussed on the next page, unions are seen as influencing governments to act on the unemployment problem during slumps, in order to protect the jobs of their shrinking membership.

The structure of the capitalist economy also includes international trade and the government sector. Kalecki throughout his writings considers the implications of these institutions to his model. Looking at government first, Kalecki (1943a) observes that the role of government is not as a 'neutral referee' trying to balance opposing conflicting interest groups for the 'common good', but, instead, having autonomy 'only relative to individual fractions of the capitalist class' (Beresford and McFarlane, 1980, p. 229). Pressure is placed on governments by 'big business', 'big rentiers' and 'their experts', including many economists. This is a development from Marx's simplistic view of the state as an 'executive' of the capitalist class and predates much theoretical work on the state by modern Marxists (O'Connor, 1973; Gough, 1979).

An important part of Kalecki's relative autonomy view of the state is 'the political business cycle'. Kalecki (1943a, p. 324) explains that during periods close to full employment (business cycle peak), capitalist groups form temporary coalitions. The capitalist coalition comes together and opposes growing government spending, due to high tax revenue and increased debt burden. They oppose public investment due to crowding out. They oppose subsidising mass consumption due to its inflationary pressure on demand, and oppose the growing social and political strength of workers during booms due to increased trade union membership that comes with increased employment. In particular, 'big rentiers' from the coalition are concerned about inflationary pressures and, thus, the lowering in value of loans being paid back. They are also concerned about the loans made for more speculative ventures. Thus, economists are hired by the coalition to 'declare that the situation was manifestly unsound' (Kalecki, 1943a, p. 330) and government must return to sound finance principles, i.e. remove budget deficits and create surpluses. This 'powerful block' or coalition of capitalist interests induces a budget tightening, causing an upper turning point in the business cycle and a contraction.[23]

The united concern of capitalists in a slump is that their business interests need support. These concerns, along with pressure from the growing number of unemployed and unions with shrinking membership, leads to the reintroduction of stimulatory budget deficits to turn the cycle up into an expansion. Such induced Keynesian effective demand intervention by the state is the result of political concerns arising from the employment issue. The modified business cycle pattern that arises is called the 'political business cycle' (Kalecki, 1943a, p. 330).[24]

Kalecki's relative autonomy view of the state is developed in a long term structural dimension through his more polemical articles (Kalecki, 1972a). These articles examine antagonisms between fractions of capital in specific historical circumstances. When such antagonisms occur, the unity of capitalist interests breaks down. In this situation, the government is relatively more autonomous to pursue economic policies.

The broadest aspect of Kalecki's institutional framework is based on Rosa Luxemburg's concept of 'external markets' and incorporates government and international trade. External markets exist when capitalism relies, for its own development, on the existence of possible realisation outlets outside the world capitalist system. Such markets are composed of underdeveloped economies, peasant (or self-sufficient) sectors of capitalist economies, and the government sector of capitalist economies. The two institutional structures identified in Kalecki (1971, chs 2, 7 and 13) as 'external markets' are imperialism and the military-industrial complex. In both structures, Kalecki (1967) notes the financing problem neglected by Luxemburg.

Kalecki maintains that Luxemburg was in error to claim that the development of capitalism depended entirely on 'external markets'. Kalecki sees investment as the major source of capitalist development. Nevertheless, external markets are an important dynamic institutional structure of the capitalist system. Pressure by various fractions of capital to obtain profits from 'external' sources affects both the cycle and growth of developed economies, with government support by the infrastructure necessary to realise such profits. Thus, the external-markets issue can be linked to the earlier discussion of the role of the state through the influence of fractions of capital on public policy-making.

In the institutional framework for investment, it is important to identify the role of firms in the innovation process. Innovation often provides the stimulus to investment, as well as possibly making obsolete existing capital stock. On this issue of technological change and innovations, Kalecki is ambiguous. Kalecki pioneered the important recognition that *endogenous* innovations 'in the sense of gradual adjustments of equipment to the current state of technology are assumed to be part and parcel of "ordinary" investment as determined by the "normal" factors [which affect investment decisions]' (Kalecki, 1954, p. 158). However, Kalecki adds a 'd' at the end of the relevant investment equation to account for 'long-run changes, in particular technical change' (Kalecki, 1971, p. 113). The equation presumes innovation to be an *exogenous* trend factor which stimulates the demand for investment over and above the long-term replacement level.

Kalecki resolves this dilemma in his last article on investment and the business cycle (Kalecki, 1968, pp. 173–4) by identifying two distinct effects of innovation on investment decision-making. This resolution is best understood by relating the two effects to the difference between the endogenous (or cyclical) and exogenous (or trend) roles of innovation. Section 2.5 below attempts to make clear this distinction.

The other confusion is Kalecki's inability to distinguish between 'innovation' and 'inventions'. In his chapter on long-run economic development, the section entitled 'Innovations' has Kalecki discussing it in terms of 'inventions' (Kalecki, 1954, p. 158). Kalecki is unable to distinguish between inventions and innovations, or to explain where such developments come from, or the respective roles of large and small firms in these developments. An attempt to incorporate these issues into a modified framework is presented in section 4.6.

2.5 STRUCTURAL ASPECTS OF INVESTMENT CYCLES

Once Kalecki adopted a damped-cycle solution to his business cycle in versions II and III, it became necessary to introduce random shocks to prevent the cycle coming to rest. Shocks to the business cycle would then act as the escapement on the pendulum of a clock to ensure its continued movement (Goodwin, 1964, p. 421). Such shocks also generate an upward growth trend, 'if it is assumed that they are asymmetric and that their action is predominatingly stimulating'. (Steindl, 1989, p. 311).

Kalecki identifies two structural features of capitalism as random shocks to the system which can generate such growth trends: the role of the state and major technological innovations. Both are exogenous to the closed investment cycle models discussed in section 2.2, but are important parts of the institutional framework of monopoly capitalism. Both are the structural aspects of investment cycles that Kalecki analyses (in the context of version III) in three articles published in 1967 and 1968. The role of the state is examined first.

Underlying Kalecki's investment decision-making is the 'state of business confidence'. Any serious erosion of confidence by the elements described in section 2.2 would turn the aggregate investment cycle downwards and increase unemployment. Kalecki (1943a) argues that maintaining full employment by the state takes from business 'a powerful device for controlling the militancy of the labour unions' (Kriesler and McFarlane, 1991, p. 14). This reduces the amplitude of the investment cycle. By opposing deficit financing and promoting 'sound finance', powerful business spokespersons lobby governments for employment to be dependent on purely private investment instability.

Kalecki (1967) observes that the 'external market' of state armaments expenditure is acceptable to business for its stimulation of effective demand and long-term accumulation without contributing to productive capacity. This is an important shock at a trough of the investment cycle to set the pendulum going again, but on a higher growth path. Such intervention can also reduce short-term investment instability if this economic role of government is sustained in the longer term. There is a political (or 'fiscal crisis') limitation to sustained armaments expenditure which eventually surfaces as demands for 'sound finance'. This limitation emerged strongly in the 1970s after a long post-war growth period of high-employment policies and reasonably stable business cycles (Kriesler and McFarlane, 1991, pp. 17–18).

Large recessions in the early 1980s and early 1990s, with a strong boom in between, provides support to Kalecki's view of social contradictions. The acceptance of 'sound finance' policies by capitalist governments from the mid-1970s reduced the demand management role of state expenditures, allowing employment to be more dependent upon private sector investment decisions, and consequently more severe investment instability arose. At the same time as exacerbating cyclical amplitudes, such monetarist and 'economic rational' policies have shown an investment growth much weaker than during the earlier post-war period of Keynesian intervention (Cornwall, 1990).

It is not clear in what respect Kalecki sees innovation as a long-term structural (exogenous) aspect of investment and as a cyclical (endogenous) element of investment. Sawyer (1985, p. 64) notes that 'Kalecki did not provide any intensive discussion on invention and innovations and . . . introduced the effects of technical change in a simple way'. A distinction between minor (endogenous) and major (exogenous) technological innovation[25] can provide a way of clarifying the innovation dilemmas in Kalecki's writings. This is consistent with Kalecki's version III of the investment cycle, in which he identifies two innovation effects on investment (Kalecki, 1971, pp. 173–4). First is the endogenous effect which relates to the speed (or rate) of technological innovation. Second is the exogenous effect which relates to the intensity of technological innovation. With the endogenous effect, go-ahead entrepreneurs are induced to introduce innovations in order to get larger-firm market share and increase their profit rate over the constant average profit rate assumed by Kalecki in the pure trendless investment cycle. This innovation can be seen as 'part and parcel' of investment decision-making, which is determined by the 'normal' investment elements (Kalecki, 1954, p. 158). It is related to the application of innovation at the firm level, which is seen as endogenous since it can be handled by individual firms adapting the latest generally available technical knowledge.

Such micro-investment behaviour determines the rate at which technical progress raises productivity over the cycle and 'causes a transfer of profits from old to new equipment' (Kalecki, 1971, p. 173). This interpretation is also consistent with a much earlier article by Kalecki which identifies technical progress as increasing 'the degree of oligopoly' through the concentration of industry. The situation is due to the more-successful innovating firms increasing market share at the expense of less-innovative firms (Kalecki, 1940, p. 179). This endogenous innovation, through its effect on firms' marginal profit rate, becomes an important element in the forthcoming explanation of the turning points in firms' investment cycles (see section 5.4.1).

The second innovation effect is a 'semi-autonomous variable' slowly changing over time in order to provide a long-term trend over a trendless (pure) investment cycle. Major new technical knowledge (in the form of innovation) is seen by Kalecki as the most important random shock for generating growth (Sawyer, 1985, p. 68), and is exogenous because it is 'rooted in the past economic, social and technological developments rather than determined fully by the coefficients of our equations as is the case with the business cycle' (Kalecki, 1971, p. 183). The intensity of the technical progress of a society is governed by the extent of major technological innovations. This becomes the major determinant of the path of development that an economy follows. A ceiling on the rate of growth of capital expenditure is determined by the level of changes in major technology. This variable, to Kalecki, is 'semi-autonomous' because the level of changes in major technology are positively related to the size of the economy (Kalecki, 1971, p. 175).

By opening up the closed trendless investment cycle to the growth trend of major innovations, Kalecki reveals another motivation of entrepreneurs to invest apart from the cyclical factors already outlined. The problem is to understand the micro-level investment motivation related to this 'semi-autonomous' variable. The motivation for introducing major technological innovations is 'to increase profitability by reducing production costs' (Kalecki and Szeworski, 1991, p. 377). Kalecki (1954, pp. 17–18) sees this motivation in relation to innovations' long term influence on raising the degree of monopoly. Kalecki (1971, p. 151) further develops this argument by identifying entrepreneurs who invest 'today' in innovations as having 'an advantage over those having invested "yesterday" because of the technical novelties that have reached them'. The same go-ahead entrepreneurs from the version III trendless investment cycle, now see long-term innovation as an 'additional stimulus for investment' (Kalecki, 1971, p. 173). This provides the motivation to adopt exogenous major technological innovation in their firms.

The analysis of investment behaviour in relation to the cycle and trend factors presented in version III was not wholly satisfying for Kalecki. Steindl (1981b, p. 133) calls this final version 'an elegant solution, but it does not fully reflect Kalecki's ideas'. Further, Joan Robinson notes that the Polish article on long-term accumulation analysis (Kalecki, 1967) 'in Kalecki's terse style, opens up a huge field of speculation in a few paragraphs' (Robinson, 1973, pp. 90–1; quoted by Osiatyński, 1991, p. 593).

The most significant concern of version III is the pendulum model of cycles. Kalecki recognises that the difficulty with this approach is 'that if the shocks are in some sense large then the time path of output and investment is largely determined by the shocks rather than by the underlying business cycle equation' (Sawyer, 1985, p. 58). This weakens the self-generating investment cycle analysis with which Kalecki started in 1933, before Frisch and Holmes had criticised his mathematics (see note 3). Goodwin (1982) is consistent with Kalecki's own essential economic elements, but has a macro-model with non-linear equations (see section 2.7) which leads to the generation of roughly constant self-generating business cycles. It is upon this Goodwin macro-model that Kalecki's investment behaviour analysis is developed in later chapters.

The microfoundations for investment behaviour that reflects Kalecki's instability of investment within the context of long-term accumulation is produced in Chapter 5. Such a detailed analysis within a modified Kaleckian institutional framework (set out in Chapter 4) can provide a self-generating investment-cycle model with structural aspects that accommodate exogenous influences determined by history and social institutions. It is clear that 'shocks are there in any case, you have no need to drag them in forcibly' (Steindl, 1989, p. 312), but the self-generating, inherently unstable nature of investment behaviour needs to be rigorously developed at the micro-level before introducing such exogenous influences. Otherwise the random shocks themselves threaten to become the central determinants of investment cycle behaviour, a result that is not in the spirit or intention of Kalecki and his significant original insights.

Kaleckian writers on the whole have concentrated on the endogeneity of technical progress, where innovation does not play a separate role from investment (Reynolds, 1987, p. 198). This stems from the importance placed on the analysis in Steindl (1952), who first developed the Kaleckian stagnation thesis. This analysis explicitly states that innovations 'affect only the *form* which net investment takes'. Once funds and demand become attainable, this 'produces additions to the capital stock, which usually, or very often, embody some innovation, simply because there is usually a stock of innovations and ideas waiting to be applied'. This means that 'technological innovations accompany the process of investment like a shadow, they do not act on it as a propelling force' (Steindl, 1952, p. 133, original emphasis).[26]

Baran and Sweezy (1968) follow Steindl by calling the above actions 'normal' innovation, arguing that monopoly capitalists tend to place restrictions on their implementation in order to protect existing capital values. This is particularly limiting on potential innovation when investment commitments are large close to peaks on the investment cycle. Any new technological systems being developed on the fringe of the corporate world tend to be ignored by monopoly capitalists. A mismatch between new technologies and monopoly power exacerbates the secular stagnation already identified by these co-authors in the previous section.

Endogeneity of technical progress is emphasised by Sylos Labini (1990b, p. 42) when he defines induced innovation as being 'stimulated by the expansion of demand or by cost increases'. The former stimulus is to product innovation, where improvement in quality or design of the product aims to provide a larger market share to the initiating firm. The latter stimulus is to process innovation, where a more efficient production method lowers the initiating firm's costs relative to its rivals. Implementation of these innovations requires investment, while their success generally contributes higher profits and a stimulation to further investment.

Sylos Labini (1990b, p. 42) explains the nature of this induced innovation as incremental advances in technical knowledge which become embedded in the new capital stock. Although 'often of secondary importance from the scientific standpoint', this knowledge-based process is important when it develops a sufficiently powerful impetus to induce an upturn in investment. For Sylos Labini, such impetus comes from the demand- and cost-based stimuli described above, but this does not render clearly any dynamic mechanism as to when and why such stimuli come about in order for cycles to emerge. Both Steindl (1964) and Sylos Labini (1990b) see such stimuli as providing a long-term improvement to the MOP and as breaking through the 'closed circle' of a trendless investment cycle in the absence of innovation. This 'sets an upward path for the capital stock' around which the investment cycle can oscillate (Steindl, 1964, p. 431).

The monopoly power theorists recognise that secular stagnation can be avoided if induced innovation destroys existing excess capacity and provides strong marginal profit rates. Only major exogenous innovations can stimulate the many necessary small, induced, innovatory steps along the path of development (Sawyer, 1989, p. 396). This integration of exogenous with induced innovation can provide a steady stream of additional demand to counter Kalecki's negative investment feedback effects (Steindl, 1964, p. 432).[27]

Levine (1981) is critical of these monopoly power theorists for positing *ad hoc* reasons for growth via exogenous shocks. He argues that firms can never be complacent about demand barriers to their own growth. Large firms are not passive in respect of market directions, but develop new products for which they create a need in the market place. Levine sees technological innovation 'as a product' developed for identified new markets, whether in capital or consumer goods, or in services. Deficient demand induces a contraction in the investment cycle. Needs creating product developments induce expansion. Long-term investment growth occurs when expansions are longer and stronger than contractions. Levine fails to provide in his analysis an explicit outline of the institutional framework in firms that successfully produces this 'social determinism', nor any idea of how failure in this process is handled (Khalil, 1987, pp. 82–4). Levine's socially based construction is used in this study as a crucial element of the endogenous investment process, ensuring that a clear institutional framework and a sound firm motivation lie behind such a process.

Levine's approach is developed further in Shapiro (1988), who draws a distinction between intraindustry and interindustry competition. In intraindustry competition, any product innovation in differentiated industries results in imitators appearing quickly. A rapid rise in investment orders results as the innovations require the build-up of new MOP to produce these new products. This form of competition is self-defeating as market shares settle back into their original positions for what have become standardised mature industries. Poor market share improvements from such innovations, however, inhibit future investment in intraindustry competition.

Interindustry competition is more attractive because 'the firm can accelerate its growth by developing new goods or diversifying into the industries that produce them' (Shapiro, 1988, p. 79). Shapiro argues that interindustry competition encourages this transition to new products and new industries by established oligopolies or rising small firms. This form of competition enables a forceful shift to new exogenous technology systems, since all new products require new technology which is embodied in process innovation. As a result, the new industries' investment orders rise through strong interindustry competition. This produces a stronger investment expansion than innovation in intraindustry competition.

The previous section noted Sylos Labini's position that innovation as a competitive managerial tool is much more important for non-differentiated oligopolies than for differentiated oligopolies. This can be related to Shapiro's view by arguing that homogeneous industries, which have limited intraindustry competition, tend to be strong in interindustry competition because they need to look to diversification out of mature industries where process innovation opportunities at cost-effective terms have disappeared. This provides the internal firm dynamics which encourage innovatory developments based on new exogenous technological systems.

From Kalecki's analysis and the above references, there is a role for exogenous innovation in investment and growth,[28] but that role has not been analysed explicitly by any Kaleckian writer except Steindl. This encourages the view that major technological advances are *ad hoc*. In Steindl (1964, p. 430) comes the first rejection of the 'extreme position' in Steindl (1952) of denying an active role for innovations in the investment process, 'which I have no wish to uphold.' Since then, Steindl has seen the random shock of innovation as the asymmetric action that delivers a predominantly stimulating effect, lengthening expansion and shortening contraction of the investment cycle. Steindl still supports the stagnation thesis, as firms' preference for safety against highly risky innovation reduces investment and 'acts as a brake on progress' (Steindl, 1969, p. 198). The only explanation Steindl gives for major technological advances is the exogenous influences of the state as it encourages the armaments race and the 'mad haste' of business to exploit natural resources. 'Technical progress is a child of war and of haphazard shortsighted business interests' (Steindl, 1969, p. 205).

Goodwin's non-linear cycles start from Schumpeter's 'vision of growth driven by the search for ever-renewed profit through technical change' (Goodwin, 1990, p. 99). So disparate is innovative technical change that no clear pattern of activity could arise. Goodwin adds the Keynesian–Kaleckian effective demand analysis to produce business cycles. The power of demand to influence investment decisions forces innovations 'to march in step' and create 'swarms' of innovatory behaviour in a step-wise process (Goodwin, 1990, p. 86). Thus, the aggregate investment cycle has this internal dynamic of successful innovation followed by imitation, which requires a strong boom in investment and leads to growth. A downturn in the cycle is short as much development is left in the innovation for a new strong investment boom to emerge. The consequent exhaustion of most aspects of the innovation produces weak booms and prolonged slumps, leading to secular stagnation.

Goodwin's analysis depicts an undamped endogenous cycle with investment as the link between innovation and demand. There are no exogenous-type shocks to stimulate the innovatory process as with Steindl. Yet major structural innovations are not induced by the short-term cyclical process. Following Hicks (1932), such innovations are exogenous. Goodwin (1986, p. 19) recognises this by noting that 'technological history, being mainly exogenous to the economy, can explain everything'. He never goes on to explain this institutional history. There is a strong institutional– evolutionary school, also inspired by Schumpeter, which does this type of analysis and is outlined in section 3.6.

2.6 KALECKI AND THE TRAVERSE

There are structural problems specifically with the nature of the time lag attached to the attainment of capital goods. This time lag – between planning for capital accumulation and the fully operational MOP that result – needs to be analysed. The aim is to understand how differential lags affect the investment cycle, and how the investment cycle alters these same lag structures. Such interdependence has been rarely identified in investment analysis, yet they are real technical issues faced constantly by investment planners.

The traverse examines a sequence of irreversible events within the structure of production. When a change occurs (or is induced by policy) to alter the level of demand or supply in the economy at a macro level, there is a sequence of slowly evolving production decisions made by industries and firms in response to such changes. This production sequence is the traverse, or path of economic growth. If a macro change affects the investment decisions of all firms in the economy, this then affects the decisions of all firms who supply these investment goods (the capital-goods-producing industries), and then affects the decisions of all firms which supply raw materials and resources to these capital-goods industries. All these reactions take time. An increase in demand, if seen as permanent, induces a higher amount of investment by many firms, which could create technical problems of bottlenecks for the capital-goods-producing industries.

At the firm level, bottlenecks extend the time to deliver and install capital goods, slowing the process of moving to the new desired investment levels. If the new capital stock (with improved technology) is necessary for a firm to compete with other firms which already have this new capital stock, any lengthy delay may lead to serious loss in market share or even to bankruptcy. This could mean that investment does not go ahead. The firm may change direction or its insolvency may negate any need for the capital stock. Any delays to a new innovating firm in getting the capital goods delivered – due to commitments by the capital-goods-producing industry to other sectors of the economy – may reduce the perceived edge which the firm believes it has, and could lead to alterations in the investment strategy of the firm.

In this time sequence of investment, an analysis of the traverse at the firm and industry level requires an explanation that involves the technical (often engineering) methods of production, including the type of plant and equipment required to accommodate changes in the economy. Some type of MOP (for example, spade and broom) are much easier and quicker to obtain than other MOP (such as specialised hi-tech equipment). This is because the technical changes required of the capital-goods-producing firm(s) by the firm intending to invest involve questions of the skills and ability needed to produce the required new equipment and whether that effort is justified in relation to the volume of orders being placed.

The traverse raises interdependent factors, where the firm's investment decisions are dependent on other firms and industries, and over which the firm has varying degrees of influence. This study adopts a broad definition of the traverse as 'the dynamic (out of equilibrium) adjustment path in historical time' (Kriesler, 1989, pp. 1–2). It is different from the notions of the traverse used by Hicks and Lowe.[29] Kalecki never formally embraced the concept of the traverse in any of his work, but in three respects it is implicit in Kalecki's work on investment theories.

The first implicit aspect of the traverse is the production lag in Kalecki's investment cycle analysis. In all versions, the parameter in the investment function 'through which an influence of supply could enter is the lag between decision and investment [delivery of MOP]' (Steindl, 1981b, p. 133). In version I this lag assumes greatest importance (see equation (2.2)), for it is only this production lag and the negative feedback from K that generates the investment cycle (see equation (2.5)). In a 1935 review of version I, Jan Tinbergen notes that a 'happy feature of Kalecki's system is the fact that he places capital goods production in the centre' (Tinbergen, 1935, p. 269; quoted by Osiatyński, 1990, p. 462). This support is expected, since version I's ' most direct and important inspiration' is Tinbergen's own 1931 article on an endogenous cycle in shipbuilding that fluctuates due to the time taken to increase tonnage construction and the intensity of tonnage reaction to changes in its volume (Osiatyński, 1990, p. 441).

Tinbergen has a micro-level cycle, but the inverse function on tonnage changes is automatic. For Kalecki, the macro-level cycle has micro-assumptions about individual entrepreneurs making investment decisions based on average profit rates and where instability stems from the assumed production lags in the system. This study constructs an endogenous micro-investment cycle model which is based on entrepreneurs' investment behaviour. This allows development of a micro-dimension to the traverse, which neither the automatism of Tinbergen nor the micro-assumptions of Kalecki can achieve.[30]

The second implicit aspect of the traverse is in relation to the path of economic growth. Kalecki's analysis in version III is described as 'life is a traverse' by Kriesler (1989, p. 14), where the long-term economic growth path is a slowly changing component of a chain of short-period situations (Kalecki, 1971, p. 165). Lowe recognised the significance of Kalecki's attempt not to split instability analysis into long-period and short-period influences (Lowe, 1976, p. 10, fn. 11). Lowe himself used this same approach in an earlier article (1955) and sees Kalecki as providing 'valuable support' for this view of growth (Lowe, 1976, p. 10).

Application of this sequential investment approach to growth is very different for Lowe (1976) and Kalecki (1968). Lowe uses it to show that the specificity of capital goods causes structural disproportionalities which affect the investment decisions of firms and the growth path. He concentrates on the effect of investment decisions when put into operation. Lags in meeting capital-stock demands occur if decisions are made to increase investment, while excess capacities emerge if investment decisions are curtailed. Such effects remain in the system for a length of time and flow back to the capital-goods-producing industries, in particular to the basic machine tool stage. This means that the growth path suffers from structural disproportionalities due to the technical requirements of producing new specific capital goods.

Kalecki uses the same sequential approach to show that the specificity of capital goods makes new capital goods more productive than old capital goods, thus capturing higher profit rates for the former. Kalecki is still concentrating on his effective-demand agenda in this analysis, showing how the determination of investment decisions is affected by profits obtained with the benefit of innovation in new capital goods. Implicit in this analysis is the supply constraint on growth. As noted in the previous section, the ceiling of an expansion in the investment cycle is determined by the technical ability to innovate, which then has a negative effect on the trend path of economic growth. It is this structural supply element which then feeds back into future and current investment decisions through modifications and alterations.

Lowe's concerns arise during the production-delivery stage, while Kalecki's concerns arise during the decision-making stage of the investment process. These two perspectives on the sequential time

path of investment by Lowe and Kalecki are incorporated into a firm-
and industry-based micro-investment analysis in section 5.5.

Kalecki adopts explicitly Lowe's structural disproportionality of
producing specific capital goods, but only within the context of
planned socialist economies. Kalecki neglects in capitalism what he
analyses in detail for socialism: that there are technical-structural
impediments in transferring investment decisions into capital stock
which could reflect back on the original investment decisions. Lowe is
aware that all societies have to develop policies to overcome structural
features of capital stock production, irrespective of the type of
economic system. Kalecki's concerns with effective demand in
capitalism concealed structural disproportionalities. Applying his
socialist planning concerns in this latter area to capitalism raises
Kalecki's third aspect of the traverse, called the shiftability of capital
goods.

Kalecki (1963) analyses the structure of investment under conditions
where the planners are aiming to increase the relative share of
investment in the national income in order to reach a higher growth
rate for the whole economy (r). To achieve this objective, it is
necessary for the growth rate of the capital goods producing sector (r_i)
to increase first, before r rises. This is necessary since accumulation in
capital goods industries is required so that such capital goods can be
used to establish a higher growth in the economy. There is a
transitional period where $r_i > r$, entailing a high share of investment
allocated to the capital goods sector, one which is greater than that
required after the new higher r is achieved. As the higher r is
approached, the relative share of investment allocated to capital goods
industries should be reduced so that a broader market of goods and
services is established.

Halevi (1981, p. 223) notes that Kalecki's analysis of the constraints
in the transitional period of a policy to increase strongly the rate of
investment growth 'serves as an important warning against the bias
towards rising accumulation rates' in Eastern European socialist
economies. This is an important policy issue, however, from a
theoretical point of view 'Kalecki's approach is subject to the same
criticism levied against the inability of two sector models to take into
proper account the structural transformations operating within the
investment sector itself' (Halevi, 1981, pp. 223–4).

Kalecki's awareness of this theoretical limitation leads him to
introduce the concept of 'shiftability of capital goods' in section 5 of
Kalecki (1963, pp. 109–11). Here he discusses the possibility of
increasing investment without having to expand the investment goods
sector more rapidly than total productive capacity. He identifies two

'shiftability' factors as allowing some relaxation of the constraining influence created by the productive capacity of the investment sector on the difference $r_i - r$. The first factor is changing the way in which some equipment is used ('e.g. the possibility of turning plant used in the manufacture of consumer durables to production of machinery': Kalecki, 1972b, p. 109). The second factor is changing the structure of foreign trade (e.g. 'increasing imports of machinery at the expense of either cutting down imports of consumer goods or increasing exports of these goods': Kalecki, 1972b, p. 109). Both factors relate to the 'shiftability of machines' (Halevi, 1981, p. 224) either from within the economy or from an external source.

Once the two shiftability factors are introduced and the goal of increasing investment more rapidly than national income (i.e. $r_iI > rI$) is maintained, then part of the difference $r_iI - rI$ results from the change in the use made of capital equipment, or in the structure of foreign trade. This part of the difference Kalecki denotes as $g(r_i - r)I$, where g is the coefficient of shiftability of machines, and is ≤ 1.

Halevi makes explicit the traverse which Kalecki has implied in this above analysis:

> In a simple two sector model the meaningfulness of the coefficient of transferability . . . [g] depends very much on the implicit assumptions about the different lengths in the construction period of capital equipment. No hidden assumptions are needed in a Lowe type model in which the period of construction is uniform and it is equal to one year. (Halevi, 1981, p. 224)

It is at this point 'that Lowe's model can be seen as supplementing Kalecki's discussion of structural problems in the investment goods sector' (Kriesler, 1989, p. 16). This can be seen in the situation when reinvestment in the capital goods sector of its own total output is inadequate to meet the planned difference $(r_i - r)$ needed to reach a particular growth rate in total production. Under such circumstances the structure of investment must be altered by varying the coefficient of shiftability (g). This is very complex in Kalecki's model due to the varying construction periods of capital equipment; however, in Lowe's model this changing structure can be analysed upon the basis of a uniform period of construction.

Halevi (1983) applies Lowe's model to examine how excess capacity comes about due to the non-shiftability of machines which are installed in the consumption-goods sector. The more specific the machines are, the lower is Kalecki's 'g' coefficient, the more dependent is growth on the simple reinvestment process. In the meantime, excess capacity and unemployment builds up in the consumption goods sector which then reacts back negatively on the capital-goods sector by damping down investment decisions and the reinvestment programme.

Lowe (1976, p. 31) splits the capital-goods sector into two subsections: 1a – which produces MOP that are applied in both subsectors 1a and 1b; and 1b – which produces MOP for the consumption-goods sector. This split adds meaning and analytical depth to Kalecki's 'g' coefficient; the higher the 'g' value, the more capital stock in sector 1 and especially subsector 1a, the more flexibility in the traverse. Yet the unstructured nature of this shiftability coefficient allows complex issues outside a uniform construction period to be discussed. For this reason, section 5.5 outlines an investment model which incorporates Kalecki's shiftability into Lowe's categories of reproduction, without Lowe's limitation of uniform lengths in the construction period of capital equipment and plant.[31] This requires an explicit investment profile of how individual investment decisions are made and then translated into actual MOP through production in the capital goods sector.

The investment profile unites Kalecki's investment-decision concerns in the 'monopoly capitalism' writings with his investment-production concerns in the 'socialist planning' writings at the micro (firm and industry) level. Lowe's reproduction schema allows this uniting of two aspects of Kalecki's work which has only been explicitly considered together in one article (Halevi, 1981), and then only in relation to the macro-issues of growth and planning. This approach has not been used to consider investment instability at the micro-level, which is at the heart of this study.

2.7 INVESTMENT MODELS: THEORETICAL BASIS AND EMPIRICAL SUPPORT

Kalecki and Keynes, in their independent analyses of output and employment, have as the central component an investment model with rudimentary firm behaviour that emphasises effective demand and financial conditions. This is the starting point for all investment models that follow these two authors. The Kaleckian view, as outlined in section 2.3, sees firms aiming for the largest surplus, given the cyclical variations in the existing competitive and distributional factors. It is on the basis of this surplus, and the related influence of effective demand and finance, that investment decisions are made. This is in contradistinction to the Keynes-based growth-maximising investment models. Investment models reviewed in this section conform to an endogenous investment cycle with microeconomic foundations compatible with this Kaleckian view.

The theoretical studies detailed below impart some insights into the cyclical nature of investment. The existence of investment cycles is based on short-term determination of investment. Another way of looking at this instability is from the long-term growth perspective. From this perspective, the volume of investment cannot grow more rapidly than the growth of technical knowledge and the size of the population. Investment instability in investment is then seen as the result of differential timing in investment commitments and modifications. Effective demand and financial conditions thus affect this timing. The long-term view sees innovation as the consequence of technical progress, but providing a feedback effect on short-term investment through capacity utilisation and profitability in the manner described in section 2.5.

Asimakopulos (1977) offers detailed microfoundations to Kalecki's investment analysis and its 'doubled-sided' relationship to profits. He begins by noting real historical time, with current investment predetermined by decisions taken in the past. Such current investment together with capitalists' consumption determine profits. This is the basis of effective demand, output and capacity utilisation. Financial ability for investment comes from this linkage. Profits also render the incentive for new investment plans, which are modified by 'current conditions', to produce actual investment commitments. Asimakopulos's model specifies the causal links in the Kaleckian investment process. This involves interdependence of profits and investment, while moving through real time towards the long term. However, by taking investment as given at the start, the analysis has some indeterminacy. The important investment upturn is associated with 'inviting opportunities for technical progress' (p. 340), but without any causal explanation. Susceptibility of investment to instability is not explained by Asimakopulos's model.

Eichner (1987, pp. 427–537) takes the investment process one step further towards determinacy in the micro-setting. He concentrates on the role of the 'megacorp' (or oligopoly) in investment planning, distinguishing between investment to expand capacity and investment to reduce costs of production. Both are an incentive to invest, due to their expected positive effects on profits. One source of investment instability comes from the timing of additions to capacity and how close such timing coincides with the growth of sales. Too much addition to capacity produces the Kaleckian feedback of overaccumulation. Too little addition to capacity concedes market share and reduces barriers to entry in a Steindlian manner. Eichner (1987, p. 456) uses a lagged sales accelerator model for this type of investment.[32] External funding only serves as a supplementary source of finance to the megacorp, unlike its crucial importance to small firms (Eichner, 1987, p. 488). Eichner sees the 'optimal' debt–equity ratio determined by the firm as crucial in controlling Kalecki's increasing risk problem (p. 480).

The other source of investment instability that Eichner identifies comes from the timing of technical progress incorporated in cost-reducing new MOP. This process can stimulate investment upturns with the destruction of old capital stock capacity. Investment downturns can be enforced by postponements in the introduction of new technology. Eichner (1987, p. 456) sees the 'rate of technical progress' as determining this type of investment. The problem with Eichner's dichotomy is that it is difficult to determine the extent to which the new machine replaces the old in order to reduce production costs and the extent to which additional capacity is involved. Often replacement machines include higher capacity due to better technology.

The SVTRP pricing model at the core of Eichner's analysis leads to a lack of microdynamic cyclical causal linkage in the investment process (as noted in section 2.3.2). His analysis of financial constraints and investment incentives, nevertheless provides an important basis for the investment model developed in Chapters 4 and 5.

Using the Levine (1981) 'needs creation' endogenous investment approach, Ong and Levine (1982) develop an endogenous business cycle with the central determinant being the investment strategy of megacorps. The timing in implementing investment projects is crucial in that early entry with new process technology or product design bestows advantages over rival firms. Competing firms follow closely the implementing leader. This results in investment clusters, as large rival corporations execute in tandem long-term strategic investment plans. Exhaustion of the main strategic investment opportunities during the hastening process, with the corresponding Kaleckian financial constraints, leads to a downturn in investment activity.

The investment upturn in Ong and Levine (1982) is based on the costs of postponing the long term investment strategy which negates a firm's primary objective of expansion in order to survive. Market share competitive pressures *à la* Steindl encourage forward movement of investment plans, especially in areas of product innovation *à la* Schumpeter. This induces the creation of new needs in weak industrial structures, as firms attempt to gain a dominant position. It can also augment the dominance of certain firms in mature industrial structures. Financial resources are decisive in allowing a firm not only to negate, but also to exploit pressures for postponement in recessions.

The essence of all the above investment models is their endogeneity, where cycles of investment are produced by entrepreneurs' decisions based on elements that are internal to the cycle itself. These elements can be grouped into three: profitability, excess capacity and financial constraints (represented by the debt–equity ratio). Given the non-linear Goodwin specification of the investment cycle (see equation (2.10)), random shocks are not necessary to produce oscillations. For this reason, Goodwin (1989, p. 250) argues that Kalecki 'was basically sound in his [version I] approach' to the investment cycle where oscillations neither explode nor become damped, despite using a very specific zero coefficient in his linear difference equation. Kalecki's aim to explain, in a Marxian tradition, that capitalism is bound to oscillate can now be shown in a mathematically generalised non-linear form.

Discrete time lag (Δt) variables are used in Kalecki's investment cycle model. Such variables illustrate the nature of the investment problem without the 'horrendous difficulties' of more realistic continuous time (non-linear) models (Goodwin, 1989, p. 251). Finite endogenous deterministic models, like Kalecki's, can illustrate highly erratic and quite unpredictable behaviour in the investment process, even though exogenous shocks are absent. Entrepreneurs must, and do, make investment decisions within a closed endogenous world. These decisions create motions of lagged investment activity which follow recognisable cyclical patterns, though these cycles have patterns that are always changing.

For Goodwin (1990, pp. 8–21), the cyclical pattern is a highly mathematical non-linear differential system. This system is free to vibrate around a wide range of motions from a slightly irregular to a wildly chaotic fashion, all within a catchment area determined by the domain of attraction or repulsion. Innovation embodied in new MOP generates this pattern, but no micro-level behaviour is specified by Goodwin which can explain the human agency behind this pattern. This study develops a qualitative analytic model of specific industry investment behaviour in terms of repellers and attractors, while accommodating for random shocks as part of a flexible cyclical mechanism of investment behaviour.[33]

Important studies provide empirical support for Kaleckian-type investment models. An early 1950s study by Hastay (1954) brings together statistical data on the magnitude and course of investment in the USA over the first 50 years of the twentieth century. Two of its conclusions are relevant. First, Hastay presents evidence of cyclical behaviour of investment at aggregate and industry level. He notes it is in 'manufacturing and mining, which in all years absorb the largest part of business fixed capital expenditures, [that] we find the closest conformity of investment outlays to the course of general business' (Hastay, 1954, p. 11). This supports the Kaleckian view of manufacturing as the 'locomotive' sector of the economy, especially in regard to aggregate investment. Secondly, Hastay sees investment cycles as reflecting the timing of investment commitments. Investment plans are long-term strategies which are executed or postponed according to effective demand and financial constraints (Hastay, 1954, p. 30).

Such observational data by Hastay form the basis for econometric studies which examine the extent of influence of various Kaleckian elements on the pattern of manufacturing investment. These studies are at either the industry-firm level or are aggregative, all of which add empirical weight to the Kaleckian approach. Kalecki (1954, pp. 109–12) made a pioneering crude empirical estimation in support of the version II investment model, with its passive role for capacity utilisation (see equation (2.8)). Chenery (1952) provides empirical support for an accelerator investment model with an active role for the capacity utilisation factor along Steindlian lines. Streever (1960) follows this line further at the industry level by reviewing a series of interview studies and then fitting an investment model with a capacity utilisation variable to data for four major US industrial sectors.

Meyer and Kuh (1957), in an extensive econometric study, incorporate the financial constraint into the 'accelerator-residual funds hypothesis'. They work with data on capital expenditures of 700 firms in 12 manufacturing industries using cross-sections within industries in one year, and cross-sections of averages across all years of data. This work strongly supported the basic Kaleckian investment approach, and it led to a series of other studies emphasising the importance of internal liquidity (depreciation charges and retained earnings) and the constraints of debt–equity ratios within an accelerator model. These studies are reviewed in Evans (1969, pp. 122–33).

Sensitivity of investment commitments to fluctuations in available internal finance is crucial to the pattern of investment cycles. This has been a strong empirical result in many studies (see Fazzari *et al.*, 1988, p. 164). Kuh and Meyer (1963, p. 383) conclude in their empirical study that 'major financing problems seem to strike manufacturing firms most often late in a cyclical recovery when large-scale plant and equipment outlays are being financed'. Sharp reductions in liquid balances at the top of the investment cycle exacerbates problems and makes firms more susceptible to an investment contraction.

Eisner (1978) surveys over 15 years of individual US firms' capital expenditure data and notes that the past level of actual profits is significant in the timing of investment. This investment can be for both expansion and replacement since they are positively correlated in the study. It also concludes that the rate of return on capital stock is subsumed under firms' savings as the cost and associated speed of adjustment of actual to desired capital stock impacts on accumulated profits (p. 113). Thus, 'firms with declining sales will represent observations with generally less secure investment programs – and these may prove quite susceptible to greater reductions the greater the sales decline' (Eisner, 1978, p. 130). This susceptibility is at the heart of investment instability in this book.

A recent detailed empirical study by Fazzari *et al.* (1988, p. 172) concludes that '[i]nternal funds help explain investment in all classes [of firms], even for firms that have much more cash flow than investment'. The study also argues (p. 183) that mature firms may be sensitive to reducing investment when cash flows fall, rather than seek more costly external finance. At the same time, small firms with low internal funds have limited access to external funds. Such behaviour by small and mature firms intensifies the financial constraints and the potential for investment instability in true Kaleckian manner.

The above studies are based on industry and firm data. Using the effective demand and financial constraint elements of these studies, some macro-investment models have been constructed for *ex post* regression analysis against actual aggregate investment activity. Sylos Labini (1967) does an early regression test based on Italian investment from 1951 to 1965. His successful regressions are built on the following aggregate (actual capital expenditure) investment [I'] function:

$$I' = \zeta \, (V, G, \dot{G}, L) \qquad (2.11)$$

The functional variables are all Kaleckian elements. The degree of unused capacity, [V], is the measure of output demand or sales; the share of current profits, G, is the internal finance measure; the rate of change of profit share $\dot{G}$, is the incentive-to-invest element; and total liquidity of the bank system, L, is the external finance constraint (especially for the needs of small firms).

The 1970s and early 1980s saw a hiatus in specific Kaleckian macro-model testing as neo-classical and Tobin's 'q' investment theories became the conventional approaches. Some comparative business fixed-investment studies over this period include accelerator-Keynesian type models. None of them look at the surplus-oriented Kaleckian approach. For example, Bischoff (1971) compares five investment models, of which two are cash flow and accelerator. In this way, output (or demand) and profit variables are examined separately rather than together. When these two models are combined in Clark (1979), the results (see p. 93) are the most volatile of the five models tested, but also the best in terms of direction and amplitude compared to actual investment.

Eisner and Strotz (1963, p. 159) criticise the accelerator–residual-funds approach on the grounds that the cash flow (or liquidity) variables are highly correlated with output (or sales) variables. Fazzari and Mott (1986–7) address this criticism in their econometric test of a specific Kalecki–Steindl investment model. Their study also uses US investment data from the more volatile period 1970–82. The noted instability feature of Kaleckian investment theory emerges more clearly over the highly turbulent period of investment experienced since the early 1970s.

The regression study by Fazzari and Mott (1986–7) is based on the following aggregate investment function:

$$I' = \xi \, (u, F/N, CC) \qquad (2.12)$$

The functional variables are capacity utilisation level, u; internal cash flow represented by the amount of internal cash flow a firm can use to finance investment, F; divided by the supply price of MOP, N; and the cash commitments to interest payments, CC, as the financial constraint on 'increasing risk' problems. The authors proxy the u variable using sales data, measure internal finance by lagged after-tax profits plus depreciation charges minus dividends, and use lagged interest expense for CC. A large pooled cross-section sample of firm data enable the authors to indicate a strong positive independent influence for internal finance over sales on investment (see also Fazzari *et al.*, 1988). External financial constraint is the third independent influence, and it is measured as a flow of committed cash flows, as against the usual stock of debt and liquidity measures used as financial constraints (e.g. Meyer and Kuh, 1957).

The strong regression results that Fazzari and Mott obtain supports the Kaleckian investment approach both at the micro and macro levels. Twenty industries estimated separately have 'almost always' the statistically significant sign predicted by the theory. At the aggregate level, the results annually produce weak sales coefficients but solid finance and risk coefficients. These results indicate 'bunching' of industry groups to produce the aggregate investment cycle.[34] Despite this bunching, Fazzari and Mott (1986–7, p. 184) found that 'internal finance is quite important for explaining why different firms invest different amounts at any point in time'.

Two problems arise from the Fazzari and Mott study. First is the use of proxies for the variables in equation (2.12), which are then 'lagged to account for the time between investment decisions and actual expenditure' (p. 178). This is an *ad hoc* approach to the time horizon in an investment pattern. For econometric empirical testing, this approach is inevitable and shows the plausibility of the hypothesis. However, lagged proxies themselves are not part of the theory, thus there is no clear behavioural analysis of how time fits into the types of theoretical variables identified. The historically interpretative analysis conducted in this study requires a clearly identifiable conception of the investment time pattern to be incorporated into the theory.

The second problem is raised by Fazzari and Mott, when they describe their results as implying 'that there is greater cyclical variation in investment than can be accounted for by changes in the independent variables alone' (p. 182). The authors surmise that Keynes's 'animal spirits' may have something to do with this. The approach taken in the susceptibility-cycle model of this book is to set out explicitly a Keynes-inspired behavioural approach, within a Kaleckian model of investment. This allows the type of variables tested in the Fazzari and Mott study to be located in a behavioural approach that makes 'animal spirits' observable in a historical setting.

Five macroeconometric models that include a Kaleckian investment function of the type described in this section have shown significant statistical results. They are the Italian MOSYL model originally set out in Sylos Labini (1967) and reviewed in Del Monte (1981); the French model by Malinvaud as described in Asimakopulos (1977, p. 351); the Eichner-based US (Forman and Eichner, 1981) and UK (Arestis *et al.*, 1985–6) models; and the US long-run survival model, using liquidity and profitability variables (Chamberlain and Gordon, 1989).

Stegman (1982) examines the two-way Kaleckian relationship between investment and profitability. He tests an investment function that distinguishes between the profits accelerator as the incentive to invest and accumulated profits as the financial constraint to invest. The Australian-based empirical results show an asymmetric relationship, with a profit share fall capable of reducing investment but a profit share rise providing no stimulus to investment on its own. This is consistent with Goodwin's approach which needs innovation as the profits incentive at the investment cycle trough. Stegman's study also explains Hawkins's (1979, p. 210) observation that an increase in the debt–equity ratio increases the willingness of firms to use debt for purposes other than capital expenditure when there is a lack of incentive to invest in MOP (as in the mid-1970s).

Carmichael and Dews (1987) examine empirically for Australia various determinants of investment. Profitability is seen as fitting best the unstable pattern of investment. Periods of poor fit in this relationship are seen by Carmichael and Dews (1987, p. 34) as being related to low rates of capacity utilisation at a time when profits have increased. This supports Stegman's study.

All the investment models referred to above provide strong theoretical and empirical support for a Kaleckian-based investment-cycle pattern. Evaluation of Kaleckian analysis of investment in this chapter identifies observable endogenous and structural (or exogenous) elements that are central to explaining this pattern. Lacking in this analysis is any underlying behavioural explanation of investment instability. The next chapter evaluates behavioural analyses that can render the Kaleckian elements highly susceptible to change.

NOTES

1. 'the institutional framework of a social system is a basic element of its economic dynamics' (Kalecki, 1970, p. 311). From this quote it is clear that Kalecki's analysis is built on the basis of observation into how contemporary capitalism actually operates. As noted by Sardoni (1987, p. 138):

    > The claim that Kalecki's analysis of capitalist economies is more 'realistic' than those of Marx and Keynes finds its justification not in Kalecki's having provided a more detailed description of the economy but in his having developed a more correct process of abstraction, one that furnishes a more rigorous model and, hence, an analysis of phenomena that corresponds more closely to reality.

2. Notation by Kalecki varies from version to version, and even within the same version notation varies from one publication to another. This is particularly the case for investment related variables; e.g. Kalecki (1935) uses I for investment orders and L for deliveries of these orders, while Kalecki (1937b) uses D for investment decisions (which in the context of his article he means investment orders, as in the previous article) and I for the volume of output of investment goods industries. The notation used throughout is based on Kalecki's notation in the original Polish monograph (Kalecki, 1933) and the abbreviated English Chapter 1 in Kalecki (1971, pp. 1–14).

3. The change was forced on Kalecki by the criticisms of Frisch and Holmes (1935) that the mixed difference-differential equation (2.7) required precise parametric values of rather remote possibility to achieve the continuously generating cycles that Kalecki wanted.

4. Kalecki (1954) in Chapter 15 analyses two other development factors apart from innovations. Rentiers' savings are seen as 'an obstacle rather than a stimulus to development' (p. 161), while population growth is discounted as a stimulus altogether (what matters is increase in purchasing power). These two factors are incorporated in Chapter 6 as exogenous factors to the susceptibility cycle model.

5. Joan Robinson and Kalecki had a long-running dispute over the role of technical progress in investment decision-making (see Osiatyński, 1991, pp. 590–3). Robinson supported Keynes's 'animal spirits', with technical progress *permitting* accumulation to go on faster than the labour force is growing, but not *causing* high profits as Kalecki argued. In Kalecki (1968), Robinson felt that he compromises to the point of recognising 'go-ahead firms are installing equipment embodying the latest inventions in the hope of gaining a higher rate of profit than the average at the expense of their rivals' (Robinson, 1973, pp. 90–1; quoted by Osiatyński, 1991, p. 593).

6. In relation to influences on his book, *Maturity and Stagnation in American Capitalism* (1952), Steindl notes that the book's issue 'was a very Marxian problem, but my methods of dealing with it were Kaleckian'. Steindl then goes on to state that Kalecki 'remains my inspiration and my reference system till to-day' (Steindl, 1984, p. 8).

7. Steindl (1952) uses what Rowthorn (1981, p. 199, fn. 8) describes as a 'brilliant analogy' for comparing the need for planned excess capacity with the need for liquidity preference in Keynes's *General Theory*. The demand for surplus capacity in anticipation of future growth in sales corresponds to the transactions demand for money. The demand for surplus capacity to meet unforeseen contingencies in future sales growth corresponds to the precautionary demand for money. 'Just what corresponds to the speculative demand for money is not entirely clear' (Rowthorn, 1981, p. 199, fn. 8).

8. The rest of the notation in equation (2.9) is same as that used in the equations in section 2.2, from which this analysis is derived. The notation in this equation, and in the rest of this chapter, varies from the original in the respective literature in order to maintain a consistent notation pattern throughout the book.

9. Measurement of u by Steindl at the aggregate level is Y/Z, whereas at the firm and industry level production is related to sales, T, so that at the micro-level $u_1 = T/Z$. Micro-level excess capacity, whether planned or unplanned, is then $1-u_1$ (Steindl, 1952, p. 13). The measure of capacity, Z, is arbitrary. Conventionally Z is an output capacity measure, which unfortunately is liable to variations simply due to changes in the intensity of use (i.e. how fast output is produced in any given time period), or in the duration of use (i.e. extension or reduction of hours of operation of the capital stock). Steindl (1952, p. 14) alternatively suggests using an input capacity measure, in terms of the maximum possible number of hours for which the machine can be operated during the year by the input of labour. He also suggests that a guide to excess capacity can be a particular type of equipment which occupies a 'strategic position' in the plant. Both alternatives involve arbitrary judgements as well.

10. The Steindl analogy of planned excess capacity to planned liquidity preference (see note 7), can be extended to take account of barriers to entry. This excess capacity is planned by a firm in order to hoard capital stock capacity in anticipation of intraindustry competitive pressures by other firms. This corresponds with the speculative demand for money, which is holding on to 'idle money' in anticipation of future competitive pressure on the bond market. When these pressures push bond prices up, speculators have the idle money ready to purchase bonds at cheap prices in order to make capital gains.

11. This same Kalecki–Steindl framework is used by Baran and Sweezy (1968, p. 66) to develop a theory of secular stagnation based on the tendency of the economic surplus and its investment-seeking portion to rise. This surplus becomes dissipated in economic waste as a result of underconsumption reflected in a secular rise of excess capacity. The resulting effect is reduced investment and long-run stagnation. Foster

(1986) reinforces Baran and Sweezy's analytical framework at a more concrete historical level. Some aspects of Baran and Sweezy's analysis is relevant to this study (see section 2.4 on monopoly power, and section 2.5 on the role of innovation); however, its overall underconsumptionist theme is a long-run trend model which is not of concern here.

12. In support of the neglect of investment in Kalecki's microanalysis, see Kriesler (1987). It is the *effects* of the mark-up and resulting profitability on investment and income distribution which are analysed. The investment decision is examined only at the macro-level in terms of the two roles of profit. See also Dougherty (1980, pp. 143–53), who points out that the role of profits is examined by Kalecki in relation to macro-investment instability and business cycles.

13. For details of these empirical reasons and why he regards the qualitative results of his model is not sensitive to this assumption, see Goldstein (1982, ch. 5). His concern about mark-up variability makes the results insensitive. A concern about the nature of the investment decision must take domestic intraindustry competition into account, see Sylos Labini (1979b).

14. A critical review that rejects the Modigliani–Miller theorem from the position of Kalecki's increasing risk concept is developed in Mott (1982, pp. 18–31).

15. Chilosi (1982) provides an account of how Kalecki's principle of increasing risk is based on the work of a Polish colleague in the mid-1930s, Marek Breit. Chilosi (1982, p. 86) quotes Breit as recognising that 'if the entrepreneur invests his own capital, . . . he calculates the risk only once, *and not twice*' (original emphasis).

16. At an aggregate economy level, Asimakopulos (1983) argues that 'finance', in terms of possessing money to effectuate expenditures, is lacking in the short term until the multiplier process works itself out fully. This, he explains, constrains capitalists' income by limiting their decisions to make expenditures, particular investment. This is a different concept of financial constraint from the micro-based arguments in the text. The Asimakopulos argument refers to the problem that the capitalist class, as a whole, has in raising the necessary funds during the construction period of investment.

This is in contrast to Kalecki's proposition that 'capitalists, as a whole, determine their own profits by the extent of their investment and personal consumption . . . [they] do not need money in order to achieve this' (Kalecki, 1971, p. 13). Asimakopulos's view created a vigorous debate, to which Kregel (1989) provides an effective resolution which takes account of the profits from sales of investment goods during the construction period. This ensures that 'the debts and credits cancel within the capitalist class . . . no "time" is required for Kalecki's multiplier to work, it is instantaneous within the defined period' (Kregel, 1989, p. 197). Thus, Kalecki's original proposition still stands.

17. Kalecki (1954, pp. 91-5) made the judgement that borrower's risk would be the earlier limiting constraint on borrowing rather than lender's risk. This is because, generally, the firm borrowing is closer to its own cash flow situation than the lender. This is, however, not always the situation. Having committed the company to a large investment project over a long period, if cash flow problems arise half-way through completing the project, lender's risk can become relevant. 'Mothballing' the project is expensive in terms of sunk costs (or even 'temporary suspend costs'). The firm may continue to borrow so as to not incur these sunk costs, thus coming up against lender's risk constraint, or at least the higher interest that may come with it.

18. Sylos Labini (1984a, p. 124) goes on to argue that:

> Financial barriers are especially important in the case of integrated groups of industry, whether vertically or horizontally, which organise finance companies for the purpose of supplying funds to the enterprises they control or granting credit to the buyers of the products. Such a practice is widespread in the automobile industry.

This aspect of financial barriers linked to integrated groups will be important in the empirical patterns identified in Chapter 7.

19. The Kaldorian view of growth provides theoretical support to this view. Kaldor's 'First Law of Economic Growth' can be stated as: 'The engine of growth hypothesis: there is a strong relationship between the rate of growth of GDP and the rate of growth of manufacturing production' (Reynolds, 1987, p. 200).

20. Kalecki's four influences on the degree of monopoly are: industrial concentration, sales promotion, tacit price agreements and trade union wage demands. Kalecki recognises that these influences have contradictory effects. However, he argues that the concentration and sales promotion influences would tend gradually to raise ϕ over time as capitalism progresses (see Kalecki, 1943b, pp. 20–1).

21. The 'industry' can only be defined within the context of the nature of intraindustry competition. This depends on the specific regional or global competitive market that is being examined in any particular industry case study. Kalecki's general cost-determined manufacturing industry is adequate for the theoretical purposes of setting up an investment cycle model.

22. In discussions with Sylos Labini (September 1990), he told me that he raised the matter of Kalecki's pricing equation with Kalecki himself. Kalecki admitted that the equation was only relevant to differentiated oligopolies.

23. In the modern Marxist theories of the state, it is the support of monopoly power by the state through the twin contradictory functions of 'accumulation' and 'legitimation' that create recurring crises for state economic policies, leading to political cycles of both short-term and long-term dimensions (see O'Connor, 1973).

24. Hayes and Stone (1990, p. 443, fn. 3) note in their review of political business-cycle literature that: 'Earlier versions of the electoral model are presented in Kalecki (1937)[sic] and Schumpeter (1939)'. Their definition of the electoral model of political business cycles, based on Nordhaus (1975), is of the political party in office manipulating the economy to win elections. Empirical evidence on the electoral model 'appears either negative or inconclusive' (Osiatyński, 1990, p. 575), which leads Zarnowitz (1985) to reject the political business cycle concept. Yet this is not Kalecki's model. Kalecki sees *capitalists* manipulating governments during booms, not necessarily when the election is out of the way, while stimulus occurs at recession, not necessarily when the election is due. Transmission of economic interests from economic classes to the state by an electoral business cycle 'is unsatisfactory, for in the latter concept the distinction between social classes and their respective interests is washed away in pre-electoral manipulations aimed at gaining universal popularity' (Osiatyński, 1990, p. 576). Hayes and Stone (1990, p. 442) develop the 'partisan cycles (persistent differences between parties)' and find that, overall, such cycles are empirically significant. This is a cycle concept closer to Kalecki's analysis, because of the relative influence of economic class interests on political parties' policies.

25. Technological innovation is the commercial implementation of new technical knowledge. This knowledge is derived from scientific or engineering developments in specific research and development (R&D) activities or in the course of day-to-day production and marketing activity (Sahal, 1981, p. 42). This ranges from epoch-making major new technological innovations (like the microcomputer chip) to minor marketing-based product innovations (like modifying a car model by adding fins to its rear). All technological innovation requires substantial investment in new MOP. Kalecki also recognises another form of innovative behaviour which 'is largely concentrated on a "scientific organisation" of the assembly process which does not involve heavy investment' (Kalecki, 1954, p. 159). This is non-technological innovation, based on improved labour practices and new marketing angles which do not involve modifying the product, and requires only a minor level of capital expenditure. Like Kalecki, for the purposes of this study, the analysis will be limited to technological innovation. Due to non-technological innovation requiring only a

small proportion of expenditure being allocated to investment, its inclusion would not significantly alter the analysis or the conclusions derived.

26. Later on in this section Steindl's rejection of this extreme 1952 position is examined. As a history of economic thought note, his 1952 position strongly influenced the Kaleckian view of innovation for a long time after 1952, as discussed in relation to Baran and Sweezy (1968) and Sylos Labini (1990b) in the following two paragraphs. See also Foster (1986, pp. 101–2).

27. As an example, the major innovation of the automobile induced many incremental minor innovations, both process- and product-related, which continued to stimulate demand and new MOP for a long time (see section 3.6 for more detailed analysis of these processes).

28. This position is rejected in the Kaldorian view of growth. Investment has embodied in it technical progress and there is no exogenous technical progress. 'The logical conclusion from this line of reasoning is that technical progress no longer has a role to play as a separate source of productivity growth since investment accounts for virtually all economic growth' (Reynolds, 1987, p. 198). The Kaldorian framework is quite different from the Kaleckian framework pursued in this study.

29. This definition describes an *observed* traverse, where a particular path of change is identified in real historic time. There are more specific definitions of the traverse. John Hicks used the term 'traverse' first (Lowe, 1976, p. 10, fn. 11), and then went on to use it in an Austrian-type model, where he defined the 'traverse' as tracing out 'the path which will be followed when the steady state is subjected to some kind of disturbance' (Hicks, 1973, p. 81). To Hicks it is an *abstract* traverse, as he is concerned with the abstract changes which occur in shifting from one equilibrium state to a new equilibrium state due to some exogenous shock in the model. Adolph Lowe describes the traverse as the 'intermediate processes required to achieve a change in the rate of growth' (1976, p. 10, fn. 11). To Lowe it is an *instrumental* traverse, where a set of policy changes are introduced in order to reach an identified goal for the economy. My thanks to Allen Oakley for providing the taxonomic classification and the explicit terms used in the three definitional forms of the traverse described above.

30. In a recent review of the economic theory of the traverse by Kriesler (1989), all the traverse models are developed at the macro (aggregate) or meso (two- or three-sector economies) level. Yet the issues underlying the traverse are basically micro (firm and industry) level concerns, that the existing models only make certain behavioural assumptions in order to develop their more aggregate models. The micro-investment behaviour is not analysed in any detail.

31. Kalecki recognises the limitations of assuming a uniform length in the construction period of investment. Kalecki (1957) explicitly examines the influence of the construction period on the relationship between investment and national income. In this article, he specifically states: 'Let us now remove our assumption that the construction of all projects proceeds uniformly' (Kalecki, 1986, p. 101). He does this to derive a coefficient of tied-up capital in the production process of capital goods. This is important for planning:

> By the coefficient of tied-up capital, we mean here the percentage by which the value of an investment project should be increased, in analysing the efficiency of that investment, in order to allow for the period of time during which capital outlays are tied up in construction. (Kalecki, 1986, p. 109)

32. The Kaleckian macro-investment function uses changes in profit level, ΔP, as the expectational factor (see equation (2.10)), while the accelerator uses changes in output levels, ΔY. Empirically the two terms have generally the same magnitude and direction. Eichner (1987, p. 441) points out that this makes it very difficult to

distinguish the separate influence of these two variables, 'despite the quite different implications for public policy depending on which is the actual determinant of investment'.

33. Goodwin recognises both the points raised in this sentence. He notes that the 'grave shortcoming of these essays is that they are aggregative' (Goodwin, 1990, p. vi). He also sees the cycle model as having 'the endogeneity of its erraticism', yet, in no way denying the importance of the large array of exogenous disturbances 'which likewise induce erratic behaviour in the economy' (p. 71). This is not to say that Goodwin would necessarily agree with the approach taken in this book. Having accepted the Goodwin endogeneity concept, this study attempts to appraise qualitative elements of investment behaviour that are compatible with his more quantitative approach.

34. Earlier studies based on the more tranquil 1950s and 1960s, reviewed by Evans (1969, pp. 114–21), also support the 'bunching' of industry investment cycles.

3. Investment under Uncertainty: Behavioural and Evolutionary Views

> Keynes' analysis of investment practices . . . may well be, as he observes . . . , at a relatively high level of abstraction. However, it is certainly not devoid of explanatory power and policy implication. Despite the indeterminism . . . Keynes' analysis can and does explain the experience of volatile investment by identifying the structures and motivations that govern possible practices, and so the actual practices, that lie behind this volatility. (Lawson, 1990, p. 26)

3.1 A 'BEHAVIOURAL' KALECKI

Investment analysis by Kalecki is in historical time. Meacci (1989, p. 236) argues that the method Kalecki uses for this historical process is what Shackle calls a 'diachronic mechanism'. This is a mechanical (or deterministic) method that is based on 'the unstated axiom that history is governed by its own past, that what happens is implicit in what has happened' (Shackle, 1972, p. 430).[1] The diachronic mechanism allows one to handle the uncertainty which arises when evaluating the '*future* outcomes of *all currently possible* decisions or acts' (Lawson, 1985, p. 916, original emphasis). This is done by the past acting as a guide to the future.[2] The major weakness of this method in relation to investment decisions, based on (un)certain expected long-term outcomes, is that by the time the long term has become the actual historical movement of society, there would have been novel developments to which the past cannot be a guide.

The role of uncertainty in affecting the course of investment from Kalecki's diachronic mechanism allows institutional factors to create instability. Incomplete knowledge about future outcomes leads to setting levels of desired excess capacity and to increasing transaction costs as the level of financing rises. In this way uncertainty is accounted for and left alone. For this reason Kalecki rarely mentions uncertainty.[3] In Kalecki's seven published versions of his 'principle of increasing risk', only in his first attempt at developing this principle (when it had yet to be called a 'principle' or given a name) did Kalecki (1937b, p. 84) mention the word 'uncertainty', and then only as a link from his critique of Keynes's inducement to invest to his own. As Kalecki's analysis reveals through the increasing risk concept, in an imperfect capital market, a rising rate of risk is faced by entrepreneurs seeking to increase their investment. This increasing risk originates from incomplete knowledge of the future outcomes of investment. Uncertainty becomes institutionalised as an instability factor when such risk is locked into rising transaction costs, or, alternatively, the more modern informational asymmetries (see section 2.3.3).

Keynes's analysis of the instability of investment demand incorporates epistemic as well as institutional factors (Runde, 1991, p. 142). Epistemic factors relate to the behavioural, or motivational, elements of entrepreneurs' decision-making. Steindl in an early article (1941) makes the only attempt from a Kaleckian perspective to look at epistemic factors on investment instability. He takes the traditional rate of return on investment method and then estimates the degree of uncertainty existing in these rates of return already calculated. In diachronic fashion, this estimation is based on a series of past observations which can be expected to provide a good assessment of the degree of uncertainty. Steindl identifies preference for safety in a world of uncertainty as the reason why 'investment will not be brought to the point where the mathematical expectation of profit is equal to interest, but only to a point which leaves a certain risk premium between the two' (Steindl, 1941, p. 50).

Risk premium in Steindl (1941) derives from probability measure of the 'degree of uncertainty'. In this sense, it is the same as Knight's measurable risk which is quantified by numerical probabilities (O'Donnell, 1989, pp. 263–4). What is different is that Steindl attempts to measure the risk in entrepreneurs' investment decisions based on similar cases in the past, whereas Knight considers such decisions as unique and non-measurable (Steindl, 1941, p. 48). Steindl takes Knight's preference for safety (a non-measurable uncertainty relation) and estimates a measurable risk premium that 'rises disproportionately with any increase in the standard deviation σ of the errors in predicting the rate of profit on private capital'. This estimation is meaningful when it is recognised that entrepreneurs feel threatened by lower than expected results the more they invest. This condition is 'based on exactly the same considerations as those on which Mr. Kalecki bases his principle of increasing risk' (Steindl, 1941, p. 51).

Steindl recognises that even such estimations are not completely adequate in accounting for the highly sensitive nature of investment: 'But this does not exclude the possibility that the subjective *attitude to risk* changes in the short run (e.g. in the trade cycle)' (Steindl, 1941, p. 46, original emphasis). Thus, uncertainty cannot totally be measured and institutionalised. Epistemically speaking, attitude to risk becomes 'subjective' and cyclically variable. These are the important beginnings of a 'behavioural' Kalecki.[4] Yet a review of Kaleckian investment literature (see Chapter 2) indicates no attempt at understanding what Steindl calls 'subjective attitude to risk'.

In the quotation that opens this chapter, Keynes is recognised for identifying behavioural motivation and institutional structures as lying behind investment volatility. The Keynes-inspired work on uncertainty is the key to developing a 'behavioural' Kalecki that leaves the mechanical diachronic mechanism for the more complex kaleidic mechanism that is sensitive to behavioural factors. Shackle (1972, p. 433) defines this kaleidic mechanism as an ephemeral pseudo-equilibrium based on some accepted practice which is often subject to sudden readjustment to a new precarious pseudo-equilibrium. The task for this chapter is to uncover behavioural relations and investment decision-making patterns of entrepreneurs which provide motivation implicit in Kalecki's surface elements of investment determination identified in Chapter 2.

Two areas of study can inform this search for motivation in Kalecki's investment model. One is the behavioural analysis of conventions and practices that are sensitive to altered information and related imagination. This is the source of investment instability. The second area of study is the evolutionary analysis of technological change that creates technical and market uncertainties in the economy. This exacerbates investment instability due to discontinuities in economic progress which lead to new patterns of behaviour. This is *not* a review of the literature in these two areas. Both areas are examined in this chapter *only* for what they can provide that is compatible with the Kaleckian model. In the following chapters these two perspectives on investment enable development of a behavioural investment model implicit in Kaleckian analysis.

3.2 KEYNES AND UNCERTAINTY

By highlighting the role of psychological factors in the determination of investment, Keynes has brought behavioural motivation to economics (Earl, 1988, p. 13), not just in terms of assumptions, but also as central to the economy's progress over time. Keynes' analysis of uncertainty is the essence of this behavioural element in investment. Keynes starts this enquiry into uncertainty where Kalecki left off. Both economists agree that investment decisions are based on entrepreneurs' rationality which is guided by past and present experiences (the diachronic mechanism).[5] This mechanism constrains the imagination of entrepreneurs; in this situation, it is the only response perceived as rational. Thus, when making investment decisions, entrepreneurs ensure that 'the facts of the existing situation enter, in a sense disproportionately, into the formation of . . . [their] long-term expectations' (Keynes, 1936, p. 148).

Keynes then examines the state of confidence entrepreneurs have with regard to the long-term expectations (LTE) formed from past knowledge. Recent studies of Keynes's uncertainty concept all agree that conventions, or simple rules, are established as devices for building the degree of confidence with which investment decisions are made (Earl, 1988, p. 13).[6] Keynes's 'chief' convention 'is to assume, contrary to all likelihood, that the future will resemble the past' (Keynes, 1973, p. 124). This attempts to preserve stability in an uncertain world. Business practices (like mark-up pricing, discounted cash flow and the pay-back rule) are established around these conventions, with different institutional frameworks giving rise to different specific motives and rules.

Lawson (1985, p. 921) argues that Keynes's investment instability stems from structural breaks, when 'moments of crisis' in confidence over reasonably steady LTE and existing conventions disrupt accepted business practices. This leads to a period of 'adaptive learning' or readjustment, 'before the process can settle down to one of knowledgeably reproduced social practices' (Lawson, 1985, p. 922). Instability to Keynes is not disorder, but order which is disturbed when the continuity of stable LTE becomes precarious. 'What Keynes is emphasizing is the *susceptibility* of LTE to change; how frequently they do change and to what degree is an important but largely empirical matter' (O'Donnell, 1989, p. 262, original emphasis). This concept of susceptibility is developed in a Kaleckian framework in Chapter 5, while the empirical evidence of frequency and degree of change in investment is examined in Chapter 7.

Increased susceptibility of LTE to change is the mirror image of decreasing confidence in existing practices. This happens when the 'weight of argument' decreases due to entrepreneurs increased incompleteness of knowledge (or information). In this sense increased uncertainty is related to lower weight. Low weight renders beliefs, based on established conventions, sensitive to new information and induces investors to trial new conventions. This is the basis of Keynes's epistemic instability of beliefs, which can be reinforced and magnified by institutional features in financial markets and in technological change (Runde, 1991, pp. 142–3).

Keynes's 'weight of argument' can be used to augment Steindl's notion of 'subjective attitude to risk'. In Steindl's analysis, the cyclical variables in the Kaleckian investment model – profits, excess capacity, increasing risk – inform the entrepreneurs on their 'subjective attitude'. This leads to raising or lowering the 'weight of argument', depending on how these variables are changing. For example, the 'weight' of entrepreneurs' subjective attitude to risk would be lowered by reduced profits. In this way, Keynes's concepts of uncertainty and susceptibility can be linked to the Kaleckian framework.

Investment instability based on 'weight of argument' places the accent on uncertainty, which has a numerically immeasurable probability. Keynes, like Kalecki, accepts that uncertainty which has a measurable probability should be incorporated into investment project evaluation as a risk premium. Such risk calculation is consistent with Knight's view of probability (O'Donnell, 1989, p. 263). Kalecki's 'increasing risk' attempts to take the 'preference for safety' element of uncertainty out of what Keynes and Knight regard as immeasurable, and give it a more institutional focus in investment instability analysis. However, Kalecki's principle is essentially a behavioural convention about constraints on financing investment which increase as the 'weight of argument' falls (and vice versa).

The analytical implication of this view of Keynes's uncertainty is the need 'to devote more resources into [*sic*] learning about institutional behaviour, norms, conventions – or, more generally, rule systems – that are produced and reproduced by people' (Lawson, 1985, p. 925). Lawson explains that such learning requires interpretative analytics to be conducted on practical primary source material derived from case studies and personal histories. This form of research has been conducted to identify empirical patterns outlined in Chapter 7.

Keynes distinguishes two forms of behaviour. One is entrepreneurial rationality based on the classical idea of enterprise as a 'way of life' (1936, p. 150). The other is speculative rationality based on short-term financial gains by 'outwitting the psychology of the market' and anticipating its movements which are governed by doubt and fear (O'Donnell, 1989, p. 258). Investors' convention is undermined by increased lack of confidence which leads to enterprise giving way to speculation. Uncertainty surrounding LTE makes new capital formation illogical, the implication being that entrepreneurs act to protect their liquidity position, while speculation abounds.

The exogenous role of uncertainty in investment instability, as outlined in the previous paragraph, is seen by Levine (1984) as inherently weak because it fails to carry through the classical idea of enterprise. Instead, Keynes falls back on the neoclassical notion that the financial market is populated by individual wealth-holders.[7] Under this assumption, firms end up using the same criteria as individual investors in deciding how to dispose of liquid assets. This ignores the 'fixity of investment within an irreversible flow of time, and the force of competition' (Levine, 1984, p. 49), both of which constrain firms' investment decisions. Levine sees past investments affecting both the current use of funds and the difficulty of liquidating existing capital stock. Once set on a path of business development, past investments limit options for future investment. Also competition, and the threat of competition, can erode market position and constrain 'the firm to funnel financial resources into the preservation and expansion of existing capital investment in particular lines even when greater short-term profits could be made by speculation' (Levine, 1984, p. 49).

Levine (1975) has a self-expansion perspective of firm development based on Schumpeter's capitalist entrepreneurial class. This investor class is affected by the uncertainties of financial markets, but its objective is the firm's survival. As explained in section 2.3, capitalists have a strategic interest in their firms. A Kaleckian class-based institutional framework, with capitalists as central ('masters of their fate') to the entrepreneur economy, can provide a structure which can then be developed to account for both oligopoly behaviour in goods markets and speculative behaviour in financial markets. Chapter 4 presents such a framework.

3.3 SHACKLE AND THE IMAGINATION

Keynes's uncertainty and consequent investment instability is the starting point for all the writings of G.L.S. Shackle. It is the kaleidic method, based on 'delicately stacked' conjectures which give way to 'sudden landslides of re-adjustment', that Shackle (1972, p. 433) argues is implicit in *The General Theory*.[8] Then Shackle adds his own crucial premise that the future, nevertheless, is imaginable. 'Uncertainty is therefore a state of mind of the decision maker occasioned by the presence of a number of *imagined* sequels to an event. It results from imaginative expectation' (Dixon, 1986, p. 586, added emphasis). The corollary of this perspective is that the durability and irreversibility of capital goods forces entrepreneurs to gain power in the market (and over the state) in order to control the consequences of their own investment decisions. This 'leads inexorably' to classical political economy (Dixon, 1986, pp. 589–90), and specifically (for this study) to the monopoly capital model of Michal Kalecki.

The standard version of a Shacklean kaleidic society demands that unacceptable outcomes are to be avoided by firms, which attempt to control the market and influence the state, and by the state itself, which provides a guiding hand through the anarchic landscape. Both aspects coalesce in the Kaleckian relative autonomy view of the state (see section 2.4). The coalition of powerful capitalist interests induces the support of the state in the management of the business cycle and in symbiotic relations (i.e. the military-industrial complex).

Lachmann (1986) has developed another version of the Shacklean kaleidic society. This is a *laissez-faire* approach (based on the Austrian school), where the state is non-interventionist since 'no centralized decision-maker could for long intervene wisely in so dynamic a world' (Caldwell, 1989, p. 51). The power of large firms is also undermined by kaleidic processes, 'in which individual plans, each consistent in itself, never have time to become consistent with each other before new change supervenes' (Lachmann, 1976, p. 61). Strong competition, without state support, ensures that no market power remains entrenched for very long.

Even though the *laissez-faire* version is rejected along the lines of Earl and Kay (1985) and Dixon (1986), this Lachmann-based methodology and its realist account of behaviour informs and makes the Kaleckian model much less mechanical (Caldwell, 1989, pp. 49–52). This is done by recognising that Shackle's concept of imagination is the motivational feature that can provide a realist

Lachmann approach to examining the fragility of investment. Imagination endogenises the world of uncertainty, placing the emphasis on the self-expansive role of accumulation. Such a strong realist position on investment uncertainty is incorporated within the Kaleckian behavioural framework of the current study.

Less well known is Shackle's empirical work on business decision-making which examines the practical frame of thought of decision makers (Earl, 1988, p. 6). From such studies, in the context of investment decisions which involve long-term commitment of large sums of money, Shackle perceives the role of imagination in the future. Decision makers cannot tell what *will* happen to their investment, but 'it may be legitimate to form judgements of what *can* happen, at worst and at best' (Shackle, 1970, p. 111, original emphasis). From this perspective, an investment indifference map is devised (Shackle, 1970, p. 123, figure 5.4), based on the same technique as a consumers' indifference map. As a static analytical device to appreciate the uncertainty related to investment decisions, the technique serves a useful device. However, in a dynamic setting of instability, the mapping technique cannot help in understanding the cumulative pressures on investment or lack of investment.[9]

Degrees of expectations are ascribed in the imagination of decision makers and shown by different contours on Shackle's indifference map. These degrees extend over a spectrum from strong expectation of gain to strong expectation (or fear) of loss. This spectrum encapsulates all possible human agents' imagined consequences of the uncertain future. Placing this spectrum within the kaleidic movement of society provides a dynamic setting for investment decisions. Shackle himself did not make such a linkage between his two concepts of 'imagination' and the 'kaleidic mechanism'. In Chapter 5 an attempt is made to do this. A dynamic systematic approach to investment decisions is developed on the basis of expectational states of the imagination.

3.4 MANAGERIALISM AND CORPORATE INSTABILITY

The managerialist view of the modern corporation developed since the 1950s has spawned a large behavioural economics literature. The basic premise of this view is the divorce of ownership and control. The behavioural implications of managerialism and the corporate instability that results provides a microeconomic industry base to the Shacklean world of uncertainty.

Marris (1964) is a classic managerialist work, examining 'what a firm must do if it is to achieve continuous growth and profitability' (Earl, 1984, p. 2). Salaried managers aim for the security and greater prestige that comes with the firm's growth. In this dynamic environment managers need to be on the look-out for growth options in existing and newly created markets. This leads Marris (1964, pp. 175–202) to the product life-cycle process in corporate growth.[10] Managers know the strengths and limitations of the skills in their company over the firm's life-cycle, with diseconomies of growth arising if managers aim for too high a growth rate. This means that managers understand what Earl (1984, p. 13) calls managerial constraints on growth. The strength of Marris's work is the detailed institutional framework that firms exist in, and which helps to establish the framework of Chapter 4 below.

The Cambridge view of investment from Keynes and Joan Robinson is based on past profits and the expectations they engender. This investment perspective is situated within the growth-based behaviour established by managers of Marris's modern stock-holding corporation. As with Kalecki, past record of profits constrains investment programmes in an uncertain business environment, with large firms able more easily to secure funds. Adrian Wood, as a student of Marris, uses the same framework to identify tolerable gearing ratios and liquidity cushions for the supply of finance constraints on investment-based growth (see section 2.3.3).

There are two problems with Marris's investment-based growth approach. First is the lack of a role for owners in the investment process, except indirectly by siphoning off internal funds through higher dividends. Second is the implied assumption, as Earl (1984, p. 19) notes, that Marris's firms never make mistakes and are very well aware of their managerial constraints. Corporate fallibility is implied in Shackle's work, but is explicitly incorporated into Marris's model by Earl (1984). This produces a model of endogenous corporate instability at the micro-level.

Mistaken decisions result in 'cycles of corporate instability' (Earl, 1984, p. 12). These cycles, unlike the diachronic business cycle mechanism, are based on a kaleidic movement. A set of conjectures or conventions establishes the desired growth path and the accompanying investment strategy. Different evolutionary paths are possible depending on the nature of the managerial and financial constraints. Earl (1984, pp. 12–16) describes the variety of possible cycles, from small damped corporate cycles to large 'catastrophic' ones. Early over-estimations by a firm can lead to much less ambitious investment plans and some relative stability over time (damped cycle). Early success can, instead, lead to euphoria and large optimistic investment plans that send the firm bankrupt as managerial constraints bite very severely and unexpectedly (catastrophic cycle). Under the latter type of cycle, after consistent failures, a revolutionary new innovation and a large new investment plan are both introduced as a 'last ditch' attempt to save the company. This strategy is most likely to fail in a depressed and inexperienced organisation with very little time for 'learning-by-doing' (for examples, see Earl, 1984, pp. 73–4).

The model of corporate instability outlined raises two matters of pertinence to the current study. The first is on methodology. The firm is seen in this model from the perspective of being susceptible to corporate instability. The investment model developed in this study is of the firm (and industry) from the perspective of being susceptible to investment instability. Both attempt to see firms not as deterministic mechanisms that can be regressed as equations, but as kaleidic mechanisms. In such an approach it is imperative to understand what are the forces that lead to reasonably stable (or damped) outcomes, and the forces that lead to major unstable (or chaotic) outcomes. Both outcomes are possible in the same general model. Also, there can be various forms of 'organisational slack' (Cyert and March, 1963, pp. 36–8) in the firms which can be tightened up during crisis periods in order to ameliorate instability. Earl (1984, p. 19) explains that instability in firms is understood by looking 'at "the ghost in the machine" . . . and examine how it thinks, how its personality constrains its adaptability in turbulent times'.

The second relevant aspect is the influence of the corporate instability model on the Kaleckian behavioural investment model developed. The financial constraints on growth in Earl's model are directly applicable to the financial constraints on the investment model. The connection is through the Marris managerialist approach adopted in the analyses of Wood and Sylos Labini discussed in section 2.3.3. The managerial constraints in Earl's model offer a particularly strong behavioural feature to the investment instability analysis. The 'ghost' of management's limitations, mistakes and available slack are major ways that investment decisions can become more susceptible to crisis or even help to ease such a crisis of instability. Corporate disasters can be interpreted in terms of entrepreneurs over-estimating, in a boom period, their ability to manage growth. This mistaken belief in their managerial abilities helps in understanding the process whereby investment transposes from boom to bust. Surface elements in a deterministic Kaleckian investment model (which has strong empirical regression results, see section 2.7) are better seen as motivating the behavioural managerial and financial processes at work in the corporate instability model.

3.5 BOUNDED RATIONALITY AND THE CORPORATE INVESTMENT PROCESS

The Carnegie school of behavioural economics, centred around Herbert Simon of Carnegie–Mellon University, is based on the concept of bounded rationality in the decision-making process within business organisations. Faced with uncertainty and the resulting costs of overcoming ignorance, this school argues that decision-makers, because of the unwieldy mathematical calculations required, find it impossible to make optimal decisions based on all potential information. This is effectively the rejection of 'rational economic man', an assumption upon which all neoclassical microeconomic theory is based (Simon, 1976, p. xxxiii).

Simon (1976) examines the psychology of administrative decisions from the basis that individuals (or agents) do not know all the alternatives and all their consequences. Such an objective rationality is impossible. Investment commitments are very long-term future-oriented decisions which are not based on an objective rationality. Instead, they are based on a bounded rationality which involves setting targets for satisfactory outcomes and using convenient rule-of-thumb techniques to meet such targets. Under bounded rationality, the use of conventions or rules of thumb entails a satisficing (rather than neoclassical 'optimal') behavioural approach to decision-making.

In a world of uncertainty where probabilities are numerically immeasurable, Keynes's view of a rationality that is based on conventions is very similar to Simon's notion of bounded rationality (Lawson, 1985, p. 918). This similarity can be seen in their views on historical (or real) time and how it affects decision-making. Keynes's conventions are guided by the past. Simon's satisficing activities involve setting rules that are based on historically determined paths. This is particularly the case with entrepreneurs making large investment commitments which set up the future path of the organisation. As Simon (1976, p. 66) explains, 'the decision [of the entrepreneur] to build the factory . . . influences his subsequent decisions'. Keynes, unlike Simon, does not provide a specific human agency process at the firm level which can stipulate how such conventions affect the investment decision.

For Simon (1976, p. 83) tension builds up in relation to crucial decisions as losses become more imaginable: 'The more vividly the consequences of losing in a risky venture are visualised − either through past experience of such consequences or for other reasons − the less desirable does the risk assumption appear.' This strengthens 'the desire to avoid the consequences of loss'. As more investment orders are made, there is a cumulative building up of tension which increases the desire to avoid loss consequences. Such desires create pressure to reduce investment orders at the time that investment orders are reaching a very high level. As investment grows, tension build-up provides a way of imagining the growing susceptibility of Keynes's LTE to change. This is the basic behavioural premise in the investment model of Chapter 5.

The task that economists who assume bounded rationality have set themselves is 'to understand how information is processed by individuals and organisational procedures in the uncertain, poorly known, complex world' in which decision-makers find themselves (Simon, 1986, p. ix). These behavioural economists have identified two approaches that decision-makers use in these circumstances. The 'passive' approach involves seeking ways to prepare for surprises and formulate plans to counter them. The 'active' approach seeks to modify or eliminate the incidence of surprises (Earl and Kay, 1985, pp. 38–43). Managerialism in corporations implies that decision-makers require strategic management to deal with both approaches. The most critical future-oriented part of strategic management is the corporate investment process because of its long-term consequences. The investment process, which consists of planning and implementation stages, involves handling both approaches.

Ansoff (1979) examines both approaches in order to discern strategies to avoid loss consequences from long-term decisions like investment. From the passive approach, firms design systems to cope with threats. Corporations confronting a highly tension-laden period, due to their own large investment commitments and concerns over the future market, employ the 'delay principle' (p. 53) and defer investment decisions until concerns are resolved. This specifies the investment process when images of loss consequences abound. From the active approach, Ansoff (1979) sees a competitive edge for firms with better devices to recognise threats when there are only 'weak signals' in the environment (Earl and Kay, 1985, p. 43). Such devices allow entrepreneurs to make investment plans and implement commitments in new developments, like innovations, when the positive expectations are only weak (see also Demsetz, 1982). This 'active' corporate investment process is the necessary stimulus to investment activity when the industry investment cycle is in a trough.

Loasby (1967) places investment strategies of the type discussed by Ansoff in a specific Shacklean context. Loasby is concerned about 'an over-enthusiastic commitment of resources' in formal long-range investment planning which would impair the flexibility and adaptability that Ansoff is supporting (Earl and Kay, 1985, p. 41). This is possible through an entrepreneur's plans being 'permeable' to new elements and amenable to revision (Loasby, 1984, p. 401). Modifying and delaying plans during the implementation stage also allows for significant revisions to occur. Such flexibility in the investment process of successful corporations allows for both the inertia-based conventions of bounded rationality and the susceptibility to expectational changes.

A balanced mixture of rules and flexibility in the corporate investment process is desirable. Bromiley (1986) contains three detailed case studies of heavy manufacturing corporations and their corporate capital investment processes. Each study presents qualitative data on the investment process from interviews with corporate officials and a quantitative data-based model. A conceptual framework summarises common aspects of the investment process in both its planning and implementation stages. This framework identifies the active and passive approaches to the investment process. Bromiley's research shows the extent to which such firms are aware of both approaches and the conflicts involved in achieving a balance of rules and flexibility.

There are two stages in the investment process that Bromiley (1986, p. 127) outlines: the aggregate planning stage, which is linked to much wider strategic management; and the project approval and implementation stage, which is more specifically linked to detailed operations. These stages tend to operate in different parts of the corporation and are closely related to what Bromiley identifies as different analytical frameworks of investment planning (1986, pp. 157–62). The corporate strategy framework aims to integrate investment plans with the overall strategic management process, including marketing, product management, finance and personnel systems and rewards. In this framework a set of executives tend to examine investment from the active approach. The financial planning framework aims to scrutinise investment from the perspective of future rates of return over a prescribed period in relation to an acceptable gearing position. In this framework a different set of executives tend to examine investment projects from the passive approach in association with financial constraints. Information is exchanged between these two planning units, but their frameworks determine a different interpretation of data.

Almost every corporation makes trade-offs between financial and strategic considerations, but often they are not explicitly recognised as such. When top management looks at assessments made by individuals from these two different frameworks, the 'conservative' position of one assessment may conflict with the 'risky' position of the other. Often top management does not perceive the ties nor see the trade-offs involved (Bromiley, 1986, p. 161). The resolution requires a balance between rules and flexibility. Lack of explicit recognition of the need for such a balance leads firms into unnecessary investment instability.[11] In section 5.4 conflict resolutions (or lack thereof) are incorporated into the investment model.

Bromiley also distinguishes between investment for expansion and replacement in terms of how flexible firms are in altering investment plans and commitments. With established firms, 'the large proportion of investment that went into replacement gave management a substantial amount of flexibility in modifying planned investment expenditures from year to year' (1986, p. 130). When firms are mostly investing in new plant, such flexibility is not apparent. Business expansion comes from expectations of future sales and capacity usage. Such expectations are often variable, and once committed to expansion, its impact is to reduce flexibility in modifying expenditures. This means that '[b]usiness expansion forms a relatively volatile component of the desire for investment' (1986, p. 131). Thus, investment expansion gives firms more tension build-up and a stronger desire to avoid consequent losses rather than undertake replacement investment.

The relevance of Bromiley's research to this study is strong, both methodologically and theoretically. At the methodological level, the empirical support comes from qualitative case-study research on heavy manufacturing in both studies. Bromiley's focus is specifically on the actual process of investment, while this study aims to understand instability through relating Kaleckian variables to Bromiley's process of investment. At the theoretical level, Bromiley rejects the neoclassical view of firm investment as being inconsistent with the conceptual framework devised from his behavioural research (1986, pp. 140–54). The importance Bromiley associates with profits and financial constraints in a model whose determinants have variable temporal effects provides support for this book's theoretical model.

One specific area of the investment process that comes up often in empirical investigation is joint ventures (JV). In the 1980s it became a popular form of cross-country alliance between established multinational enterprises. Casson (1990, p. 24) notes the reduced flexibility in the investment process which comes with large expansions and increased uncertainty due to major structural changes in world manufacturing. Corporations feel a stronger desire for loss avoidance which can be ameliorated by entering into JV. Such 'compromise contractual arrangements' allow increased flexibility and reduce the tension of major expansions. Casson (1990, ch. 7) reviews the many recent behavioural studies of JV arrangements and concludes that there are two major forms: The transitional form which is aimed purely at minimising tension; and the co-operative form which is aimed at a creative permanent alternative by reducing cross-cultural transaction costs.

3.6 EVOLUTIONARY VIEW OF TECHNOLOGICAL CHANGE

From the behavioural perspective, innovative and imitative strategies require firms continually to enlarge their quantity of commercially successful technical knowledge, in relation to both new techniques (process innovation) and new products (product innovation).[12] Technological change is thus defined as the search for increase in the known set of scientific production techniques and products, in terms of both quantity and quality of inputs.[13] 'The motive driving the firm's search for new technologies is profit' (Verspagen, 1992, p. 53). The process of innovative search at the firm level is not the issue here (see Dosi and Chiaromonte, 1990). This section is concerned exclusively with the effects that such innovative search has on investment behaviour under uncertainty.

Technological change, derived from specific research and development (R&D) activities or in the course of day-to-day engineering (production and marketing based) activities, needs to be implemented by investing in new plant and/or equipment. This distinctive form of investment creates a non-quantifiable uncertainty which is outlined in this section, and is based on the views of the new evolutionary school on technological change.[14] As Dosi (1988a, p.

222), a prominent member of this school, acknowledges, 'innovation involves a fundamental element of uncertainty'.

Two specific types of uncertainty are identified by writers of this school. One is 'technical uncertainty' which relates to innovation and its ability to satisfy a variety of technical criteria while being commercially viable (Freeman, 1982, p. 149). Such uncertainty arises because procedures to solve these techno-economic problems are unknown and the time path of these solutions cannot be precisely traced (Dosi, 1988a, p. 222). The other is 'market uncertainty' over the success or failure of new products. Product innovation involves both types of uncertainty. Process innovation for in-house application involves only technical uncertainty. Selling a new process on the market suffers both uncertainties, as it effectively becomes a product.

The degree of innovative uncertainty depends on the level of technological change involved in the innovation process. When the level of scientific input is minimal, the degree of innovative uncertainty is 'very little'. This is the case with process innovation in minor technical improvements and imitation of established techniques; and with product innovation in new 'models' and product differentiation. Investment in such innovation tends to be a more mechanical or goal-driven process, governed by normal business investment uncertainty, than other forms of innovation. A 'very high' degree of uncertainty relates to both radical product and process innovation; while 'true' uncertainty relates to fundamental research and invention (Freeman, 1982, p. 150).

In the evolutionary school literature, innovative uncertainty renders the search for profits from innovation a non-optimising behaviour. This is because under innovative uncertainty, 'neither rational expectations or full certainty applies nor the chance distribution of an event is known' (Verspagen, 1992, p. 55). Instead, this reasoning implies that firms perform profit-seeking (satisficing) behaviour based on Simon's bounded rationality. Conventions based on 'standardized rules of thumb are used to make decisions about investment in [the search for] new technologies' (Verspagen, 1992, p. 55). This form of innovative behaviour perceived by the evolutionary school can be linked to the behavioural literature set out in the previous sections: the consequences of innovative-based investment decisions result in the firm making 'mistakes' (*à la* Earl) or in successful growth (*à la* Marris). 'Imagination', as conceived by Shackle, takes these experiences into account in the next innovative endeavour.

The rules are not the same for every firm in the industry. However, the actions of entrepreneurs may look co-ordinated, as they tend to use the same rule-of-thumb procedures and there is the existence of some general 'market expectations' (Verspagen, 1992, p. 55). This links in to the Goodwin view of the power of demand influencing investment decisions that forces innovations to create 'swarms' of innovative behaviour in a step-wise process (see section 2.5). Both reflect 'the Schumpeterian view of competition' that to improve the firm's market position requires a search for better techniques and products (Nelson and Winter, 1980, p. 183). This search under uncertainty needs experimentation and selection with rules that provide market coordination. In the early stages of searching, uncertainty is at its strongest. Thus, it takes some time for the industry or market to reach the necessary degree of co-ordination needed to see 'swarming' behaviour.

Cumulation and selection are the two aspects of technological change that lead to reduced uncertainty and more market co-ordination. Cumulative technological change occurs because firms use Keynes's 'chief convention' of 'the past as a guide to the future'. 'What the firm can hope to do in the future is narrowly constrained by what it has been capable of doing in the past' (Dosi, 1988b, p. 1130). Successful past innovation tends to limit future options, bringing some co-ordination even if firms are taking different investment decisions. The growth in market power through successful competitive past and present innovative (and imitative) behaviour establishes the long-term viability of firms adopting such behaviour. These firms reduce uncertainty by attempting to create a 'stable' co-ordinated market (Boulding, 1981). Firms without this power are eventually either forced out of the market altogether or sidetracked into a niche market.

This selection process determines the structure of industries and the path of economic change. To continue in power, firms need to have entrepreneurs who have the ability to learn from experience and respond to changes. A micro-level evolutionary theory emerges from this analysis, with innovation seen as a learning process. Experience in innovative and imitative behaviour increases over time, inducing the evolution of more efficient and powerful firms (Verspagen, 1992, pp. 60–1).

The evolutionary view – inspired by Schumpeter – has taken this firm-based innovative behaviour to the macro-level, where it aims to explain the take-off of a new scientific revolution in terms of a common method and pattern of solution to selected technological problems. This new 'paradigm', if it has a pervasive effect on the structure of most major production sectors, will require new investment and the creative destruction of old MOP in these major sectors. Such a techno-economic paradigm shift, in the Kuhnian sense, produces structural change in market economies. Discontinuity in economic progress occurs and 'a new pattern in the location of investment both nationally and internationally' (Radosevic, 1991, p. 99). Refinements and further adaptations of the paradigm (incremental innovations) sets off a large expansion in investment expenditure and what some authors call a new long wave of boom and prosperity (Kleinknecht, 1987).

The emergence of a new technological paradigm is *exogenous* to a single firm or industry. It manifests itself only when a whole set of firms, over a few major industries, begin to apply the new basic scientific principles to their investment decisions. The combined effect of all the shifts in investment decisions, due to competitive pressure to lead or quickly follow, creates the 'swarming' behaviour.

At the aggregate economy level, the technological change process is *endogenous*. Availability of the new scientific revolution comes from a large body of continuous investigation which has many failures and a few successes. Its discovery is linked to many small developments in various laboratories and informal networks between them, eventually coming to fruition in some way divorced of individual firm or industry competitive behaviour. There are, however, given scientific principles (or laws), like gravity and the speed of light, which establish the technological possibilities. This, to a certain extent, sets an exogenous constraint on the evolutionary innovative process (Verspagen, 1992, p. 49).

A new technological paradigm is more likely to replace the old paradigm as the latter becomes less competitive. Freeman (1991) has identified technological, economic and institutional factors that influence the competitiveness of paradigms. Each of the three factors need to be examined separately. First, the technological factor involves the development of a 'critical mass' of successful innovations in the new paradigm with a sufficient network of externalities to make it a viable competitor (technology-push effect). From the old paradigm's position, the threat of a new paradigm stimulates minor innovations in the old paradigm, allowing the latter to 'rule' for a while longer, until the former is better developed ('the sailing ship' effect, see Rosenberg, 1976, pp. 205–6). Eventually limits to innovative potential make future profits of the old paradigm suffer decreasing marginal returns. The consequence of this is depression, which triggers more R&D effort in reducing the uncertainty of the alternative paradigm (Freeman and Perez, 1988, p. 49).

The second factor is economic. Economic competitiveness, based on the demand-pull hypothesis, implies that innovation is a function of market demand (Schmookler, 1966). Saturation of demand for the old paradigm's basic products, and stimulation of demand for the new paradigm's basic products, encourage a product innovation-based paradigm shift. Growth in demand for the new paradigm's products decreases production costs which helps to lower prices. This further stimulates new paradigm demand, and results in a process innovation-based paradigm shift.

The third factor is institutional. The institutional setting of the economy influences relative paradigm competitiveness. Long postponements of new innovative investment tend to inhibit changes in the legal, political, industrial, education, transport and communication systems. This produces an entrenched old institutional structure, with a mismatch between the new technological paradigm and current investment practices. Competitiveness of the new paradigm is in this way stymied (Freeman and Perez, 1988, p. 49).

Pavitt (1984) draws up a taxonomy of sectors on the basis of their current innovative characteristics (see Table 3.1). At the centre of Pavitt's taxonomy are science-based small scale firms (sector 1), no larger than 1,000 employees, who are the main source of innovation based on the new technological paradigm. These firms are mainly in chemical and electronic/electrical product areas, symbiotically linked to the large firms in other sectors through new product and process applications. Investment is software- and equipment-oriented, and required for major innovations. There is a very high degree of innovative (both technical and market) uncertainty. As a result, complementary and synergistic links to large corporations (such as IBM) are developed. These links help to provide needed 'patient' funding, since the time frame for producing innovative information is never known, given the high level of failure in any particular approach taken. Kaleckian analysis has generally ignored this new role for small firms. Only Sylos Labini has noted their role and linkage to oligopolies (see section 2.4).

Productive intensive firms are the second sector in Table 3.1. These are large oligopoly firms, with strong scale or information economies. The technology-push process exploits these economies and keeps market share intact against other large firms who are doing the same. This is where application and diffusion of science-based innovations chiefly occurs. The largest investment commitments are made in these firms, particularly in new plant and computer hardware equipment. Incremental product and process innovations are often occurring, related to mastering complex systems and developing scale or information economies. Innovative uncertainty is only 'high' (cf. science-based firms), and strategies (as noted in Table 3.1) are needed to alleviate some of this, including patents, profit centres and vertical (dis)integration (co-operation with suppliers further down the input chain). There is a strong emphasis on R&D related to incremental innovation, but nowhere near the depth of R&D in the science-based firms.

Scale-intensive firms are the manufacturing firms of Kaleckian models. There are the 'assembly-based' industries which make product-differentiated consumer durables using Taylorist and Fordist automation processes, e.g. the motor vehicle industry (Dosi, 1988a, p. 232). There are also the 'continuous process' industries which make basic materials, e.g. steel and aluminium industries. Such industries are central to old technological paradigms (Freeman and Perez, 1988, pp. 50–3). In the late twentieth century, these industries have had problems adapting to a less central position under the new electronics-based technological paradigm. Their sharp reduction in investment after the 1960s growth boom was a period of readjustment, or 'structural break', when the degree of innovative uncertainty increased greatly and previous conventions were no longer suitable. Chapter 7 charts their post-war course of investment and their recent investment expansion by adopting the new paradigms.

Information-intensive firms are service-based oligopolies, particularly in finance and retailing. Economies are achieved not from pure scale of production, but from the intensive use of information and communication. Quick adoption of the new electronics-based paradigm leads to very large investment in new computer-based hardware. Powerful information-intensive differentiated oligopolies emerge. There is strong technology-push competitive pressure to create new software packages and form links with science-based firms to develop the appropriate hardware. Firms in this sector have many conventions which are aimed at adapting to a high degree of innovative uncertainty.[15]

Supplier-dominated firms are the final sector in Table 3.1. These firms are found in traditional areas of manufacturing (e.g. textiles, printing), agriculture, construction and professional services. Firms are generally small suppliers, contractors and consultants who are involved mainly in the adoption of process innovation – embodied in the best-practice MOP and innovative intermediate inputs – originating generally outside this sector. Firms are principally concerned with the incremental efficiency improvements of such innovation (Dosi, 1988a, p. 232). The level of investment in this sector is relatively low and dependent on servicing the needs of other sectors (see Figure 3.1). The degree of uncertainty is relatively 'little' in both general business uncertainty (due to low level of investment) and in technical uncertainty (due to minor process innovation), with no market uncertainty (due to lack of product innovation).

Table 3.1 Taxonomy of firms based on the nature of their innovation

Sectors	Source of innovation	Trajectory (relation to the economy)	Typical product groups	Strategic problems for management based on uncertainty
1. Science-based firms	R&D Laboratory	Synergetic new products Applications engineering	Electronics Chemicals	Complementary assets Integration to exploit synergies 'Patient' money
2. Productive-intensive firms				
2.1 Scale-intensive firms	Production engineering and specialised suppliers	Efficient and complex production and related products	Basic materials Durable consumer goods	Balance and choice in production technology among *appropriation* (secrecy and patents), *vertical disintegration* (co-operation with supplier), and *profit centre*
2.2 Information-intensive firms	Software/ systems dept and specialised suppliers	Efficient (and complex) information processing, and related products	Financial services Retailing	'Fusion' with fast-moving technologies Diffusion of production technology amongst divisions Exploiting product opportunities 'Patient' money
3. Supplier-dominated firms	Small-firm design and large-scale users	Improved specialised producers goods (reliability and performance)	Machinery Instruments Specialty chemicals Software	Matching technological opportunity with user Absorbing user experience Finding stable or new product 'niches'

Source: Adapted from Pavitt (1990, p. 6a)

Based on Pavitt (1984, p. 364), Figure 3.1 shows technological linkages between the four sectors. Supplier-dominated firms obtain most of their technology for innovation from science-based and scale intensive firms (e.g. power tools and transport equipment from the latter; consumer electronics and plastics from the former). Science-based firms transfer technology to scale-intensive firms, who depend on the developments in the former (e.g. the use of plastics and electronics in automobiles). Both science-based and scale-intensive firms accept and receive technology from information-intensive firms (e.g. banks' new software assists both sectors, while the hardware from science-based firms sustains the banks computer programs, and new transport security supports banks armed-guard needs). These linkages are the life-blood of small firms, and identifies how they have increased and prospered (Sylos Labini, 1990a).

Figure 3.1 Technological linkages between sectors

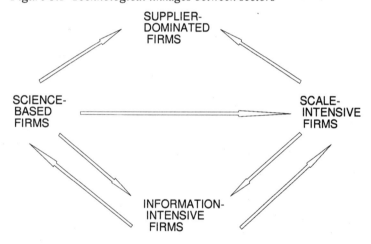

Source: Adapted from Pavitt (1984, p. 364)

The diffusion of new technological paradigms depends on the rate of adoption of the new innovation principles in specific industries and specific countries. Industries and firms that are resistant to adopting new innovation principles, due to particular cultural, educational or sociological backgrounds, are liable to extinction if the new technological systems become so pervasive as to create a new paradigm. Also, the rate of adoption varies from one industry to another depending on the tendency to imitate each other in that industry. In some industries (for specific reasons due to background) one firm quickly imitates another; in others this is slow.[16] The diffusion of innovation depends on the capabilities of the 'receiving' firms (and even countries) to 'assimilate' the new technological knowledge and the ability to have the funds necessary to invest (Verspagen, 1992, pp. 104–7). The difference that results from the process of diffusion means that each industry's investment cycle is influenced in terms of speed and amplitude by the specific nature of the acceptance of innovation (see section 6.3).

Taking into account all the technological, economic and institutional factors, as well as the linkages between firm sectors, the rate of diffusion of a new technological paradigm is variable. As an exogenous element, the point at which new technological systems enter into the firm or industry and the subsequent endogenous (incremental) innovations have a strong impact on its investment cycle. This is incorporated into the Kaleckian investment cycle model developed in the following chapters. The evolutionary view has the dynamics and the related behavioural uncertainty contributing significantly to the development of a behavioural Kalecki.

NOTES

1. Shackle (1972, pp. 430–3) distinguishes three other methods of analysing time. The achronic mechanism is the general equilibrium approach where changes are handled in logical time only. The pan-chronic mechanism is where two kinds of time are handled together, one for the all-seeing analyst and one for the participant making trial-and-error judgements without the benefit of overview. The kaleidic mechanism is where ephemeral pseudo-equilibrium based on some accepted practice is often subject to sudden readjustment to a new precarious pseudo-equilibrium.

2. There are many other possible ways of attempting to mitigate uncertainty, even though it can never be removed. The neoclassical approach is by calculating stochastic risk, which fits neatly into the achronic mechanism. The behavioural approach is by examining the type of practices or conventions that firms use to adjust and readjust their behaviour in a kaleidic environment. Other ways of handling uncertainty include the 'gypsy approach' by consulting respected fortune tellers.

3. In the first two volumes of Kalecki's *Collected Works*, which analyse capitalism, there is no reference to uncertainty in either detailed Index of Subjects (see Osiatyński, 1990, 1991).

4. Kalecki (1943b) in footnote 40 refers to Steindl (1941) for further analysis of risk. Steindl (1941, p. 40, fn. 1), in return, strongly acknowledges 'Mr. Kalecki for his advice and criticism which alone enabled me to give the article its present shape'. Kalecki's own references to an entrepreneur economy reveal a behavioural orientation to his Marxian base (Sardoni, 1987, p. 133).

5. Keynes's rational economic person is wider than the conventional neoclassical view of rationality which is purely based on known and measurable probability, even if that measure is less than full certainty. The bulk of Keynes's discussion on uncertainty relates to known probability relations, but which are 'numerically immeasurable' (Lawson, 1985, p. 89).

6.   See – in alphabetical order – Carvalho (1988); Fitzgibbons (1988); Lawson (1985, 1990); O'Donnell (1989); Runde (1991).

7.   For Carvalho (1988, p. 80), Keynes's 'long-term expectations are, thus, exogenous, because they cannot be definitely related to any current economic variable'.

8.   Lawson (1985, p. 915) and O'Donnell (1989, p. 371, fn. 17) suggest that Shackle has 'misrepresented' Keynes's analysis of uncertainty. They argue that Keynes's social rules and conventions are rational and objective responses to uncertainty, while Shackle's conjectures are subjective responses to uncertainty. As Rowley and Hamouda (1987, p. 54) argue, this objective/subjective nexus is a crude distinction and not self-evident. Lawson (1985, p. 915) himself admits that 'Shackle's own contributions on the subject [of uncertainty] are not overly different, in some respects, from the account [of Keynes's uncertainty] outlined above'. The analysis in this section shows that this debate is not relevant for the purposes of this study.

9.   Similarly, consumer indifference mapping is inadequate in understanding the processes of consumer behaviour over time as it is affected by cumulative pressures of advertising (see Katona, 1980) and the intensity of the pain/pleasure spectrum (see Scitovsky, 1976).

10. This resembles the innovation-based growth in Levine (1981) derived from a macro-Schumpeterian perspective (see section 2.5). Unlike Marris's model, Levine's work lacks a detailed institutional framework at the micro-level.

11. Such instability from the poor resolution of conflicting advice, or lack of balance because both groups provide (say) wildly optimistic 'risky' investment assessments, relates very closely to the Earl (1984) corporate instability model of mistakes.

12. This is in contrast to the neoclassical view that technical knowledge is taken as a datum of microeconomic theory, where firm analysis cannot explain the behaviour of firms' agents in relation to how technical change comes about. From this perspective, change in technical knowledge is defined as the increase in productivity of all techniques available, in terms of the quantity of capital and labour factors used. This ignores the important quality differences in these two factors that arise out of technical change (Verspagen, 1992, p. 53).

13. Innovative behaviour involves technical change of two types: technological change and non-technological change. Process innovation is chiefly based on technological change of scientific research and development (R&D) and engineering activities. Process innovation can also be due to non-technological change consisting of improvements in organisational structures, labour practices, management practices and training. Technological change is also crucial to product innovation, since non-technological change does not typically lead to any product changes. Technological change requires a much higher level of investment than non-technological change due to scientific-engineering knowledge generally requiring implementation by new MOP, whereas other knowledge is normally implemented in existing MOP.

14. The evolutionary or neo-Schumpeterian literature was initiated in the early 1980s by authors like Nelson and Winter (1980, 1982) and Dosi (1982). For a detailed 'state of the art' reading list, see Dosi *et al.* (1988).

15. As noted in a recent theoretical paper on banks coping with uncertainty, 'behavioral rules [of thumb] are established through supervisory pressure, bank experience, innovations, and "whirlwinds of optimism and pessimism"' (Wray, 1992, p. 306). The financial sector boomed in the 1980s with a series of new 'optimistic' conventions to fit the new electronics paradigm and the related diminished central bank supervision. The century-old conservative banking conventions were no longer thought to be appropriate to the new technologies. The severe 1990s financial crises of the deregulated banking systems in USA, UK and Australia appertain to the failure of these new conventions to justify the optimism generated by the new technology (and related deregulation). For details on the financial crises in USA, see Mayer (1990); and for Australia, see Martin (1991).

16.   Salter (1960), from a neoclassical perspective, tackles these same issues. He examines the different rates of productivity between industries and finds that they are due to differential rates of investment in technical advance. Technical advances have no marked biases, but are affected by factors that induce relatively quick adoption of technical advances (notably high cost of labour and economies of scale) and by factors that discourage quick adoption (notably oligopoly power). Salter's study has been unfortunately ignored by neoclassical and evolutionary economists alike. His neoclassical framework and his neglect of uncertainty makes this excellent study irrelevant to the current chapter discussions.

4. Institutional Behaviour of Firms

No 'general' theory of economic growth is conducive to understanding economic realities of different social systems; for the institutional framework of a system exerts a profound influence upon its dynamics. (Kalecki, 1970, p. 311)

4.1 FROM THE FIRM'S PERSPECTIVE

The institutional framework and its implications for the behaviour of manufacturing firms is presented in this chapter. It forms the basis of the investment decision-making model developed in the following two chapters. Since investment decisions are made at the firm level, the framework is expressed from the firm's perspective. There are two aspects to this firm perspective. First is the self-repeating aspect. Second is the structural aspect where there are changes to the pattern of long-term production.

Sections 4.2–4.4 concentrate on the short-term self-repeating features. Specifically the form of competition and the role of various agents within firms are set out. This is followed by the structure of entrepreneur's investment decision-making and the financial behaviour of lenders and borrowers. All these features are self-repeating because they tend to be repetitive over the business cycle and are instrumental in developing the endogenous investment cycles. The final two sections outline the roles of innovation and the state. Both these latter two sections have self-repeating aspects that can support the endogenous investment cycle process, but it is changes in the roles that they perform that bring about structural (exogenous) shocks to the investment cycle and in this way alter a long-term development process.

Fundamental to the way manufacturing firms operate in this study is Kalecki's monopoly capitalism. This structure is dominated by cost-determined markets which have constant prime costs and a mark-up for pricing up until normal capacity utilisation. The mark-up allows payments of overheads (e.g. interest, salaries, rent), depreciation of capital equipment, and net profit which needs to be divided between dividends and retained earnings for planned investment.

Kalecki's basic institutional framework is modified in this chapter to take into account the criticisms of the Kaleckian monopoly capitalist analysis in Chapter 2, and the behavioural aspects discussed in Chapter 3 which centre around the uncertainty nature of investment. The result is a 'behavioural Kaleckian' institutional framework that establishes the basis for a cyclical model of investment.

4.2 FIRM COMPETITION

Kalecki asserts that capitalism is 'monopolised' with a high degree of concentration in manufacturing industries. This is the prevalent market structure in manufacturing for all developed western economies (Sylos Labini, 1984a, pp. 87–9). Manufacturing can be divided into three types of oligopolies, following Sylos Labini (1984a, p. 186): concentrated (or non-differentiated) oligopoly in industries producing major basic producer goods like steel, glass, chemical products; differentiated oligopoly in industries producing non-durable consumer goods like soap, breakfast cereals, soft drinks; and mixed oligopoly (concentration *cum* differentiation) in industries producing durable consumer goods like refrigerators, stoves, automobiles. As will become evident below, the difference in the type of oligopoly has implications for the way investment decisions are carried out.

Most resources are mined by large global firms that are highly concentrated in a worldwide market (Caves *et al.*, 1987, p. 25). Processing minerals into higher value added resources (e.g. bauxite into alumina and aluminium) is part of manufacturing, and is conducted by the same large mining-based firms. Within manufacturing, these firms form powerful oligopolies that operate as 'concentrated oligopoly' types (see section 2.4).

The pricing behaviour model is price leadership. Such a model is the most consistent within the Kaleckian framework of monopoly capitalism. This consistency is outlined by Bloch in section 2.4, with Kalecki's pricing equation being depicted as a case of price leadership with the possibility of having an uncompetitive fringe of small firms. It is quite possible that the leadership may switch from one large firm to another depending on the changing market shares. Such 'arrangements' may be informal and tacit or within a formal cartel structure.

The cost pattern behind price leadership behaviour is basic Kaleckian. Prime (or direct) costs consist of the cost of labour, raw materials and produced variable input goods and services (such as power). They all vary with the changes in the level of output produced by the firm. Prime costs decrease per unit of output until the technical scale of minimum efficient production is reached, then prime costs per unit are constant for levels up to full capacity level of production – forming an L-shaped marginal prime cost curve (which at the horizontal level is also equal to average unit prime costs). Overhead (or fixed) costs consist of depreciation, interest, administrative expenses (including managerial and senior clerical salaries), research and development non-capital costs (e.g. laboratory staff). These costs only alter at extremes of production levels. Nearing peak production, these costs tend to rise slightly due to pressures on demand (higher salaries and financing). Nearing trough production, these costs bear proportionately greater importance and short-term finance may rise due to the cash flow problem.

Sylos Labini's strategic price hypothesis is combined with Goldstein's cyclical profit squeeze on mark-ups (see section 2.3.2) to provide a modified Kaleckian variable mark-up hypothesis that applies to all three types of oligopolies. Although the mark-up remains relatively stable over the long term, the mark-up in the short term varies due to reasons external and internal to the firm. The external reason relates to foreign competition. As domestic prime costs rise after mid-expansion of the business cycle, a constant mark-up would raise the price relative to imported products that are similar or identical, which would reduce the domestic firms' market share. For this reason, domestic firms' price will not rise proportionate to prime costs and the mark-up will fall until the business cycle trough. Internal oligopolistic rivalry will also induce a fall in the mark-up at mid-expansion. Internal to the firm is concern that new entrants or anti-trust authorities may recognise too high a price and attractive profits (especially if there is an expansion of demand at the time prime costs rise – which often happens with wages near the top of the business cycle).

Kalecki's 'degree of monopoly' factors (see section 2.4) are still relevant in this reconstruction. They are the crucial factors behind the action of the price leaders. The 'degree of monopoly' factors determine the strength of the oligopoly structure in the industry. The first factor is industrial concentration. Firms with predominantly non-differentiated products form the most concentrated markets. These large firms form a 'natural' oligopoly due to the basic producer-oriented nature of the product, e.g. steel. A common homogeneous product which is basic to most producer goods and services provides strong market strength that allows a large mark-up. The large and 'lumpy' nature of investment in these industries also demands a large mark-up. All the firms face virtually identical cost curves and thus the 'strategic price' is easily agreed upon (most likely tacitly). Short-term cut-throat competition can reduce the mark-up when there is a government-sponsored public firm set up for nationalistic reasons and which is being publicly subsidised to reduce prices.

In differentiated oligopolies the second and third 'degree of monopoly' factors (sales promotion and price agreements) play an important role. The greater the ability of large firms to differentiate their own consumer non-durable product and hold huge slabs of the market, the stronger is the price leadership. All large firms in such industries recognise that their own differentiation is only strong as long as there is no cut-throat competition. It is a strong reinforcement of the mark-up. The weaker the differentiation (or brand loyalty) of the large firms, and the weaker the differentiated oligopoly, the greater the opportunity for the uncompetitive fringe to be competitive at least in the short-term through variations in output, and the more chance to break the 'strategic price' position. Mixed oligopolies are somewhere between concentrated and differentiated oligopolies, exhibiting features of both. For example, the automotive industry has some 'natural' attributes which give it a 'concentrated' look – 'a car is a car', but differentiation through sales promotion is strong.

The final 'degree of monopoly' factor is the power of the trade unions. Here the issue becomes much more complex than in Kalecki's system. Powerful union action on wages during booms can reduce the 'degree of monopoly' of any oligopolistic industry, leading to reduced mark-ups. However, unions also play a role during recessions in trying to maintain employment (and their membership), which means less pressure for increased wages and more pressure to maintain levels of production through agreements with firms to keep down wages so that there is less pressure on prices via the mark-up. These tendencies can be aided or thwarted by the state in terms of the nature of industrial relations established in its jurisdiction.[1] General propositions regarding the links between the state and trade unions in this model are set out in section 4.6.

Pressure on wages, with the inability fully to mark up on price, provides an inducement for firms to plan investment strategies involving more labour-saving MOP. This would not only reduce wages but increase productivity. Both factors work towards increased 'degree of monopoly' for firms as their subsequent larger mark-up enables them to pay for even more labour-saving investments in the future. If, however, at the beginning the pressure of wages is easily passed on (say in very concentrated oligopolies), then there is less incentive to raise productivity through labour-saving MOP.

The ability of firms to stay as price leaders (or gain ascendancy as such) needs to be considered. In all the discussions on non-price competition the investment strategy issue has been at the forefront, whether in relation to trade unions (and wages), level of mark-up, new entrants, even sales promotion (much of which requires capital investment in marketing sections, etc.). Investment planning is an important part of non-price competition in all types of oligopoly structures. Firms will attempt to react to objective changes by altering their investment decisions, as shown in the next two chapters. Some firms will be more adaptable in reacting to such changes and they will make investment decisions more quickly, efficiently and accurately with more efficient lines of credit and finance. Such firms can be assured future leadership (whether or not they are currently in that position).

Under this price leadership model, excess capacity acts as an expensive, but necessary, co-operative threat by the current large 'players' in the industry. This ensures that new entrants are deterred and also provides a credible threat to any established firm which thinks it could increase market share by breaking out of the co-operative approach. In both cases the threat is that extra output can be produced and prices dropped for a short time, forcing firms back to the co-operative situation where large firms in the oligopoly tacitly determine price and output. Excess capacity threat has been incorporated into Kaleckian microeconomic analysis (see section 2.3.1), and is important for the development of the story of the investment cycle to be presented in the next two chapters.

4.3 ROLE OF AGENTS IN THE FIRM

The role of various agents within the company needs to be clearly delineated for the investment cycle analysis in the following chapters. This position is evident from discussions of the behaviour of agents under uncertainty in Chapter 3. Instability of beliefs by various agents involved in the investment decision-making process, and how they relate to each other, sets up the endogenous investment cycle. The role which each agent plays affects the way investment decisions are made and then carried out. Further, the role of these same agents in corporate evolution under innovative uncertainty determines major exogenous shifts in technology and subsequent influence on the investment cycle.

The managerialist simple separation of owners and managers is rejected, while Kalecki's original formulation of the 'controlling group' is inadequate for modern diversely owned corporations. Kalecki's 'controlling group' is now modified for modern corporations, taking into account the managerialist view of the important role of managers. The 'controlling group' in this analysis pertains to the joint-stock corporations which dominate the oligopolistic structures outlined in the previous section. This group is made up of (a) Kalecki's original 'entrepreneur-owners' who typically control closely knit ownership corporations (often based on kinship ties or interlocking directorates between a few corporations); and (b) 'entrepreneur-managers' hired to make the major decisions in diversely owned (or loosely knit ownership) corporations. The two types of entrepreneurs make up the newly redefined 'controlling group'.[2]

In the rest of this study the term 'entrepreneur' is used to refer to both owner and manager types. This term indicates the controlling group in the corporation which makes the investment decisions. Either of the sub-groups is referred to by its full description (i.e. entrepreneur-owners or entrepreneur-managers) when there is a need to note differences between actions or implications of the two sub-groups.[3]

The advantage of this taxonomy of entrepreneurs is that the role of 'capitalists' becomes clearer. There are first the industrial capitalists, made up of what are now identified as entrepreneurs, who control the important investment decisions. The second group are the financial capitalists, made up of rentiers who are either shareholders not within the controlling group of entrepreneurs or lenders of finance. The role of the 'shareholder rentier' is clear, it identifies members of the corporation who are only in the corporation for dividend returns (long-term shareholders) or capital gains on shares (short-term shareholders). Capitalists in this model, both industrial and financial, have strategic interests in the investment decisions of the companies with which they are involved. In Kalecki's terms, they are 'masters of their fate', who influence investment decisions in ways discussed below. This clarifies the capitalists' role within the Kaleckian capitalist/worker dichotomy.

This taxonomy of entrepreneurs enables the incorporation of the managerialist view of the corporation within the broader Kaleckian framework. Entrepreneur-managers see themselves as part of the company and are as committed to its reproduction as the entrepreneur-owners. This is consistent with the view by Wood (1975) that the senior management level makes the crucial decisions which in effect 'control' the corporation. There is also recognition of a still important group of entrepreneur-owners who take 'control' of their corporation by the major decisions they make (even if they do not handle the day-to-day affairs of the company). Such corporations are 'run' by significant powerful owners who, while not holding a majority ownership, have enough to control the company board and make major decisions from this position. Cubbin and Leech (1983) show that as little as 2 per cent of shares is often enough for such control.

Entrepreneurs control the investment decision-making process through a sequence of investment decisions. This sequence can be dissected into three separate influences: (a) profit determination; (b) profit distribution and (c) investment planning. Each influence has a compounding effect on the next, creating an interdependent investment decision-making sequence. The manner in which entrepreneurs handle the three influences determines their control over investment, relative to other agents within the institutional framework. Each of the three influences is examined below.

The Kaleckian profit-determination process and its influence on investment decision-making is discussed in section 2.3.2. The conclusion from that section is that mark-up, price and output are decided in order to achieve the necessary profit to maximise reproduction of the corporation through reinvestment. The entrepreneur decides on the mark-up in relation to what Sylos Labini calls long-run profit maximisation to ensure that maximum investment and growth is possible.[4] The co-operative process in price leadership models is carried out by entrepreneur-owners through either tacit understanding between owners or direct links between corporations (interlocking directorates). Entrepreneur-managers can also develop tacit understanding within markets, or in the case of fairly new corporations, through trial-and-error strategies (*à la* game theory, see Ulph, 1987) which end up reaching the same co-operative position.

The second major influence on investment decision-making is profit distribution between dividends and retained earnings. Through this decision, the controlling group in effect determines the income of all the shareholders. Due to the increasing risk involved in external financing (see section 2.3.3), entrepreneurs prefer a high retention ratio.[5] Rentier-shareholders prefer a high dividend payout rate (or low retention ratio) in order to satisfy their advertising-induced, high-consumption needs.[6] Entrepreneurs control dividend policy and their concern is for the long-term reproduction and growth of the corporation, thus rentier-shareholders generally have no choice but to accept low payout rates.

The position of long-term shareholders is more complex than that of short-term shareholders. The latter require high payout rates which add to the higher valuation of the shares in the stock market and thus their aim of capital gains. Long-term growth and possible long-term higher valuation of stock is not relevant to these short-term shareholders, but it is relevant to the long-term shareholders. The potential internal conflict of long-term shareholders for high dividends *and* growth is usually resolved in favour of long-term growth. These shareholders are willing, through loyalty and support, to see long-term expansion providing future higher profits and *then* higher dividends – even on the current high retention ratio.[7]

In extraordinary times the interests of all rentier-shareholders and entrepreneurs coincide with respect to the same corporation. Such times relate to when market valuation of shares becomes a crucial issue for survival in the short term due to takeover raids or stockholder revolts. In these circumstances entrepreneurs are constrained from meeting their long-term objective of growth and give in to high payout rates in the hope of raising the share price. Once the crisis is resolved, entrepreneurs can revert back to their long-term investment based strategies. If there are continual raids and revolts due to a wildly fluctuating stock market prone to massive speculative uncertainty, then entrepreneurs continue to concentrate on the short term. Investment decisions under these circumstances are continually put off. If many major sectors of the corporate economy are involved, economic development is threatened.[8] Such stock market crises are 'exogenous' to the basic investment cycle analysis and are examined (along with other exogenous shocks) in Chapter 6.

The third major influence on investment decision-making is investment planning and implementation. This influence builds upon the previous two influences. In section 5.3, the whole-time profile of investment (from planning strategies to operation) is outlined. Here the concern is about the type and nature of control which entrepreneurs have over investment in the corporation and what factors (if any) can undermine this control. The separation of rentier-shareholders and entrepreneurs can create a theoretical problem due to the short-term vision of the former. In reality, rentier-shareholder 'power' is more the exception than the rule. The constraint of dividend payout to rentier-shareholders is weak except for designated periods of market valuation crises.

Rentier-lenders are a more serious constraint on investment planning. Borrowing is subject to 'increasing risk', which means that attempts to increase investment through external finance puts a constraint on the firm. The 1970s low (and negative) real interest rates and the 1980s leveraged stock buyouts both increased corporate debt–equity ratios such that further investment decisions were constrained if external finance was required. Financial lenders increased their influence over investment decisions in the 1980s and early 1990s as corporate gearing (or leverage) grew. The implications of higher gearing is examined systematically in the next chapter.

A related 'increasing risk' constraint on investment, and one which increases rentier-shareholders' influence, comes from any attempt to escape the gearing constraint with the issue of new shares. Kalecki was the first to identify the constraint of losing 'control' over all the three major decision-making influences as more shares are issued. This is a potential constraint which is easier to realise in diversely owned corporations where entrepreneur-managers could be controlling with only 2 per cent of shares. For entrepreneur-owners the constraint is difficult to realise, such that in tightly knit corporations, the concerns of small shareholders can be, and often are, ignored.

It is appropriate to call the 'controlling group' entrepreneurs, because all investment decisions imply some innovation, however small. They are more than just managers, they more than 'manage', they steer the corporation into an unknown future where technology is always changing. To be successful, entrepreneurs must be able to cope and succeed in this technologically competitive struggle. Now, there are other senior salaried administrative staff who are really managers in the sense of handling day-to-day affairs (e.g. accounting, personnel, industrial relations). Once the investment decisions are made, these other administrative staff need to be involved to implement the decisions (e.g. hiring the right staff with technical skills, arranging short-term (wages fund) finance, etc.).

To the extent that administrative managers have the ability to frustrate the long-term investment plans of the entrepreneurs, then control can be constrained (or weakened) by their actions. Lack of co-operation can delay, but not stop, investment decisions. The ability to change the decisions is extremely limited because the technical needs of investment are in the hands of engineers and technicians. Their future in the firm (and as professionals) is based on their ability to deliver the best technology in the investment, even to the point of improving on the investment plan already developed.

Two arguments can be used to support the view that 'short-term managers' only have, at the most, a weak effect on reducing the controlling power of entrepreneurs. First is that the firm's planning and implementation is generally 'chaotic', with short planning horizons (maximum three to four years). This reduces any possible conflict with short-term managers because the time horizons of entrepreneurs is not all that much longer than their counterparts in short-term management. Also, there is no real attempt by short-term managers to frustrate well-thought-out 10–20-year plans by entrepreneurs, because 'chaos' in planning ensures that such plans do not exist.[9]

The second argument is based on the application of game theory strategy to the firm's internal operations. A few top managers in each section of the firm give instructions. For their own survival, any attempts by managers not to co-operate with each other lasts only a short time. There is a tendency to devise co-operative strategies which make life easier and more efficient for all the managers concerned. There is no future for managers trying to operate outside co-operative (explicit and implicit) strategies devised in the corporation. Threats are devised to prevent such occurrence. Frustrations still remain, especially with new short-term managers, but 'learning by doing' should solve this. As for entrepreneur-owners, their overall control of closely knit corporations ensures that conflicts in internal management which frustrate their plans are extremely limited.

So far in this chapter, an institutional framework of monopoly capitalism with its implications for the role of agents in investment decision-making has been developed. At this stage, it can be concluded that 'megacorps': (a) control the manufacturing sector and propel the economy; (b) use co-operative mark-up pricing for long-term growth; and (c) are controlled by entrepreneurs who have relative autonomy in achieving this long-term growth.

4.4 FINANCIAL BEHAVIOUR

The financial behaviour of megacorps and the implication of this behaviour on the financial market is examined in this section. This is an important aspect of the investment analysis in the following chapters, since investment behaviour is impinged upon by both the real sector and the financial sector. The implications of financial behaviour for the stability (or lack of stability) of the financial market, and how in turn the market develops overtly political and oligopolistic behaviour to overcome this instability, are also outlined in this section.

All companies establish a gearing (or leverage) limit using the debt–equity ratio. This limit depends on entrepreneurial expectations of both the future course of profits and the risks (and disadvantages) of borrowing in relation to the degree of risk aversion by the entrepreneurs. These expectations are 'not only conditioned by the knowledge of data and risks but also by the initiative and the ability of managers' (Sylos Labini, 1984a, p. 133). The gearing limit set is an internal 'increasing risk' constraint on investment decision-making based on the borrower's own estimation of this risk. The lenders' perspective on what this gearing limit should be may not accord with the firm's own gearing limit. Kalecki sees borrower's risk as generally the prior constraint to lender's risk, but particular circumstances can reverse this order.

In Kalecki's analysis, only entrepreneurial capital is considered as equity in the gearing ratio, since other shareholders' equity to rentiers is a 'risk' to the controlling group. However, the framework has been expanded to include diversely owned companies with entrepreneur-managers controlling the organisation with little (or no) shareholding equity. Thus, Kalecki's specialised gearing ratio (debt to entrepreneurial capital) is not general enough to take account of diversely owned companies, which are very prolific due to institutional shareholdings. The following analysis of gearing is based on the more conventional simple-debt–total-equity gearing ratio.

As set out in the previous section, the dividend policy of entrepreneurs requires the maintenance of a stable level of dividends with a low payout rate. This dividend should remain stable at the lower end of the possible range for maintaining investor confidence.[10]

There is no simple 'rate of profit' target for investment. The target derives from mark-up policy and, thus, net profit return over the long term. This net profit return target is based on the rate of expansion of sales in the near future (given the tacit or formal understandings between the large firms in the industry), the critical gearing limits, and the decision on dividend payout rates (and hence partially the rate of return on share capital, see below). For this reason, net profit becomes an important financial indicator in the empirical analysis of Chapter 7.

Now the perspective of the financial behavioural framework is broadened to look, first, at the share market, then at other financial institutions which are principally lenders to firms, and finally to the broader power role such financial institutions play in modern capitalism.

Shares are traded in an extraordinarily volatile and uncertain market due to the dominance of speculative activities by short-term shareholders. This speculative behaviour relates to the need for quick responses by these shareholders who seek capital gains upon the basis of the very limited amount of 'hard' information available. This 'causes an exaggerated importance to be attached to isolated scraps of information and unsubstantiated rumours' (Wood, 1975, p. 43). Thus, the short-term price of a company's shares reflects much more these speculative activities to a greater extent than the company's own dividend policy.

The latter is only of concern to long-term shareholders who do not move the share price significantly and who became notably less important in the 1980s.

Lenders to companies are only concerned with rates of return, as are ordinary shareholders. Lending companies seek maximum sales revenue through high rates of return from their loans. Due to lender's risk, obtaining a loan gives the financier a much more powerful position than ordinary shareholders. As discussed in section 2.3.3, to cover such risk lenders require security on the loan as well as a higher interest rate as the gearing ratio of the company rises, until a too-high gearing ratio leads to outright refusal at any interest rate (see Vickers, 1987).

There are two power-related implications of financial fragility which create important self-repeating institutional developments impacting on the endogenous investment analysis. Both implications feature in the investment cycle when financial indebtedness becomes severe. The first relates to Kalecki's political business cycle, where rentiers become concerned that an inflationary situation is unsound as Ponzi financing becomes common, leading to a Minsky-type fragile financial system. This induces governments to end such inflation with short-term deflationary policies. At this stage the rentiers' interests conflict with the entrepreneurs' interests. These conflicts between fractions of capital create their own uncertainty.

More important is the political power that puts pressure on governments for longer-term deflationary macro-policies. The rise of monetarism as a 'social doctrine' is a particular case of this general principle (see Bhaduri and Steindl, 1983). Financial institutions do not want financial fragility based on Ponzi financing to continue once major debt non-repayments begin to become a serious problem for them. Given the oligopolistic nature of finance business, no one financial corporation stops lending because that threatens its market share, its image and the future loyalty of customers. It is better done via the government instead, with the attendant advantage of reducing the growing deficit of public budgets which siphon funds away from private financial interests.

The second element is based on financial institutions encouraging industrial concentration. This strengthens firms' financial repayments due to fewer bankruptcies, less price-cutting leading to losses and delays in repayments, and more cost-determined markets so that the cost of interest can be accounted for explicitly.[11] The need of large corporations to refinance indebtedness when the financial system is fragile leads to stronger co-operative efforts between corporations in different industries. This is supported and encouraged by banks through strong interlocking directorships, where banks' own leading entrepreneurs (i.e. general managers and board chairmen) are also involved in these linkages. Carroll (1990, p. 14) describes the 'power and influence' exercised by banks through networks such as 'the Money Relations Club'. These positions of power enable banks to organise financial rescue packages, oversee financial decision-making and encourage complementary strategies between corporations to overcome any threats of financial instability.

4.5 ROLE OF INNOVATION

Kalecki identifies two structural features of capitalism that affect the pattern of investment cycles (see section 2.5). They are innovation and the state. The respective role of each in the above institutional framework is outlined in this and the next section.

The role of (technological) innovation developed here is Kaleckian-based, modified by the influence of the new evolutionary school (see section 3.6). Essentially, at the firm level innovation is the search for profit which has significant implications for investment. From this perspective, innovation is not forced on any firm, but the competitive forces in each particular industry significantly affect the rate of adoption by firms of new innovation principles.

New technological systems have the potential to change the pattern of long-term production, and in this way to alter the structure of the economy and industries within it. New systems are an exogenous element to any single firm. Subsequent endogenous (or incremental) innovations based on these new systems have short-term effects on the investment cycle. Quick adoption in one industry, due to strong competitive factors, ensures a larger cyclical investment expansion than in weak competitive industries. Such differing adoption rates are a self-repeating aspect of endogenous investment cycles. Increasing the rate of adoption of new innovation principles into industries changes the role of innovation itself. This brings with it stronger long-term structural exogenous shocks to the investment cycles of the respective industries.

The distinction between endogenous and exogenous underlines the causes of innovation. Endogenous innovation is based on the Kaleckian notion of 'part and parcel' of the investment process itself. This is innovation 'as a product', used to enhance capital and consumer goods when competitive pressures force firms to invest by utilising the stock of innovations on hold (see section 2.5). This 'endogenous' approach recognises that innovation is not simply an addition of a trend line to cycle behaviour, but has a crucial role to play in affecting profit returns at the margin (new MOP versus old MOP). The amount of endogenous innovation affects productivity, profit returns and investment order patterns.

Invention is the devising of something new, as by ingenuity. There is no implication in the process of invention for the commercial introduction of inventions. This latter commercialisation process is innovation. Yet, Kalecki (1954, p. 158) stated that 'a steady stream of inventions adds to investment' in his analysis of 'long-run economic development'. Since only commercial viability of innovations adds to investment, Kalecki's 'steady stream' can be understood as endogenous innovation. From this explication of Kalecki's confusion of terms, this framework adopts the logical extension that invention's introduction into the commercial world is through endogenous innovation.

Endogenous innovation consists of 'incremental innovation' that reflects fluctuating rates of investment due to learning by 'doing' and 'using', and 'radical innovation' due to deliberate R&D activity as a 'potential springboard for growth of new markets, and for surges of new investment associated with booms' (Freeman and Perez, 1988, p. 46). R&D investment in the past, or buying out smaller uncompetitive firms during the contractionary phase, prepares 'radical innovations' for implementation.[12] For this study, endogenous innovation relates to both incremental and radical innovation. Both forms of innovation involve minor technological change that becomes embodied in MOP.[13]

Exogenous innovation is the random shock which delivers an asymmetric effect to the investment cycle, lengthening expansions and shortening contractions (see section 2.5). The evolutionary school establishes the forces which produce a technological paradigm shift such that the newly adapted technological systems pervade the whole economy (see section 3.6). Such a shift creates the random shock to the investment cycle. The rate of adoption of the new paradigm in different industries, as determined by the endogenous competitive forces described above, ascertains how strongly and how quickly the random shock develops into a long-term secular force.

Based on Levine (1981) and Shapiro (1981), interindustry competition produces strong product development as a platform for robust investment expansion (see section 2.5). Through stimulation of demand (needs creation) for the new paradigm's basic products, a product innovation-based paradigm shift occurs. Such innovation entails considerable technical and market uncertainty for the firms involved, which explains the idea of 'searching for profits'. As this uncertainty reduces with stronger demand construction, greater market co-ordination and swarming behaviour occurs in relation to these new paradigm product innovations.

The introduction of new techniques of production which lower costs is process innovation. Limitations of a techno-economic paradigm (e.g. inflexibility and high energy intensity of post-war mass production methods) induces research. The availability of new technological (scientific) principles allows process innovation and forms the basis of an emerging new technological paradigm (Verspagen, 1992, p. 49). To one particular megacorp, such new techniques are exogenous and, if successfully adopted widely, would lead to lower production costs. It does not stop there. New techniques tend to spawn endogenously opportunities for new products, which, if successfully introduced (minor product innovations), entrench the new techniques further. Minor process innovation improvements also are endogenously induced within firms that have already adopted the new paradigm.

There is also the exogenous influence of the state in encouraging new technological advances through the military-industrial complex and support for natural resource exploitation. Specifically, the state is directly involved in enhancing the adoption of new techniques by the funding of basic research and large spending on procurement-related R&D (see Nelson, 1990, p. 209). In this way, the role of the state is to support the role of innovation in shifting to a new paradigm, by reducing costs of private sector research in a highly uncertain endeavour.

The effect of innovation is two-fold. At the micro-level, innovation is used by firms as a managerial tool to maintain and increase market share in the short term with survival and growth in the long term. The strong endogenous role innovation plays in homogeneous industries acts as a stimulus to investment during periods of low economic activity. Often such innovation involves interindustry competition and diversification out of mature areas of the industry (e.g. basic steel manufacturers developing new consumer-oriented products like 'colorbond roofing'). During booms, 'safety preference' reduces the pace of induced innovation.

The new computer-based technological paradigm has introduced great flexibility and co-operative networking in production. This has allowed the development of a strong synergy between small firms (science-based and supplier-based) and large oligopolistic firms (scale- and information-intensive). The megacorps are still dominant in the economy, but the new technologies enable strong innovatory behaviour by small firms in order to satisfy a larger part of the megacorps' needs. The linkages are outlined in detail in section 3.6.

At the macro-level, the success of a new paradigm creates a swarming of innovatory behaviour, leading to a strong growth in aggregate investment. The exhaustion of most aspects of the technological paradigm and the growing limitations on its continued use lead to weak aggregate investment booms and secular stagnation. In this model, these successes and exhaustions provide the exogenous random shocks to the firm and industry investment cycles, which manifest themselves by variations in cycle amplitude. For example, strong growth in aggregate investment due to new technology, if diffused quickly into a particular industry, would produce large amplitudes in firm investment expansions and small amplitudes in firm investment contractions. This then produces an upward investment growth trend that is quicker and stronger than in industries where adaptation to the new paradigm is slower.

4.6 ROLE OF THE STATE

The role of the state developed here is Kaleckian-based with a specific public sector structure based on O'Connor (1973). The O'Connor state sector involves both the production and provision of public goods. This consists of public authorities (or enterprises), public services (e.g. education, health, social services) and private companies which supply public goods in areas like armaments, capital goods construction and transport construction. The private companies tend to exhibit relatively high capital to labour ratios, but productivity in all areas is difficult to measure due to unique or individual productions, non-market services and cross-subsidised pricing and investment decisions. Also, some private companies in the state sector (especially in armaments) are also in the monopoly sector (e.g. General Electric), which creates empirical problems that can only be handled on a case-by-case approach.

Interdependence between public and private sectors is an important structural feature of modern capitalism and forms part of the institutional framework of this analysis. The state of private investment behaviour cannot be divorced from what the public sector is doing because of the way in which powerful private oligopolistic firms in O'Connor's 'monopoly sector' have developed co-operative strategies between themselves which require government support for social investment (infrastructure support for private industry) and social consumption (private social cost outlays).[14]

In this model, the state is linked to powerful trade unions (or peak union bodies) chiefly through the industrial relations system. This link can support union actions for wages during booms and maintaining employment during recessions. In general, the state strongly supports the mutual interests of large oligopolistic manufacturing firms and strong industrial unions. More recently, in post-industrial society, there has been a relative shift of corporate power away from industrial capitalists to finance (and other service-based) capitalists whose workforce is much less unionised.[15] In these circumstances, the manufacturing-based industrial relations system (with its award structures and comparative wage justice principles) becomes an impediment to the rising capitalists. Some governments have attempted to eliminate these impediments by introducing policies that undermine union power and the system that supports it.

The relative autonomy view of the state underlies relations between the public and private sectors in this Kaleckian structure. When there are disagreements between fractions of capital, especially during periods of considerable structural change, the state can more autonomously pursue economic policies that are different from the needs of the monopoly sector. Fundamental disagreements also develop between capitalists (together with their managers) and unions in modern monopoly capitalist economies which are undergoing major post-industrial structural change. This provides the state with the ability to initiate new industrial relations structures which may not be in concert with the established monopoly sector's needs, but more in support of either the rising capitalists (by conservative governments) or the humanist/socialist objectives of left-based governments.

A capitalist economy exhibits growth of both surplus (excess) capacity and surplus population (unemployment) in the monopoly (oligopolistic) sector based on the Kaleckian principle of expanding capacity to employ existing capacity (Beresford and McFarlane, 1980, p. 231). In this case, 'monopoly capital must create expanding markets (which it can control) in order to utilise productive capacity that otherwise would be idle' (O'Connor, 1973, p. 27). This expansion is supported by a growing state sector, which also absorbs the surplus population from an increasingly capital-intensive monopoly sector.

The public sector resolution of the problem of effective demand (through Keynesian macropolicy and 'external markets') creates a growing state sector which is squeezed from further tax revenue due to growing public tax resistance. Increased government debts needed to overcome the fiscal shortage exacerbates the growing fiscal crisis. The conventional conservative forces, following the other Kaleckian principle of the political business cycle, demand sound financing of government by reducing budget deficits and turning them into budget surpluses. This principle has been recently extended to demand that certain elements of public infrastructure, which have now become profitable in a post-industrial society, should be given to the private sector (e.g. communications, air transport, banking). The fiscal crisis, it is argued by conservatives, cannot support the massive capital investments by government that are needed in these areas, and also provide basic social consumption for an ageing society (Aubin, 1990).

In Kalecki's political business cycle, the 'stop–go' mechanism of macropolicy ensures that there is a self-repeating aspect of the role of the state which adds further to the cyclical nature of investment. The 'stop' mechanism of increased deflationary fiscal policies reduces capacity utilisation and raises direct costs which squeezes profit margins, leading to reduced investment. Tighter monetary policies raise overhead interest costs, further squeezing margins. The 'go' mechanism tends to have the reverse effect, which stimulates investment. In Chapter 5, the endogenous investment cycle analysis can be influenced by Kalecki's political business cycle.

With the increasing oligopolistic nature of capitalist economies, the surplus capacity and surplus population problems not only fluctuate, but also grow over time. This means that each boom becomes more serious with correspondingly more pressures for public finance stringencies. This is a secular factor overlaying the cyclical 'stop–go' mechanism. The secular movement to more stagnatory policies over the longer term, involving the increasing trend to smaller public budget deficits (even to budget surpluses), and implications for the investment cycle are discussed in Chapter 6 with other secular or exogenous factors.

Institutionally, the state establishes 'external markets' through imperialism or a military-industrial complex. This aims to create realisation outlets outside the pure capitalist economy in order to secure long-term growth and accumulation. A drive by the state for expansion of foreign demand in order to create a trade surplus or to reduce a trade deficit is an extension of the 'external markets' approach. Sylos Labini (1984a, p. 140) details how the 'push has come from public decision centres' to initiate the Common Market, Japanese export-orientation, USA firms' subsidiaries overseas, and Third World expansion into world trade markets.

State manipulation of foreign demand has led to its own peculiar political business cycle. An expansion of foreign demand by the state (e.g. export incentives) increases profitability and stimulates investment. A contraction of foreign demand due to serious current account deficits, by deflationary macropolicies, results in more 'stop' mechanism effects and its investment consequences. Kalecki (1971, pp. 15–25) notes the identical investment implications of export deficits and the earlier discussion of budget deficits. Again, such self-repeating state manipulation of foreign demand influences the endogenous investment cycle analysis in the following chapter. Secular and random factors in the international economy (e.g. the collapse of Bretton Woods, increased protectionist policies, reduction in the military-industrial complex after the collapse of communism in Eastern Europe) are exogenous influences on the investment cycle analysis and are examined in Chapter 6.

NOTES

1. There is the added complexity of overlapping industrial relations jurisdictions between federal (or national) government and various province (or regional) based governments. Intergovernmental conflict occurs when a sub-national government aims to thwart the power of unions while the national government develops industrial relations policies in concert with the unions. The model in this study does not formally include this aspect of the role of the state. Jurisdictional conflict may become relevant in specific capitalist economies under empirical investigation.

2. Pitelis (1986) provides evidence to support the rejection of the separation of owners and managers. The argument is not ownership *or* control, but ownership *and* control by what Kalecki calls a 'controlling group'.

3. Lawriwsky's (1984) study of the different roles of owners and managers in Australia, Europe and the USA applies the same distinction to entrepreneurs, noting different motivations between owners and managers but also noting fundamentally the same survival and growth techniques of both types of entrepreneurs.

4. The mark-up is based on a proportion for fixed costs (including managerial salaries and stipends) and the remainder as net profit. The decision on managerial salaries and stipends for board members are based on the consumption needs and personal savings requirements of entrepreneurs. Higher salaries and stipends would, *ceteris paribus*, require a higher mark-up in order to maintain the same long run profit and investment stance (see Cowling, 1982, pp. 52–6).

5. The (gross) retention ratio is defined as the ratio of internal finance to (gross) operating profit. Internal finance consists of charges assigned as depreciation allowances and retained earnings (Wood, 1975, p. 39).

6. See Duesenberry (1967) and Cowling (1982) on this point. Duesenberry calls it 'the demonstration effect', while Cowling calls it 'the advertising induced effect'.

7. Research by Wood (1975, pp. 39–40) supports this view of high retention ratios by 'megacorps'.

8. For detail discussion of investment instability based on these concerns of owners and managers, and their manifestation in low investment during periods of stock market uncertainty within a Kaleckian framework, see Crotty (1990).

9. Robin Marris, in discussions on the role of entrepreneurs, pointed out to me the 'chaotic' nature of investment planning. These discussions were held in Trieste on 27 September 1990 during the Ninth International Summer School of Advanced Economic Studies. For written support, examine the writings of Shackle (see section 3.3), in particular Shackle (1969).

10. If in one year a higher payout is provided and the next year a lower payout is provided, the second-year decrease often creates a loss of investor confidence and a lower market valuation of shares. For this reason, it is better if a lower but stable payout is provided over the two years, then the market valuation would not fluctuate as much. The risks entailed in having a high payout ratio is revealed by the data which show a positive correlation

between payout ratio and the gearing ratio (Wood, 1975, p. 48, footnote).

11. This argument has its intellectual origins in Hilferding (1981), originally published in German in 1910.

12. R&D investment increases the productive capacity of the firm, enabling it to increase investment that is innovative (see Kay, 1979, for detailed discussion on the behavioural aspects of the innovating firm). R&D investment may be constant throughout the investment cycle, or may vary under the same susceptibility pressures of other investment commitments. Which of the two it is depends on how important R&D is for the firm and industry. In an industry where innovation is a regular competitive tool, R&D investment is large and variable under the same susceptibility pressures as other investment. In an industry where innovation is only occasionally implemented, R&D investment is small and constant over the cycle. Non-differentiated industries tend to conduct R&D investment in process innovation work, while differentiated industries tend to conduct R&D investment in product innovation work. The exception is firms in homogeneous industries attempting to use R&D investment to diversify out of mature areas of their industries (see later in this section).

13. Salter (1960) examines this form of technological change in terms of long-term productivity gains and structural change.

14. From a non-Marxist perspective, Sylos Labini (1984a, p. 21) supports this interdependence thesis.

15. Such a relative shift of corporate power does not contradict the 'engine of growth' Kaleckian view of manufacturing set out in section 2.4. The shift refers to the relatively increased concentration in finance and other service industries of a post-industrial economy. In such an economy, manufacturing still plays a significant role as the 'locomotive' force for economic growth, given the established large capital stock base and the strong multipliers derived from this base (Reynolds, 1987, p. 200).

5. The Susceptibility Cycle: an Endogenous Model

> The relative importance of the various elements responsible for the cumulative expansion and contraction processes determines the exact nature of the upper and lower turning points . . . Changes are to be expected over time according to the character of investment and according to the psychological attitudes of those responsible for investment decisions. (Matthews, 1959, p. 83)

5.1 CYCLICAL BEHAVIOUR OF INVESTMENT

In a survey of investment and its role in business cycles, Matthews (1959, pp. 7–97) emphasises the endogenous nature of investment instability. This is based upon past investment levels and the cumulative implications such past historical conditions have for crucial elements in the investment decision-making processes currently being conducted. The quotation above notes that changes in investment occur because of two aspects of the investment process: the 'character of investment' and the 'psychological attitudes' of decision-makers. Matthews' survey of past investment theories and his own analysis do not unite these two crucial aspects. In this chapter an investment model is developed which does unite both aspects. The dynamic character of investment is interrelated with the decision-makers' psychological attitudes to the cumulative investment process, as specified by the susceptibility cycle, to provide an integrated endogenous investment cycle.

Angell (1941, p. 5) notes that self-generating (endogenous) factors give the essential characteristic of business cycles in that 'each process and phase leads on to the next in an unceasing self-repeating round, and that

114

in at least their broader characteristics the several recurring sequences are fairly uniform as between one cycle and the next'. Investment is the central self-generating factor in major business cycles. Angell makes an early attempt at understanding the linkage between investment and business cycles, which has been developed theoretically by the Kaleckian literature outlined in Chapter 2.

The investment–business cycle linkage is understood. It is the cyclical self-repeating behaviour of investment which has lacked an adequate explanation. The reason is two-fold. The first is that investment functions use one monocausal investment theory to explain self-generating business cycles. This is evident in the review of investment theories in Chapter 2 (e.g. Mott and Minsky on financial commitments; Sylos Labini and Goldstein on profit squeeze; Steindl on excess capacity). Behaviour is multifarious, and *all* the theories examined previously have a role to play in the development of a highly sensitive behavioural approach to investment. The 'highly sensitive' state of investment, noted but not explained by Zarnowitz (1985, p. 556) in his review of modern business cycle theories, is a behavioural description which leads to cyclical activity.

The second reason is that investment theories do not recognise how self-generating investment behaviour links with exogenous factors that are seasonal, secular or random. All three factors may alter the duration, amplitude, intra-cycle trend and even some of the internal sequences of the principal components of the actual investment cycles, 'but they do not and cannot alter the essential and self-generating character of the cycles themselves' (Angell, 1941, p. 5). The next chapter describes how such exogenous factors affect the endogenous investment cycle model developed.

This chapter brings together uncertainty-based antecedents to form the behavioural concept of susceptibility. The Kaleckian analysis of investment is then built around this concept to produce a schematic model of cyclical behaviour in investment. This model incorporates the innovatory process and the traverse to provide an internally generated path for the investment cycle. All the analysis in this chapter is at the firm and industry level, although macroeconomic issues often inform this disaggregated level.

5.2 THE CONCEPT OF SUSCEPTIBILITY

Keynes's epistemic instability of beliefs is developed, with Minsky's work on euphoric (Ponzi-style) behaviour followed by financial fragility and collapse, into a cumulative process of expansion and contraction in investment decision-making. Then, by introducing Loasby's idea of flexibility and adaptability in investment planning into Simon's convention-based satisficing behaviour, a specific Shacklean kaleidic susceptibility to expectational changes in investment is conceived. This makes investment decisions highly sensitive and subject to change. Decisions are regularly revised to satisfy changing expectations, while investment orders at the implementation stage are subject to modifications and delay.

For this study, the complex multifarious Kaleckian elements and their effect on Loasby's investment planning approach produce the highly sensitive cyclical nature of investment activity. Sylos Labini provides the micro-Kaleckian structure of oligopolistic firm processes with endogenous innovation, while the Evolutionary school's innovating process has the effect of triggering investment expansion and the potential for innovative 'swarms' that alter investment paths.

Entrepreneurs are sensitive to the varying degrees of confidence held for expectations generated from investment decisions. This confidence is based on degrees of belief that investment commitments are likely to turn out to have the results originally expected. Threats to this confidence generate a degree of psychological tension about undesirable consequences for entrepreneurs, inducing a search for new conventions that alter investment behaviour and mitigate the source of these growing risks and uncertainties.

Susceptibility refers to the psychological tension felt by entrepreneurs in relation to their fragile confidence about a particular investment decision, given the level of investment orders already committed. The fragility of this confidence in convention-based investment decisions explains unstable investment behaviour. Increasing fragility arises when tension related to current investment decisions escalates as confidence is eroded. This cumulative process renders entrepreneurs' confidence increasingly fragile (or sensitive) as investment order levels rise. When investment order levels are falling, cumulative pressures are being eased on the fragile confidence of entrepreneurs. In this formulation, the level of investment orders is susceptible to change. This susceptibility is a function of the tensions generated by the degree of fragile confidence felt by entrepreneurs from exposure to risk and uncertainty.

The fragile confidence formed by entrepreneurs in their investment decisions is based on the objective evidence from the three Kaleckian elements (profits, increasing risk and capacity utilisation) identified in Chapter 2 as central to investment. Growth, in terms of firm size or market share, is the wellspring that dominates optimistic confidence formation. This drive for growth, built on the three Kaleckian elements, is the *raison d'être* of investment. A firm also aims to 'avoid threats to its decision-making autonomy or its financial security' (Crotty, 1992, p. 491). This safety objective erodes confidence when the three Kaleckian elements provide information that the push for growth has resulted in serious safety-threatening problems. At such a level of investment orders, further planned investment commitments are increasingly susceptible (or prone) to postponement and even (if the threat to safety is perceived as serious enough) modification or cancellation of current orders.

The outcome of this relation between investment decisions and experience of psychological tension by entrepreneurs is to establish a duality of interdependence between susceptibility and investment orders. At a given level of investment orders, an increase in investment commitments generates increasing susceptibility. A threshold of response occurs when rising susceptibility reaches such 'panic-stricken' proportions that tension needs to be released. A structural break ensues at a certain high level of investment orders, such that a turndown in investment orders occurs which releases tensions and reduces susceptibility. At a given level of investment orders, a decrease in investment commitments generates decreasing susceptibility. This is the key means of reducing the risk and uncertainty exposure that causes tension. Such a reduction in susceptibility allows for the possibility of investment orders rising due to the competitive drive for growth, this rise once again increasing susceptibility levels.

From this interdependence, an endogenous cyclical effect on investment orders is formed by entrepreneurs, making due allowance for the qualifying influences of entrepreneurs' characteristics and environmental factors. The existence of susceptibility is the central psychological mediation between observable economic (and other variables) that influence investment commitments and the entrepreneurs' reactions to them. This analysis reveals how susceptible entrepreneurs vary their investment decisions when confronted with a given set of pertinent expected factor changes and what form and pattern such variations exhibit.

The cumulative building up and easing down of tensions ensue from the objective data of the three Kaleckian elements, giving rise to *susceptibility cycles*. These cycles map the feelings of susceptibility in relation to current investment decisions that originate in the building up of tension as businesses are exposed to more uncertainty and higher costs, and the breaking down of tension as businesses are exposed to less uncertainty and lower costs.

In all cycles, the explanation of turning points is crucial. Turning points in susceptibility cycles occur when entrepreneurs' susceptibility is such that current conventions used for investment decision-making are rejected, leading to structural breaks in patterns of investment behaviour. This echoes Keynes in his view that 'a *conventional* judgement . . . is subject to sudden and violent changes . . . [when] certainty and security, suddenly breaks down' (1937, pp. 214–15, original emphasis). The difference is that with Keynes such breaks are exogenously induced (see section 3.2), while in this analysis they are endogenously based on given levels of investment orders already committed.

If the three observable Kaleckian elements can create the objective preconditions for strong confident investment ordering, this leads to the building up of tension as investment orders are increased. Investment expansion generates cumulative tension which manifests itself as an inclination to decrease investment commitments and postpone investment plans. This is called increasing susceptibility. Entrepreneurs' capacity to absorb cumulative tension has a limit (or threshold of response) determined by their own characteristics and environmental factors. Once that limit is reached, the rate of increase of investment commitments are prone to being reduced in an attempt to keep the tensions within acceptable limits.

Despite the decreasing rate of investment commitments, the level of investment orders continues to rise with increasing susceptibility resulting. At some point the investment orders are so high that further investment commitments are extremely susceptible to shattering the buoyant investment mood. The process runs from increased tension created by objectively observed conditions of rising investment orders (higher costs, increased risks, falling utilisation rates) to a subjective feeling of increased fragility in the confidence of current investment decisions. This makes new investment decisions highly susceptible to postponement and investment orders already committed susceptible to downward modifications. At this point, some factor (seasonal, secular, random or self-generating) or a combination of factors leads to reducing investment commitments by postponing planned investment decisions and/or modifying downwards current investment orders. Such a structural break releases tension and reduces susceptibility. The susceptibility cycle begins its contraction phase, reflected by decreasing investment orders.

In the contraction phase, there is a cumulative reduction of tension as uncertainty and costs are lessened due to lower investment orders. Entrepreneurs' investment confidence is less fragile as a result, this being identified as decreasing susceptibility. Continued need to restructure the financial state of firms, which suffered high and increasing risk during the expansion, leads to continued lower levels of investment orders. Decreasing susceptibility reflects a lowering of the degree of psychological tension due to the existing level of investment orders and renders entrepreneurs receptive to any otherwise induced prospects for a higher amount of investment commitments.

When the level of investment orders has sufficiently decreased compared to recent macroeconomic activity, some factor (seasonal, secular, random or self-generating) or combination of factors induces increased economic activity. This inducement is generally very weak on its own, but if it can provoke a higher level of investment activity, then the recovery phase is more strongly based.

Towards the trough of the business cycle, large corporations of most industries have substantial undesired levels of excess capacity. Under such circumstances, there are two possible inducements to increase investment activity. First, due to low susceptibility, entrepreneurs are prone to take more risks with new investment challenges. The high costs of postponing strategic investment plans, as outlined in the next paragraph, places competitive pressure on entrepreneurs to reintroduce such plans so that the growth potential of the firm can be maximised.[1] Secondly, excess capacity does not deter new investment if susceptibility is sufficiently low and the factor (exogenous or endogenous) which affects economic activity creates sufficiently strong optimism for the future to create competitive investment ordering. The ability to engage in such behaviour depends on: (a) innovations making some of the old capital effectively irrelevant, and eventually being 'decommissioned',[2] and (b) the support of the state sector in utilising the existing excess capacity.[3]

Decisions are made to postpone investment plans for the firm's long-term growth during the contraction phase of the susceptibility cycle. This means holding off from major new investments that often incorporate innovations not yet implemented. In oligopoly industries, firms that postpone such plans suffer the cost of not taking a competitive advantage over other firms in the industry. As the level of investment orders continue to fall, the period of low investment extends further, postponement of strategic plans become longer and the related costs of postponement increase. The longer a firm postpones investment commitments, the greater is the opportunity for competitors to obtain similar innovations. The firm's chance to increase market share and long-term growth is lost. These are the costs of postponing investment plans. To the entrepreneur, as susceptibility decreases, these costs of postponement loom larger. Eventually, the costs of postponement become too great relative to the falling susceptibility. At this point, the entrepreneur has increased resilience to the uncertainty of higher investment orders. Also, as investment orders increase again, the new MOP enable much of the existing excess capacity which is not decommissioned by innovation to be employed productively again.[4]

This inducement to reinvest at higher levels creates new tension as uncertainty begins to increase with such commitments. The pressure of deciding to increase investment brings its own tension. The trough of low susceptibility is a situation of increased resilience which induces higher risk-taking from the more adventurous entrepreneurs, making their current levels of investment orders prone to upward modifications and higher new investment commitments. In this 'low susceptibility' trough the more resilient firms are now susceptible to larger investment commitments. For competitive reasons, other entrepreneurs in the same industry tend to follow. Each firm's entrepreneur (and the industry as a whole) experiences the starting up of the susceptibility cycle again, with a corresponding rise in tension.

It is important to notice the asymmetry between the susceptibility to changes in investment orders in the expansion and in the contraction phases. While increasing susceptibility provides the basis for the explanation of an endogenously generated upper turning point, it is the receptiveness of entrepreneurs at low susceptibility to taking greater risks when the costs of postponement become large that induce an increase in investment orders.

Each individual firm's entrepreneur experiences his/her own susceptibility cycle. Given such variations, the best possible approach to defining an industry susceptibility cycle is to hypothesise an ideal type for each particular industry. The stronger the oligopolistic competitive pressure among firms in the one industry, the closer each firm's susceptibility cycle resembles its competitors, because each entrepreneur quickly follows the investment decisions of competitors so as not to lose any market share. In this way, with a strong Kaleckian institutional framework, the ideal-type susceptibility cycle is a reasonably good representation of the state of the industry as a whole.

The concept of susceptibility requires that the investment cycle analysis of an industry's temporal behaviour include the duality of interdependence between a susceptibility cycle and an investment orders cycle as the basis for explaining the observed industry investment (activity) cycle. This duality of firms' investment decisions, as it applies in specific industries, determines the character of industry investment cycles.

Investment behaviour is susceptible to specific factors which are based on the distinctive capitalist institutional structure of a particular economy. Susceptibility cycles vary with different economies because each economy's institutional structure affects the endogenous and exogenous factors differently. This variation creates, in the same industry, distinct peaks and troughs of susceptibility cycles for different countries.

Investment order levels are the objective reflection of the susceptibility of entrepreneurs to investment commitments. In this way, analysts can acknowledge increasing susceptibility when investment orders rise and decreasing susceptibility when investment orders fall. It is important to recognise that susceptibility is not *measured* by investment orders. Investment orders merely *reflect* what is happening to the 'feeling' of susceptibility. There does not have to be a one-to-one relationship between investment orders and susceptibility – i.e. when investment orders increase by 10 per cent; it does not necessarily mean that susceptibility to investment decisions also increases by 10 per cent. For the endogenous analysis presented in this chapter, the relationship can be assumed to reflect a one-to-one ratio between orders and susceptibility, unless otherwise specified. In the next chapter, when exogenous factors are introduced, this one-to-one ratio alters due to changes in seasonal, secular and random factors.

Susceptibility of a firm, as reflected by the level of investment orders, needs to be addressed by the firm's entrepreneurs in the way they make investment decisions and modify current investment projects. If firms themselves do not address their susceptible condition, then other firms who are more adept at reacting to susceptibility are likely to make investment decisions which may threaten the existence of firms who do nothing. The more proficient firms have efficient lines of communication to recognise and administer needed investment changes, and have good lines of credit and finance to implement such changes. There are also firms who recognise tensions but do nothing in the belief that it will turn out all right in the end. Reactions based on poor lines of communication and credit or with an attitude of 'do nothing' will not endure. The firms which survive in the industry are those which continue to make investment decisions and continue to participate in the investment cycle.

5.3 DYNAMICS OF SUSCEPTIBILITY

Investment decisions occur in historical time that render them irreversible, affecting the susceptibility of investment over the time period of the cycle. Kalecki clearly sets out a time pattern for the investment process:

> Three stages should be distinguished in the investment activity: (1) investment orders, i.e. all types of orders for investment goods for the sake of reproduction and expansion of the capital equipment, the volume of which per unit of time will be denoted by I; (2) production of investment goods A which, according to the above, is equal to the gross accumulation; (3) deliveries of finished equipment per unit of time D. (Kalecki, 1971, p. 2)

Kalecki's investment time pattern provides a basis to the dynamics of susceptibility. What this pattern neglects is the time involved in making the decisions which generate the investment orders. The susceptibility of investment model developed here has Kalecki's investment time pattern, but also incorporates long-term strategic investment planning from Levine (1984). This allows the time frame of investment to be extended back to strategic plans and optimal decisions. Entrepreneurs set up this strategic planning by taking account of the internal resources of the firm (e.g. liquidity cushion, retained earnings, skill of staff) and how best these resources can be harnessed to be used most competitively in future investment. This reinforces the view that investment orders are based on investment decisions which use as their basis this strategic planning – either explicitly set up or intuitive planning of an entrepreneur-owner (see section 4.3).

Figure 5.1 shows a time horizon within which the Kaleckian elements of investment can be seen as dynamic forces leading to susceptibility. Such dynamics are not instantaneous but operate with the time lags specified in the figure.

Figure 5.1 Stages of investment activity

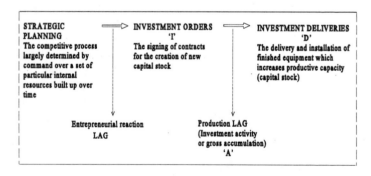

The two lags identified in Figure 5.1 require clarification in the context of a Kaleckian model. The entrepreneurial reaction lag consists of three separate time lag sequences that entrepreneurs face within the firm before making investment orders. There is, first, a recognition lag by entrepreneurs between observing the changes in any Kaleckian element (e.g. excess capacity) and making a decision as to what the desired MOP should be, consistent with the long-term strategic objectives and the internal resources available to that firm. Then comes a decision lag, when entrepreneurs have to determine the level and type of new investment as a result of identifying desired MOP. Finally, there is an administration lag between the investment decision and the actual signing of contracts. Perceptions of what is needed is turned into action. All three lag sequences together form the entrepreneurial reaction lag. Taking this combined reaction lag into account, the investment process arrives at Kalecki's investment orders 'I' (in versions II and III, Kalecki uses the notation D_t for investment orders).

The entrepreneurial reaction lag involves all the internal organisational activities (observation, determination, administration) which take time and finally lead to the investment order contracts being signed. Across this lag structure the concept of susceptibility applies. Entrepreneurs observe changes in any Kaleckian elements, make decisions and sign orders which affect the perception of (imagined) consequences resulting from such investment orders. How agents feel about such consequences determines the level of susceptibility. For this reason the level of investment orders only reflects the level of susceptibility developed in the process of making certain investment decisions.

The observed changes in the Kaleckian elements may signal to the entrepreneur that the continuation of full contractual investment orders threatens the viability of the business. Modification or cancellation of investment orders necessitates the variation of already-signed contracts.

This is a costly exercise which only occurs when the threat to safety creates a high level of susceptibility. In such circumstances, the entrepreneur makes a decision to reduce the desired MOP quickly by stopping investment activity which is currently adding to the level of MOP above the revised desired level. This then reduces the level of investment orders. The entrepreneurial reaction lag includes all such decisions which involve alteration of contracts.

The production lag relates to four time lag sequences in the actual production and installation of the capital goods, right up to when the new MOP is in full operation, denoted as 'D' in Kalecki's version I (in version II it is F_{t+x}, in version III is I_{t+x}, where x is this production lag). The first sequence is the capital goods production lag between receiving the order and constructing the capital stock. Then there is the delivery lag in having the capital goods transported to the firm which orders it. This is followed by the installation lag at its permanent position in the production process. Finally, there is the operational lag (or commissioning problems) involving staff familiarisation with the new MOP and ironing out the bugs hindering their full operation (see Penrose, 1959).[5]

The production lag looks at the irreversible events within the structure of producing the capital goods agreed to in the contracts signed. The production process which creates this production lag is identified as the traverse (see section 2.6). Issues in the traverse are not restricted to internal organisation. There are the requirements that other organisations build, deliver and often install capital goods for the firm. This can take the lag structure outside the control of the ordering organisation and its entrepreneurs (except for the operational lag which reflects the ability of the staff to operate the new equipment and plant).

The level of investment activity (A) is a reflection of the traverse in terms of the production lag. A longer production lag reduces the flow of investment expenditure (A) per period, indicating that within the traverse there are increased supply constraints on the producers of MOP. Out of this production lag come two implications for the investment cycle analysis. First, investment activity is measured in dollars of capital goods produced over a period of time after the investment orders have been signed. This means that (say) a turndown in investment orders takes some time before it affects actual production in the capital goods sectors, with the machine tool (or basic capital goods) subsector (1a) taking longer to be affected than the broader capital goods subsector (1b) which is specific to consumption goods sector needs. Secondly, there are important feedback effects from the production of capital goods back to the entrepreneurs' decision-making internal structures. Delays in the production lag affect the entrepreneurs' susceptibility. These feedback effects relate to the capacity of the two capital goods subsectors.

Full capacity constraints induce quantity and price responses. The length of the production lag grows, reducing the quantity of flow-through of capital goods into the industries requiring these machines. When there is a large spurt in investment orders, the capital goods industry feels the pressure – first in subsector 1b, then in subsector 1a. Of particular concern are supply constraints in subsector 1a, which significantly limit the reproduction process of investment. There is also the short-term price response identified by Keynes (1936, p. 136), where the price of MOP rises for a particular industry in the short-term, due to the pressure on facilities for producing the capital goods. This occurs at the time, towards the top of the boom, when profit margins are getting squeezed in megacorps (see section 4.2). Such quantity and price pressures add tension to the already fragile state of high investment commitments.

Supply constraints add to the growing susceptibility of investment as economic activity moves towards a peak.

During a contraction in investment activity, excess capacity emerges in both capital goods subsectors. Thus, when investment orders increase, there is a very quick response with a very short production lag and even possibly cheaper (discounted) prices for capital goods by some sectors of the capital goods industry (especially by uncompetitive fringe firms desperate for business). This quick and cheap response to new investment orders at the bottom of the investment cycle has a feedback that reduces any nascent susceptibility tensions, providing strong confidence in future investment. The negative aspect is that the high excess capacity and attempts at discounting by fringe firms damps incentive for the large firms in the capital goods industries to invest in new MOP themselves. In effect, susceptibility tensions remain high, leading to delays in scrapping old MOP. Postponement of investment in the capital-goods-producing sector makes the structure of production overall less efficient at the margin than if such firms had put in the available new advanced technology.[6]

Both the quantity and price effects of the traverse, in particular close to the turning points, lead to readjusting previous investment contracts and altering future investment plans. In the analysis of the following section, the susceptibility cycle is developed without these feedback effects in order to show clearly the endogenous self-generating nature of each Kaleckian observed element on investment. The investment (activity) cycle is introduced in section 5.5, in order to observe the feedback effects on the susceptibility cycle of capacity constraints and excess capacity in the capital goods sector of an oligopolistic capitalist economy.

5.4 SELF-GENERATION OF SUSCEPTIBILITY CYCLES

The susceptibility cycle is *reflected* in the level of new investment orders being created during the entrepreneurial reaction lag. The investment cycle *measures* the actual investment activity occurring during the production lag. Both cycles are represented as flows of dollars in investment in the form of 'orders' and 'activity' respectively. When firms in an industry have very strong levels of investment ordering, this reflects high susceptibility to downward modifications due to the increased tension created by the three elements. At this highly susceptible position, any changes to seasonal, secular, random or self-generating factors (or a combination of these factors) can lead to a decision to modify current investment orders downwards and to reduce planned new investment decisions. Only self-generating factors provide purely endogenous turning points. These modifications and reductions in decisions are reflected in investment activity with a time lag. For this reason the peak in investment cycles follows the peak in susceptibility cycles. Lower investment commitments reduce tension created by the three elements, reaching the trough in susceptibility cycles, followed by the trough in investment cycles.

The three observable Kaleckian elements and how they are individually responsible for increasing and then decreasing susceptibility of investment orders of a typical oligopolistic firm are set out in this section. Each of the three elements is examined separately to see how that particular element affects susceptibility. Systematic contradictory pulls (see section 2.3) develop with each element to produce, on its own, a highly abstract self-generating susceptibility cycle. As a result, three distinct notional generalised susceptibility cycles of the firm are described below.

5.4.1 Profits Element

Profit is the crucial element in all three versions of Kalecki's business cycle. The role of profits in the susceptibility cycle, as it is modelled here, is based on Bhaduri's instability model (see section 2.3.2). Bhaduri's notion of systematic contradictory pulls is used to show how, in the abstract, the basic susceptibility cycle can be developed endogenously with only this profits element. The contradictory pulls occur because profits reflect both an inducement and an ability to invest. While the change in profit levels acts as the inducing expectational factor, the current profit level provides the internal finances to invest (and also the basis for external finances).

These contradictory pulls can be used to illustrate pressures on the susceptibility cycle because of the expectational nature of Bhaduri's analysis. The susceptibility cycle places these contradictory pulls within a historically based susceptibility phenomenon where downward modifications and cancellations of investment orders in the forthcoming period occur at the top of the cycle and upward modifications and restarting mothballed projects occur at the bottom of the cycle.

Contradictory pulls are resolved by creating turning points in the self-generating susceptibility cycle. Rising profit levels at a constant or increasing rate add to investment orders, reflecting growing susceptibility. Profits at a high level means that susceptibility is also high. At this point, any decrease in the incremental profit levels would cause a contradictory pull, at first only strong enough to reduce the rate of increase of investment orders, but then (as incremental profit levels decrease further, even down to zero) strong enough to induce a downturn in investment orders. The opposite effect can work in the trough of the susceptibility cycle when the profit level is low and any small increment in the profit level is enough to start an increase in investment orders in a period of low susceptibility. At the trough, the firm is highly susceptible to moving into a better competitive position *vis-à-vis* other firms in the industry. This leads to an upward modification of investment orders. A new susceptibility cycle starts up with a corresponding rise in tension.

The final (version III) business cycle treatment by Kalecki (1968) depicts a complex interaction between the increment in total profits (ΔP) and the increment in profit on new MOP (see section 2.2). This version of Kalecki's investment cycle model identifies the increment in profits from newly installed MOP as the better expectations guide to further investment decisions than the increment in total profits. The newly installed MOP, incorporating technical change, embodies new and efficient methods of production and new products related to innovation. This efficiency means that there is a stronger increment in profits from newly installed MOP relative to the total increment in profits.

Incorporating this version III analysis into the susceptibility cycle provides an even more sensitive variable of incremental profits from newly installed MOP, as a guide to the fragility of confidence in investment decisions. Two firms (or industries) may exhibit the same ΔP and profit levels, but if one firm (or industry) has a much higher amount of ΔP coming from recently installed MOP than the other, then a variation in their respective susceptibility cycles occurs. The firm (or industry) whose ΔP comes relatively more from new MOP suffers considerably more in increased fragility as investment orders increase than the other firm (or industry) whose ΔP comes relatively more from old MOP.[7]

Following the susceptibility cycle upwards, a firm invests in more new MOP yet also exposes itself to greater tension as the marginal increment in profit (on new MOP) creates an increased fragility. Self-generation of the susceptibility cycle is evident when the rate of new investment orders slows down due to this increased fragility (firms wanting to maintain some old MOP with more stable and predictable rates of return). This slowdown in new investment orders leads to reduced marginal increments in profit (on new MOP), which further induces slowdown in new investment orders, creating a turning-point eventually as investment orders level off and finally decrease. Such a turnaround in the susceptibility cycle causes the investment cycle also to follow the same pattern.

The type of entrepreneur may also create further differences in susceptibility cycles between firms. Entrepreneur-owners tend to have a weaker preference for safety than entrepreneur-managers (see section 4.3). This means that in the same situation, entrepreneur-managers are more susceptible to a downturn in investment ordering than entrepreneur-owners. The significance of this during a boom is that a slowdown in new investment orders tends to occur first in more diversely owned oligopoly companies.

On the downswing of the susceptibility cycle, fragility of confidence is reduced as increments in profits (ΔP) are relatively more attributable to old MOP with more predictable rates of return. In the trough of the cycle, the ΔP becomes very low but predictably stable. As entrepreneurs have low susceptibility (or are more resilient to uncertainties and risks of investment), some firms modify investment orders upwards, competitively attempting to appropriate new markets and new methods of production. Even a quite simple innovation (such as placing fins on an established car style) may create this competitive advantage, which enables the ΔP to rise. This generates a turning point at the bottom of the susceptibility cycle, with new tensions slowly developing from the decision to lift investment orders out of the trough.[8]

The investment order upturn begins to cumulate fragility as the new MOP, with more unpredictable rates of return, contribute proportionately more to ΔP than the old MOP. The upturn in the susceptibility cycle occurs in spite of what could reasonably be expected to be a very high level of excess capacity (since a low level of aggregate economic activity exists when the susceptibility cycle hits bottom). Slowdown in the rate of decline of the susceptibility cycle and its eventual upturn is related to ΔP from new MOP relative to old MOP.

A distinction again can be made between types of entrepreneur during the trough of the susceptibility cycle. The entrepreneur-owner in tightly owned companies leads the slowdown and eventual upturn (reversing the position from the cycle peak where it was diversely-owned companies leading). Entrepreneur-owners tend to become aware earlier of reduced susceptibility as the cycle turns down. Their weaker preference for safety and their determination to grow quickly induces moves through innovation for some small marginal ΔP rises, when most other firms in the industry are still reducing investment orders. This slows down the contraction of the industry susceptibility cycle. Further innovations introduced by entrepreneur-owners induce higher ΔP from new MOP coming on stream. Throughout the whole cycle, tightly owned companies tend to have relatively lower amounts of old MOP. Thus, their ΔP depends much more on obtaining new MOP and being more inclined to scrap (or decommission) existing excess capacity such that a higher market share can be more quickly obtained.

Non-differentiated oligopolies with more aggressive price-cutting leadership can remove the uncompetitive fringe more quickly than in differentiated oligopolies. Thus, excess capacity is reduced sooner in non-differentiated oligopoly-type structures. This removal of excess capacity, while the majority of manufacturing industry is still in high excess capacity, induces such companies (and industries) to recover their profits quickly after their aggressive price cutting. They become leaders in slowing down the contraction phase of the susceptibility cycle and bringing on the upturn as they introduce new methods of production.

The profits-related mechanism incorporates both systematic contradictory pulls between ΔP and total profit levels, and conflicting pressures on ΔP related to concentrations of new MOP relative to old MOP. The negative feedback of higher capital accumulation in this analysis operates through changes in profitability rather than from the levels of actual capital stock which is the crude acceleration mechanism which Kalecki found unacceptable in his second version of the business cycle. The advantage of introducing the concept of the susceptibility cycle into this analysis is that it provides an understanding of the dynamic nature of investment decision-making: how investment decisions create and break down tension leading to instability in investment cycles.

The 'stop–go' mechanism of state macropolicy (see section 4.6) adds a further dimension to the profits-based susceptibility cycle. The mid-expansion decline in the share of income accruing to profits, arising from the cyclical profit squeeze described above, induces entrepreneurs to pressure the state into damping effective demand (and weakening the state's commitment to high employment) so as to limit the rising wage share. Such induced macropolicy further squeezes profits (as weaker demand generally rises slower than wages at the top of a business cycle) and endogenously exacerbates already rising susceptibility tension. Pressure is exerted again on the state to pursue expansionary macropolicies once the profit squeeze starts to abate at the business cycle trough. The objective of successful macropolicy expansion is to augment rising profits share and thus ease susceptibility tension emanating from the acceleration in investment commitments.

5.4.2 Increasing Risk Element

The debt-to-equity gearing ratio limitation on investment is identified by Wood (1975, p. 30) as being dependent on: (a) managerial expectations of future company's profits, and (b) the attitudes of entrepreneurs towards 'increasing risk' factors outlined in borrower's risk[9] and, to a lesser extent, share issue risk. The former relates back to the first element of profits; the latter takes us directly to Kalecki's 'increasing risk' concept and the second element in the susceptibility cycle.

Mott (1985–86, p. 73) identifies increasing risk as connecting Keynes's emphasis on the volatility of investment spending and liquidity-preference with Kalecki's mark-up pricing behaviour. This integration provides the second notional self-generating susceptibility cycle process. In summary, '[t]he necessity of congealing wealth into fixed capital in order to earn income carries with it a danger of illiquidity which limits the amount of investment spending and sends the economy on a growing but unstable, cyclical path' (Mott, 1985–6, p. 73). This cyclical path is explained by the building up and breaking down of tension as represented in the susceptibility cycle analysis.

During an upswing of the business cycle, the growth in internally generated funds allows a firm to increase its borrowing and share issue. As outside funds become more easily available during the upswing, the increasing risk involved in committing funds to MOP seems to rise only minimally. Under these circumstances, the firm (or industry) is well below gearing ratio limit. Tension builds up only slightly as it relates to small borrowers' risk, when financial (liquid) assets that earn income are turned into illiquid MOP with a long gestation period before any income is received. As the boom continues, greater borrowings and share issue bring the principle of increasing risk into operation.

There is increased susceptibility as tension builds up much more rapidly due to the increasing illiquidity of investment. Mott (1985–6, p. 73) notes that '[c]oncern over the greater degree of illiquidity resulting from borrowed financing may drive industry price-leaders to raise mark-ups, when an increase in investment spending seems desirable'. This tension is further built up either by nominal wage costs rising to maintain real wages due to widespread mark-up price rises, or mark-up price rises not being widespread due to potential competition frustrating any such pricing behaviour. Both events militate against relieving increasing risk. Greater (or enforced) indebtedness and wider share ownership occur as investment orders are being realised into capital stock, just as such illiquidity-type pressures occur. Some smaller firms in the uncompetitive fringe and some industries (as a whole) may even suffer bankruptcy pressures. Enforced indebtedness, often seen by gearing ratios rising above what firms consider are safe limits from increasing risk, create such high tension.

At this stage of the susceptibility cycle, with high gearing ratios (often above gearing ratio limits), any short run fluctuations in profits would create short-term liquidity problems (i.e. meeting interest payments). Then, 'a high gearing ratio makes banks more reluctant to provide additional short-term credit, because of the greater burden of outstanding debt' (Wood, 1975, p. 19). Lender's risk now becomes a serious short-term issue. The firm then must ensure a larger financial assets ratio (holding of financial assets relative to investment), in order to cushion liquidity constraints. Shifting investment funding to equity finance, so as to relieve lender's and borrower's risk, leads to rising share issue risk. Concerns by the controlling entrepreneurial group of all the negative implications of issuing more shares, including share price falls based on the relatively lower positive ΔP, further increases tension as the equity finance alternative creates its own cumulative pressures.

These increasing risk factors force entrepreneurs to reduce the rate of new investment commitments. Susceptibility continues to rise (even if at a slower rate), threatening the firm's liquidity position. Again contradictory pulls emerge. In relation to this element, continuing long-term competitive pressure to earn income through investment in illiquid MOP eventually creates the need to protect the decreasing short-term liquidity position by doing the exact opposite – reducing investment orders and cancelling (or modifying) current investment orders. This lowers the very high tension related to increasing borrower's and lender's risks (and share issue risk), which reduces susceptibility and, with a lag, reduces investment activity.

In the downward phase of a business cycle, increasing risk generates a reverse susceptibility behaviour cycle to the one outlined in the previous paragraph. Immediately following the downturn in investment activity, there is an initial period when the gearing ratio remains relatively high. As investment activity continues to decrease, entrepreneurs concentrate on using still relatively high profits to pay off debts and thus lower their gearing ratios. Share price falls (which had initially started when investment was being 'overextended' with rising share issue risk) may still continue deep into the investment contraction period, although successful restructuring of debt tends to weaken this fall and to allow continued lowering of gearing ratios. Low profits make new borrowings more difficult to obtain and allows for increasing the financial assets ratio.

These actions to reduce the increasing risk also decrease susceptibility, until very low susceptibility encourages some risk-taking in order to take some competitive advantage. Again, contradictory pulls between the need to maintain a strong short-term financial assets ratio (and thus limit investment decisions) conflicts with the need to raise gearing ratios in order to create long-term competitive advantage by the development of new income-earning illiquid MOP. Firms with a lower preference for safety, especially tightly owned companies and non-differentiated oligopolies, are the first to increase their investment orders. Lenders willing to take risks in order to increase their own earnings capacity support these aggressive entrepreneurs, building up gearing ratio pressures again. How low susceptibility needs to be before there is a preparedness to take on such new increasing risk (both by lenders and borrowers) depends on the specific institutional structures within individual economies.

From this analysis, gearing ratios and their limits are guides to increasing risk at the firm and industry levels. The gearing ratio can be looked at over time to see how changes to it alter tension in relation to individual firm and industry commitments for investment. Susceptibility can be associated with growing pressure from increasing risk as investment orders increase, and then pressure easing off from increasing risk as investment orders decrease. Increasing risk on its own, via gearing ratios, has the ability to create in the abstract a self-generating susceptibility cycle.[10]

The increasing risk element traces out an unstable cyclical path of investment orders. Financial commitments to such investment orders, in the form of borrowing and share issue, affect gearing ratio levels in a way that identifies the susceptibility related to increasing risk. The gearing ratio and its limits create susceptibility to borrower's, lender's and share issue risks which, in isolation from other issues, generate this unstable path of investment orders. The links between profits and increasing risk are important, and the combination of these two elements gives a much stronger basis to the susceptibility cycle path.

5.4.3 Degree of Capacity Utilisation Element

The degree of capacity utilisation of any plant at any particular time is based on two factors. First is the level of demand. Second is the degree of planned excess productive capacity which can be utilised immediately without the long time delay involved in building new capacity. The *actual* degree of utilisation may be above, equal to, or below the *planned* excess capacity, depending on the state of demand for the commodity and the level of MOP.

No entrepreneur can guarantee that a planned degree of excess capacity will be always realised. Unplanned excess capacity can and often does occur. It is a situation where the utilisation rate varies from the planned (or normal desired) excess capacity due to the conjunction of time lags and variations in demand. Firms order the capital goods, and the expectation is that solid sales will continue. However, by the time the capital goods are delivered and in operation, sales may have fallen, leaving utilisation rates at a lower level than prior to the investment decision. This is how unplanned excess capacity can emerge. On the other hand, increasing utilisation rates above planned levels (even to over 100 per cent in the short-term) occur in order to take advantage of realising profits from rising sales while capital goods are being produced and have not yet come on-stream. Also, the entrepreneurial lag means that firms take some time to recognise and decide what to do about situations of utilisation rates above and below desired levels.

A self-generating capacity utilisation susceptibility cycle is first developed from Kalecki's own implied view of unplanned excess capacity, which remains consistent in all three versions of his business cycle theory. In all three versions, it is the increasing MOP coming out after a production lag that reacts on future investment decisions due to a build-up of MOP. This relation between capacity utilisation and the susceptibility cycle can be seen graphically in Figure 5.2.

Kalecki's version II investment equation (equation (2.8)) can be used as the aggregate indicator for the self-generating susceptibility cycle at the firm level caused by unplanned excess capacity. Starting from time 'o' in Figure 5.2, increasing investment orders up the susceptibility cycle generate (after a production lag) an increasing rate of increasing MOP. Just after time 'm', deliveries of capital stock become greater than what is needed as desired capacity utilisation (u_o). Given the time lag in the investment process, such overinvestment is quite possible. Higher-than-desired excess capacity increases tension, especially with a boom in progress and increasing fears of a slow-down in sales. This makes the latest large investment orders highly susceptible to cancellation. Thus, a rise in the rate of increase in MOP slows down the rate of rising investment orders I_t.

Figure 5.2   Relation between capacity utilisation and the susceptibility cycle

1. CAPACITY UTILISATION

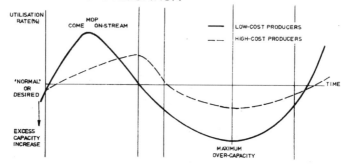

2. SUSCEPTIBILITY CYCLE

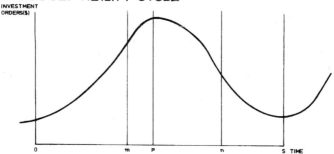

Kalecki saw unplanned excess capacity appearing mid-way through a boom as MOP rises at an increasing rate due to investment orders being completed and demand not being able to keep up with the boom in MOP. In Figure 5.2, this concern with unplanned excess capacity begins after time 'm' for the powerful low-cost (oligopolistic) producers. This excess capacity keeps rising past 'm', its influence becoming greater as the rise in demand (and thus realised income) slows down towards the peak of the business cycle. The combination of contradictory pulls between capital production lags and economic activity creates unplanned excess capacity, and thus tension builds up within a self-generating susceptibility cycle.

The slower increase in investment orders eventually slows down investment activity. In the meantime, tension is still growing as sales increases slow down and inventory investment rises, leading to even higher undesired excess capacity. This pressure continues to reduce the rate of increase in investment orders until it becomes zero at the peak of the susceptibility cycle. The entrepreneurial reaction lag ensures that there is no instant downturn in investment orders upon the appearance of unplanned excess capacity.

With the production lag, the susceptibility cycle peak leads to investment activity ceasing to increase. MOP continue to add to the capital stock so long as investment orders are greater than simply replacing depreciated MOP. Thus, at the investment cycle peak there is even more tension as more MOP come on stream, sending excess utilisation rates even higher above desired rates (see solid line at time 'p' in Figure 5.2). Entrepreneurs' confidence is extremely fragile, with high but constant levels of investment orders which are unsustainable. This fragility leads to a break under extreme pressure. Investment orders decrease, and although productive capacity continues to increase, the *decreasing rate* at which MOP come on stream starts to ease susceptibility.

In the context of undesired excess capacity at the upper turning point of the susceptibility cycle, the technical problem of lumpiness in scale of new capital projects that occurs in some capital-intensive industries (especially the non-differentiated raw material processors), creates particularly severe susceptibility. In their strategic planning, a certain amount of lumpiness can be useful for future demand and as a barrier to entry, thus forming part of planned excess capacity. However, the contradictory pull mechanism outlined above throws such planning into disarray towards the top of the susceptibility cycle, when lumpy MOP come on stream and very quickly add a large level of undesired excess capacity. This is a strongly unsustainable position of very high susceptibility.

A reduction in investment orders greater than originally planned for reduces susceptibility more than it otherwise would have done. The persistent increase in undesired excess capacity continues as demand slows down, and then possibly falls in absolute terms. As investment projects currently in progress (past committments) threaten to come on-stream and worsen further the utilisation rates, modifications of such investment projects occur. 'Mothballing' the project totally; a 'go slow' approach which intentionally stirs up trade unions so that strikes and work-to-rules occur; selling off part-ownership in the specific project; decommissioning the project before it starts, are all possible modification actions. The advantage of the susceptibility concept is that modifications to current investment projects can be incorporated into a specific analysis of investment behaviour.

The contractionary susceptibility phase occurs as investment orders are decreasing in absolute terms from the peak of the susceptibility cycle. At the start of the decline in investment orders, utilisation rates continue to fall as the previously ordered MOP come on-stream. More seriously, economic activity by now has fallen, partly due to reduced investment ordering itself forcing more unplanned excess capacity up to the maximum overcapacity at time 'n'. Eventually investment orders decrease to below replacement requirements, so that the level of capital stock falls. Also, methods of removing unplanned excess capacity at a faster rate than allowed for by the decrease in capital stock are devised (see discussion below). These actions result in the capacity utilisation curve turning upwards (see solid line as it passes time 'n') towards more desired capacity utilisation rates. This further reduces entrepreneurs' tension and sends the susceptibility cycle close towards the trough.

Having reached low susceptibility, there is a lack of tension (or stronger resilience to uncertainty) due to the disposal of 'old' inefficient capital and the removal of any uncompetitive fringe of high-cost producers that may exist. Under these circumstances, entrepreneurs with low preference for safety want to take a competitive advantage with new improved capital, even though utilisation rates are still relatively low. This induces some small new investment decisions, or at least the unmothballing of partly completed plants, by such entrepreneurs. A small increase in accumulation pushes investment orders back up. Other entrepreneurs follow to remain competitive. These decisions again build up tension as investment orders rise, forcing a rise in susceptibility (see time 's'). The positive influence of rising investment activity, with a time lag, begins the process of MOP adding to the level of capital stock. Eventually, as capital stock levels increase, the mechanism of a negative feedback of accumulation drives tension up to high susceptibility when capacity utilisation rates are very high (even over 100 per cent). This begins the cancellation of investment orders and the cycle repeats the process again.

Steindl's 'fear of excess capacity' analysis (see section 2.3.1) is another dimension of the susceptibility cycle and the tension in decision-making that this entails.[11] The growing fear of excess capacity, when investment orders increase, is reflected in higher levels of susceptibility for two reasons. First, each firm in an oligopoly is large, and thus its major investment decisions to increase capacity have a significant effect on the potential capacity of the whole industry. This is particularly the case when much new investment embodies innovation that is more efficient per worker used in production. Secondly, each firm is clearly aware of what its competitors' new investment commitments imply for the whole industry.[12] Both these reasons extend the entrepreneurs' susceptibility to what increasing investment commitments in the industry as a whole are prone to do to their excess capacity. This is the 'fear' of growing excess capacity in the industry at the time when their own excess capacity is increasing.

A third dimension to this fear concept can be examined if high-cost producers (the uncompetitive fringe) are added to the oligopolistic structure of the industry. Such producers have much more fear about the effects of the major firms' increased investment orders on overcapacity than their own investment orders, which have a relatively small effect on the overcapacity of the industry.

Figure 5.2 shows, in the form of a dotted line, the high-cost producers' utilisation over the cycle compared to the larger low-cost producers. To high cost producers, excess capacity is a serious cost and less of a competitive tool (if at all). Also, their fear of overcapacity is much greater. This results in a decreased chance of reaching very high utilisation rates, as their investment commitments are more measured in response to demand increase than those of low-cost producers. It also means less chance of reaching very high excess capacity rates. To achieve more stable utilisation rates, these high-cost producers are prepared to have less-stable pricing. They are willing to reduce prices (and mark-ups) in order to keep capacity utilisation higher than that of the major firms. However, given the institutional framework outlined in the previous chapter, the high-cost producers' pricing behaviour does not influence the investment decisions of the major firms.

Fear of overcapacity among high-cost producers is at its highest at time 'p', when major firms have substantial undesired excess capacity, when high-cost firms are at their desired 'normal' capacity levels, and when there is the prospect of large investment commitments continuing to come on stream for the major firms. The 'fear of excess capacity' pressure on susceptibility is at its highest at this point for high-cost producers, which corresponds to the same 'p' point at which the low-cost producers have such high actual excess capacity that they are also at the peak of their own susceptibility cycles. Since this fear is a perception, there is no entrepreneurial lag for fringe producers. From this point in time 'p', high-cost firms begin immediately to decrease their new investment orders so as to relieve their fear-based susceptibility.

During the early contraction period of the susceptibility cycle, when MOP are still coming on stream at a high rate in the industry due to the production lag, high-cost firms experience increasing actual undesired excess capacity. This induces even lower levels of investment orders. By time 'n', high-cost firms are also at maximum overcapacity. Strenuous efforts to remove their own excess capacity, apart from allowing depreciation to take its course, enables excess capacity to move back towards desired levels without becoming as high as in low-cost firms. This permits susceptibility pressures to ease off reasonably quickly in an effort to stay in the industry and enter the new investment order cycle with prospects of increasing their market share.

All firms want to remove unplanned excess capacity that is building up in the contraction phase of the susceptibility cycle. Simply allowing the level of new investment orders to fall below depreciation rates is generally a very protracted approach which adds to the 'costs of postponement'. Pressure to minimise such costs leads to other, more immediate measures to remove excess capacity. There are three such measures: (a) price cutting to absorb unplanned capacity by increasing output and by removing the uncompetitive fringe; (b) cancelling or modifying previous investment decisions and reducing current investment orders; (c) 'de-commissioning' old, less-efficient capital stock.

The first method is limited to operations in oligopoly industries with an uncompetitive fringe that is attracted into the industry by innovations and high profit margins (see section 4.2). Dominant firms cut prices back to the original (pre-innovation) mark-up, or slightly lower, in order to remove fringe competitors and reduce excess capacity. In industries which are closer to perfect competition (i.e. monopolistic competition), or which are oligopolies with high-cost producers, the price-cutting can be used to maintain (or increase) output, thus absorbing unplanned excess capacity. In the Kaleckian structure where a few firms exist, such actions are very limited and generally impractical (see Cowling, 1982, pp. 29–30).

The second method applies to oligopolistic industries in the time period between 'p' and 'n' in the susceptibility cycle. In this situation, entrepreneurs cancel or modify investment commitments that are partly completed. Once this avenue of excess capacity reduction has run its course, the industry reaches maximum overcapacity at time 'n'. Then the major method of reducing existing capacity is by decommissioning old capital stock, made possible by the recent introduction of new (more-efficient) MOP. This third method is in concert with any new demand growth occurring in the industry, enabling the new MOP to reach an efficient level (through 'learning by doing') by the time sales have picked up quickly and capacity utilisation has reached around the desired level.

A self-generating susceptibility cycle is notionally developed with the degree of capacity utilisation acting as a 'controller of the rate of investment'. Increase in the level of unplanned excess capacity inhibits future, and modifies current, investment plans.[13]

5.5 THE TRAVERSE AND ITS IMPLICATIONS FOR SUSCEPTIBILITY

Changes to the traverse (production lag sequence) increase or decrease the time delay between the susceptibility and investment (activity) cycles, and alters the amplitudes of both cycles. Lowe's analysis of the traverse is based on aggregate and sectoral effects of production lag changes to long-term growth. By adopting Lowe's sectoral structure (see section 2.6), this section examines the implications for the susceptibility cycle of changes in the production lag. Short-term instability in investment orders of firms and industries is exacerbated by changes in the production lag sequence, providing a micro-dimension to the traverse and its impact on susceptibility.

The time frame between when a susceptibility cycle reaches (say) the peak of its investment orders and the investment cycle of capital goods production reaches the corresponding peak depends on the ability of capital goods producers to satisfy the investment orders coming through. At different points of the susceptibility cycle this time frame can alter. At the bottom of the susceptibility cycle, any upturn in investment orders produces a quick response in investment activity due to excess capacity in the capital goods sector. Towards the top of the susceptibility cycle, high capacity utilisation levels in the capital goods sector lengthens the production lag. This prevents any quick response from the capital-goods-producing sector to new investment orders.

Variable production lags over the period of the business cycle generate variable time delays between the susceptibility cycle and the investment cycle. Figure 5.3 schematically models this time frame between susceptibility and investment activity for a representative Kaleckian monopoly capitalist industry. At low levels of investment activity (see solid lines in Figure 5.3), the investment cycle rises as quickly as investment orders reflected in the susceptibility cycle, because there are no constraints in the capital-goods-producing sector. With more investment dollars (in orders and activity), supply constraints begin to lengthen the production lag and the investment cycle shows a slower rate of increase than the susceptibility cycle. The former is concave from below, while the latter is convex from below.

With investment activity rising, the subsector which produces specific capital goods for the consumption sector (1b) increases investment orders as profits increase. This leads to increasing investment orders in the machine tools sector (1a). As the boom in investment activity reaches towards the peak, the machine tool sector reaches supply constraints with full capacity. This slows down movement of basic investment goods to subsector 1b, which in turn means even a longer slow-down in the delivery of capital goods to the consumption goods sector. Such delays extend the period between the peaks in the two cycles even further. The tendency is for time period 'a' in Figure 5.3 to extend further, with the supply constraints in the machine tool sector slowing the whole reproduction system.

Figure 5.3 Time frame of susceptibility and investment cycles: a schematic representation of an industry

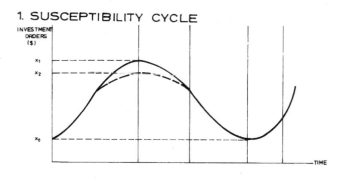

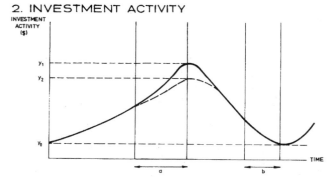

In Figure 5.3, rate of contraction of the susceptibility cycle is closely followed by a similar rate of contraction of the investment cycle, since there are no supply constraints reducing investment activity. The traverse issue arises again at the trough of the susceptibility cycle, when large excess capacity builds up in the investment goods sector. Thus, any turnaround in investment orders quickly results in the production of investment goods with the excess capacity existing. For this reason, Figure 5.3 shows a larger time delay between orders and activity at the peak of the cycles (distance measured as 'a') than at the trough where the distance is only 'b', thus a > b.

The traverse also affects the amplitude of the investment cycle. Throughout this theoretical analysis it is assumed that $x_1 = y_1$, and $x_o = y_o$ in Figure 5.3. This means that the amplitude of the investment cycle always coincides with the susceptibility cycle. The rationale behind this assumption is that no investment activity can be made without a corresponding investment order. Any investment action (e.g. to cease construction mid-way through the project) requires an investment decision to be made regarding that investment order. The investment order always reveals, with the time delay mentioned above, a certain level of investment activity.

This assumption does not rule out changes in the amplitude of the investment cycle. Changes occur as a result of a feedback from investment activity going to investment orders which react back on the investment cycle. Such changes occur due to the production lag. Supply constraints in both subsectors 1a and 1b lead to lengthening time delays which affect firms' investment decisions throughout all the three sectors. A firm's decision to increase investment orders is based on the three Kaleckian elements (see section 5.4). Yet waiting for MOP to be produced may threaten a firm's market share if other competing firms have already gained their MOP. This delaying of MOP *intensifies* susceptibility, which means that at the same level of investment orders, the level of susceptibility becomes higher. To the entrepreneur waiting for MOP, each dollar in investment orders now has a higher level of tension than previously.

Such intensification of susceptibility leads entrepreneurs to alter their investment strategies. The options are to change the way in which existing MOP are used or to change the source of new MOP to overseas. Both options describe the 'shiftability of capital goods' (see section 2.6). Adoption of either option relieves the supply constraint problem, and reduces domestic investment orders for the firm and the industry. This reduces the intensity of susceptibility during the late expansion phase of the susceptibility cycle. In Figure 5.3, it is depicted by a shift of the susceptibility cycle downwards, reducing the amplitude as it moves towards a lower peak of x_2 (see dotted line). Such a change is transferred to the investment cycle, correspondingly shifting investment activity down by the dotted line reaching a peak at only y_2 (such that $y_1 - y_2 = x_1 - x_2$).

Serious supply constraints reduce domestic investment orders, and the amplitude of the susceptibility cycle, by an amount depending on the coefficient of shiftability (g). The more specific the MOP in use, the less able is the industry to take advantage of this shiftability. Subsector 1a, with the least specific MOP, is best able to reduce domestic investment orders, followed by subsector 1b, and finally the consumption goods sector with the most specific MOP. If an industry has no options for shiftability ($g = 0$), then the intensified susceptibility cannot be alleviated, and the susceptibility cycle does not shift. This means that the cycle will be affected over the next few short-term periods by increased intensity of susceptibility and not by a sudden shift in the cycle.

The intensifying effect on susceptibility of supply constraints when $g = 0$, makes forthcoming expansion phases of the susceptibility cycle shorter and weaker. These future expansion phases will be shorter in duration because the time delays raise the rate of susceptibility with increasing orders (i.e. moving from a 1:1 ratio between investment orders and susceptibility to, say, a 1:1.5 ratio). The expansion is weaker because the time delays add a further component to the tension of new investment orders, reaching the peak of the susceptibility cycle at a lower level. In this way, the amplitudes to the cycle peak are slowly reduced over the next few periods due to a lack of shiftability options.[14]

Raising the price of new MOP, due to capacity shortages at a time of very high demand, squeezes ordering firms' profit margins if fixed-price contracts were not arranged. Expected rates of return on future MOP fall as well. Both these profit considerations increase directly the susceptibility of investment orders already committed. This intensification of susceptibility leads to the same shortening and weakening effects on the susceptibility cycle's expansion phase. Entrepreneurs become more susceptible to revising their investment orders downwards than before the price rise in MOP. The susceptibility of high investment orders is further intensified by this price effect, bringing on the downturn quicker and at a lower level of investment orders.

Inputs that subsector 1a needs have less value added and more basic resources than sectors 1b and 2. Thus, the basic nature of MOP in 1a provides some room for the shifting options to relieve supply constraints and weaken price effects, leading to the least intensification of susceptibility. At the other extreme, the specific nature of MOP in the consumption goods (2) sector induces few shifting options, leading to high intensification of susceptibility. Subsector 1b constitutes an intermediate position between the two extremes.

The implications of this sectoral breakdown is to locate where the downturn in investment activity tends to come from. Sector 2 is strongly prone to downturn, since it is the one closest to the retail market. Any slow-down in this market during the boom is quickly transferred into a downturn in investment activity in sector 2 and, through a chain reaction, flow through to the other sector. The susceptibility suffered by sector 2 when inventories build up towards the top of a boom, is intensified due to the nature of MOP supply constraints during a boom period. Investment order reductions by this sector generates unused capacity and increased susceptibility in 1b and then in 1a subsectors. Consequently in subsector 1b, followed by subsector 1a, there is a downturn of both susceptibility and investment cycles. This is consistent with Halevi's traverse analysis at the sectoral level (see section 2.6).

Examining the lower turning point of the investment cycle provides a different story. The actual contraction phase does not have exactly opposite repercussions to that of an expansion phase. There are no problems in reducing investment activity by the capital goods sector. The problem which does arise is the build-up of excess capacity, but this does not limit the downward reduction in investment activity. Not even decommissioning old MOP in the investment goods sector should pose any problems for delivering new MOP to the consumption goods sector. No capital-goods-producing firm will intentionally make it difficult to meet investment orders by decommissioning so much capital stock that it reaches supply constraints due to full capacity of existing stock.

Problems related to the traverse reappear at the trough in investment orders. An above-average downturn in investment orders by most sectors of the economy depresses any inducement for new MOP within subsectors 1a and 1b. As a consequence, neither invests in more advanced technology, but instead remains with current capital goods. Being at the furthest distance from final consumption, 1a in particular can wait for obvious signs of an improved outlook in sector 2 and subsector 1b before 'costs of postponement' pressures start to induce some more positive mood towards reinvestment in new MOP.

Two effects of such lack of investment by the capital goods sector can be identified. First, it makes the possibility of an investment ordering upturn by any sector much more problematical. The lack of reinvestment stimulus in the capital goods sector places the onus for investment turnaround on sector 2. Inventory accumulation in the capital goods sector, built up as a result of most industries having very low investment orders, means that overcapacity becomes a severe barrier to any upturn in investment orders in the capital goods sector itself (Halevi, 1983, p. 354). Without any upturn in investment orders in 1a and 1b, and no reason for stimulus to investment in sector 2, the susceptibility cycle tends to skid along the bottom (at level x_o in Figure 5.3). Sector 1, in such circumstances, is hit hard with large excess capacities and low profits (both rate and level) – the two key elements that need to improve in order to stop the skid.

The second effect of the lack of investment by sector 1 operates during the next investment boom. Leaving the reason to the next section, assume that an upturn in investment orders occurs in sector 2 (where it is most likely). The large excess capacity in 1a and 1b ensures a quick response to initial orders from sector 2. The lack of new investments in 1a and 1b takes its toll when industries in sector 2 increase their investment orders further up the susceptibility cycle. Excess capacity is removed in 1a and 1b, increased efficiency is required to meet growing investment demand from sector 2. The problem of inadequate reinvestment in MOP needed to meet growth requirements arises (a problem Kalecki identified in socialism, see section 2.6). Poor investment ordering in 1a and 1b during the contraction and trough of their own investment cycles magnifies the supply constraint problems in the new investment boom. This intensifies the susceptibility of industries (especially in sector 2) that are dependent on receiving new MOP at the appropriate planned time for competitive reasons during an investment boom. Time delays that result can be further extended by past poor reinvestment in new technology in 1a and 1b.

The irony of the situation is that sector 2 suffers most from the delay effect and the related poor reinvestment of the capital goods sector, leading to an intensification of susceptibility. Yet this is the same sector which has less ability to alleviate this susceptibility by the lack of shifting options. For this reason, the downturn in the susceptibility cycle tends to occur first in sector 2. The poor reinvestment (or 'skidding' at the trough of the susceptibility cycle) by subsectors 1a and 1b merely intensifies further the tendencies, already noted, towards the top of the expansion stage of investment ordering.

The traverse analysis by Lowe and in another context by Kalecki, on the structure of investment, has been linked to the concept of susceptibility in this section. The supply constraints in sector 1 via the traverse lead to an intensification of susceptibility, which then heightens the probability of a downturn in investment orders. To reduce susceptibility, investment orders decrease, which lowers capital goods production and results in an investment cycle downturn. Applying

Kalecki's version III business cycle to the traverse, the increasing inability to meet new MOP requirements as the boom progresses intensifies already growing susceptibility. This occurs as firms (especially in sector 2) are forced to rely on old MOP, which provides a lower profit rate due to the use of less-efficient MOP compared to competitors with newer MOP.

A second issue comes in as feedback from susceptibility to the traverse. Firms suffering from intensified susceptibility due to the supply constraint problems look to Kalecki's two shiftability factors for relief. Only limited relief, notably in subsector 1a, comes from shifting use of existing MOP, because there is no 'putty-putty' MOP model in the Kaleckian institutional framework. The second factor of shifting to foreign-sourced MOP is a more viable option. Small open economies (like Australia) source much of their MOP from overseas, which means that their relatively small orders from foreign MOP producers cannot alone cause any traverse problems. However, in concert with increased MOP demand from other economies the traverse problem could also arise in foreign sources.

The relative strength of supply constraint problems as well as solutions such as shiftability vary with the specific structure of industries. Each industry has a different story. Historically based general empirical patterns of supply constraints are presented in Chapter 7. It is adequate to recognise here links between the traverse and susceptibility so that such problems and the extent of modification and alteration to investment strategies can be identified.

5.6 THE INTERACTION OF SELF-GENERATING ELEMENTS

Interaction of the three elements outlined in section 5.4 (profits, increasing risk, capacity utilisation), within specific industry conduct and institutional macroeconomic structures, produces distinctive susceptibility cycles for each industry. Each element operates on tension build-up and breakdown, and is theoretically able to produce its own self-generating susceptibility cycle. However, it is the interaction of all three elements that produces a complete endogenous susceptibility cycle which is a powerful analytical guide to understanding investment behaviour.

At the outset it should be recognised from the examination of each element separately that there are two essential and common features of all three analyses. First is the contradictory pull mechanism, causing negative feedback on accumulation when investment orders are very high. This is the basic feature of rising cumulative tension in investment ordering, and the corresponding higher susceptibility to such contradictory pulls. This turns the level of investment ordering down by cancellation of previous investment orders. The second is the competitive long-term pressure experienced by firms at low levels of susceptibility, forcing firms to increase market share, create barriers to entry and take advantage of expected demand improvements. All these actions require new efficient MOP. Thus, competitive pressure induces an increased rate of investment ordering at a time when susceptibility is low and tension is relatively low. By responding to such pressure to increase investment orders, entrepreneurs begin to encounter renewed tension build-up and rising susceptibility.

Figure 5.4 is a generalised schematic representation of all the elements that are involved in the investment decisions of firms in an industry within the modified monopoly capitalist Kaleckian institutional framework of Chapter 4. The figure combines the essential aspects of Figures 5.2 and 5.3, to derive short-term cyclical patterns over time. Only measurable parts of the theory, based on the Kaleckian elements, are drawn in Figure 5.4. The behavioural aspects of fear, tension, euphoria and fragile feelings come out of firms attempting to handle the Kaleckian elements through a variety of rules of thumb which exhibit various adjustment processes to investment ordering. These adjustments differ according to specific entrepreneurial characteristics and environmental factors.

Graph 1 depicts a generalised cycle of capacity utilisation. Graph 2 illustrates a generalised susceptibility cycle. By drawing together the three self-generating elements, a schematic representation of a susceptibility cycle which follows a fluctuating dynamic path can be sketched. Susceptibility is *reflected* in the level of investment orders: the higher the monetary value of current investment orders, the higher the susceptibility of investment commitments to collapse. For this reason, the vertical scale of the susceptibility cycle in graph 2 shows investment orders. Graph 3 portrays a generalised cycle of investment activity, measured in terms of actual value of production of capital goods, reflecting the time delay after orders and the traverse involved in producing capital goods.

5.6.1 Expansion of Susceptibility (Phases 1 and 2)

To appreciate the interaction of the three self-generating elements in this cyclical behaviour, a generalised explication of dynamic susceptibility is presented, following this path on Figure 5.4, graph 2. When investment orders in an industry are growing, entrepreneurs experience an increasing susceptibility derived from cumulative tension. Entrepreneurs commit themselves to greater investment orders because they expect the resulting investment to deliver increased market share and growth in the industry. Such optimistic investment decisions are implemented to take advantage of potential markets relative to existing capital stock. Increasing susceptibility is the growing countertendency to optimistic expectations.

Figure 5.4 Schematic representation of industry investment decisions

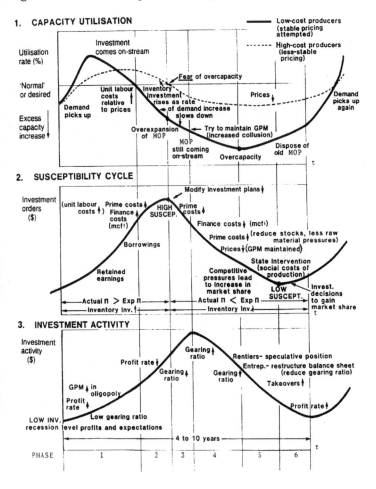

As noted in section 5.3, the firm's investment strategy is developed independent of the state of the economy, but the firm's decision when to undertake projects in specific time frames depends on the state of the economy, and in particular the state of the industry in which the firm exists (or wants to enter). This is the basis of entrepreneurs' expectation – knowledge of the past with its application to the future (Shackle, 1970, p. 106). This expectation is shaped by experience of how the aggregate economy behaves in relation to the specific industry in which the firm operates. Investment orders are on the rise at the beginning of the graph 2 cyclical path because of the past period's success, with increased growth coming from higher demand. However, such decisions can not completely anticipate an uncertain future (Shackle, 1970, pp. 109–110).

The susceptibility cycle is an *ex ante* 'economic counter' which aims to map out behaviour that leads to adjustments in investment decisions. It does this by measuring the sensitivity of investment commitments to uncertainty as disturbances become more strongly anticipated. This cycle can identify the elements that build up tension in a firm's investment decision-making and in this way anticipate a major disturbance to the economy when susceptibility is at an historically high level in relation to past cycles. The build-up of susceptibility via contradictory pulls occurs with all three self-generating elements.

First, utilisation rates go well above desired rates due to aggregate demand (and industry demand) pick up. During this early period, called Phase 1, investment orders rise sharply. In graph 3 of Figure 5.4, the level of investment activity follows the rise in investment orders with a time lag, this being depicted as a slower rise than in graph 2 (see section 5.5). Once MOP begin to come on-stream from these early period rises in investment orders, capacity utilisation rates start to fall (follow solid black line in graph 1). Initially, rates fall to desired levels (end of Phase 1), but then excess capacity continues to increase as more capital goods come on-stream with a lag (Phase 2). Assuming the majority of final goods industries can be represented by this schematic diagram, during Phase 1 there are no supply constraints from the capital-goods-producing sector. Most of the final goods industries are only just picking up on their investment orders and undesired excess capacity exists in the capital goods sector. Only in Phase 2 do some supply constraints begin to occur.

Secondly, the profit rate increases during Phase 1. This coincides with the rise in the degree of monopoly (reflected in the gross profit margin, GPM) due to success in sales promotion, new improved capital stock (innovation), and increased concentration through higher market share of dominant firms. The cyclical effect in the mark-up (or GPM), where it rises until mid-expansion of the typical business cycle and then declines until the business cycle trough, is supported by the theoretical and empirical studies discussed in section 2.3.2.

With a rising gross profit rate, the available retained earnings increase based on a reasonably stable gross retention ratio. This allows investment orders to increase, reinforcing the rise in susceptibility from a low base. Overheads, such as salaries and interest, remain constant during Phase 1 so that there is no pressure on the GPM. The actual increment in realised net profit provides a positive feedback on past investment decisions, inducing higher short-term expectations that the rate of return of new improved (innovatory) capital stock will rise. During this phase, entrepreneurs' expectations of increased profit levels in the near future are greater than the actual (current) profit levels realised. This positive environment encourages further investment order increases, moving at an increasing rate up the black line in graph 2 through Phase 1. Tension related to the contradictory pull of the negative feedback inherent in greater capital stock is low at the start of Phase 1. This increases somewhat during this phase, but with only limited effect on investment ordering, due to extremely high expectations and the low base of susceptibility.

Thirdly, the financing of investment orders is not a constraint during Phase 1. Rising retained earnings due to dividends generally increasing more slowly than profits (Wood, 1975, p. 48) allows internal accumulation to occur. The low gearing ratio inherited over the previous slump is of little effect. Some increase in borrowings towards the end of Phase 1 raises the gearing ratio a little, but not enough to provide any serious negative feedback to current high expectations and investment ordering.

In the shorter Phase 2, the contradictory pull of negative feedback from all three self-generating elements results in investment orders increasing at a decreasing rate. During this phase, entrepreneurs' expectations of increased (future) profit levels are still greater than actual realised profit levels. However, problems are beginning to arise with the three elements, which generates increased tension in entrepreneurs' investment decisions.

First, tension arises from excess capacity increasing above the desired level from the beginning of Phase 2. This is due to the time lags involved in the very large investment ordering during Phase 1, which now comes on stream very quickly. Also, inventory investment becomes positive, as the rate of demand increase slows down, creating increased stocks that lower future capacity utilisation. In Phase 2 the traverse becomes an issue, on the assumption that most industries in sector 2 are in this phase of the schematic diagram. As excess capacity rises in sector 2, sector 1 becomes more constrained. Sector 1 reaches the high capacity utilisation rate of mid-Phase 1 at the time when sector 2 is in mid-Phase 2. From the analysis in section 5.5, assuming no shiftability options are available, such supply constraints intensify susceptibility (at a given level of investment orders). Towards the end of Phase 2, the supply constraints may actually reduce the throughput of capital goods compared to the anticipated levels. In spite of the large level of capital goods being produced and the levelling off of final goods demand, there is little reason for supply constraints to alleviate in any way the excess capacity tensions.

Secondly, tension arises due to the reduced actual profit rate as unit labour costs rise, creating pressure on firms trying to maintain the Phase 1 'high ratio of profits to wages' (Kalecki, 1954, p. 17). This pressure mounts as profit mark-ups are reduced to levels experienced at the start of Phase 1 (Goldstein, 1982), in order to remove the uncompetitive fringe and excess capacity (Bloch, 1990, p. 449). The adoption of such lower mark-ups by firms depends on the industry structure and the relative costs of producers. As shown by graph 1, low-cost producers attempt to maintain stable pricing (resist price-cutting rivalry); this means that excess capacity increases much quicker and goes much further than with high-cost producers, where price-cutting occurs to maintain higher output production and correspondingly lower excess capacity. In low-cost tightly controlled non-differentiated oligopolies, the tension of negative feedback on large investment orders filters through to a greater extent from excess capacity than from profit reductions; while, in high-cost loosely controlled differentiated oligopolies, tension filters through more from profit reductions and less from excess capacity.

Thirdly, tension arises as pressure mounts for increased distribution to rising overheads from gross profits. Higher gearing ratios raise the marginal costs of funds to firms due to increasing risk. This raises financing overheads, reducing actual profits. Pressure also comes from executives who see success as needing to be rewarded by higher salaries, including management's own desire for higher remuneration. This raises overheads to the managers and senior executives.

With this increased susceptibility, investment ordering faces negative feedback from capital stock, profits and increasing risk. There is also the increasing frustration of supply constraints suffered by many industries in sector 2 over the large levels of investment ordering. All these pressures lead to progressively decreasing the upward *rate* of investment orders through Phase 2. Investment orders are still rising because expectations of future profit levels, despite being reduced, are still greater than the levels of actual (net) profits. Also, there is the entrepreneurial reaction lag of low-cost producers to recognising that having achieved desired excess capacity at the beginning of Phase 2, by the end of this phase these firms are well below desired utilisation rates. Optimism has not been totally destroyed, although it is increasingly weakened by all these tensions through Phase 2.

The peak of the susceptibility cycle occurs at the end of Phase 2. The combined contradictory pressures of overexpansion of MOP, increasing risk, and (net) profit levels rising at a decreasing rate, all contribute to an extremely fragile investment environment. The reduced rate of increase in both investment orders and capitalist consumption through Phase 2 places a strong squeeze on net profits. Further, the peak of the susceptibility cycle exhibits a heightened intensity due to supply constraints on sector 2, unless firms are able to shift supply constraints away. Old capital stock is not prone to such susceptibility, as it can hold on to markets with older more stable products and methods (Steindl, 1981b, p. 128).

All this fragility is reflected in expectations of future profit levels (i.e. the rate of return on new future capital stock) which alter from being greater than actual profit levels (on old capital stock) to less than actual profit levels. It is at the peak of the susceptibility cycle that this reversal between expected and actual profit levels occurs. This profit reversal is the 'final straw' which turns a highly susceptible position into a collapse of potential investment commitments, reducing investment orders. These reduced orders relieve both tension and the highly susceptible position in which firms had placed themselves.

5.6.2 Contraction of Susceptibility (Phases 3, 4 and 5)

Entrepreneurs modify downwards both present and future investment plans as a result of the turnaround in the susceptibility cycle. This contraction is based on the factors which create fragility and also the responses to it by firms reducing future investment commitments and modifying downwards current investment orders through mothballing, stalling, seeking government support or simply cancelling projects. When investment orders begin to fall through Phase 3, unfavourable aspects of all three elements are still operating.

First, excess capacity continues to increase (see graph 1) as MOP come on- stream with a time lag from the period of rising investment orders. It should be noted that there is still a relatively high level of investment orders in Phase 3, but the direction is towards continually decreasing such orders. The level of industry demand is still increasing through this phase, but at a continuing slower rate which causes more excess capacity problems. High-cost producers in the uncompetitive fringe, having a fear of overcapacity, modify downwards their investment plans and reduce prices to maintain production and utilisation at a higher level than low-cost producers (see dotted line in graph 1).

Secondly, the profit rate continues to fall due to continued pressure on prime costs. These pressures come from higher labour and raw materials costs which are associated with the continued rise in economic activity (MOP still coming on-stream and industry demand still high). Pressure also comes from maintaining the lower mark-ups of Phase 2 and the continued rise of overheads. However, as investment orders fall during this phase, the above cost/mark-up pressures begin to ease.

Thirdly, the gearing ratio (debt-to-equity) continues to rise as more borrowings are required. In particular, short-term lending increases strongly for what is seen as temporarily high interest rates. For entrepreneur-owners the need to continue to issue shares and, with it, the increasing potential for loss of control is also a problem.

Supply constraints still remain in Phase 3 as investment cycles for industries in sector 2 move towards their peaks. Some relief comes from sector 1 itself producing its own MOP necessary to overcome supply constraints. This very growth and success in sector 1 adds its own intensification of susceptibility for the capital-goods-producing entrepreneurs, now at Phase 2. The advantage that sector 1, and especially subsector 1a, has is the ability to shift its structure of investment in order to reduce the intense susceptibility being built up.

The significance of the susceptibility cycle is to distinguish between when the three elements are creating tension so that pressure is placed on entrepreneurs to modify downwards or postpone investment plans and when the same three elements (together with the traverse) are exhibiting effects of time lags. In the latter case, they still exhibit strong negative measures (e.g. high gearing ratios), but tension has already been reduced as a result of falling investment orders. Tension is not measured by the elements themselves, nor by the extent of supply constraints, but by the level of investment orders. The length of this Phase 3 depends on the length of time lags involved in the production of MOP. A long time lag prolongs the pressures placed on the three elements and on supply constraints, leading to a long Phase 3. A short time lag results in a comparatively shorter Phase 3.

Turning a highly susceptible position in Phase 2 into a collapse of investment commitments at the start of Phase 3 results in a postponement of long-term investment strategies by entrepreneurs. Observable in graph 2 is the reduction of investment orders. To understand why it is occurring, it is necessary to appreciate the nature of susceptibility during Phase 3 as noted above.

Problems related to the production–delivery stage of the traverse intensify susceptibility, chiefly during the late part of Phase 2. These problems continue during Phase 3 as investment activity is still rising. This situation adds further urgency to postponing investment strategies and reducing investment orders in Phase 3. Such actions ease the susceptibility of investment, first in sector 2 which is highly vulnerable to the traverse during the boom. Sector 1 follows sector 2 with a downturn in investment ordering; first subsector 1b, then subsector 1a reduce their investment orders in a chain reaction. The 'shiftability options' are increasingly available through this chain of sectors from 2 to 1b to 1a. This means that subsector 1a in particular has relatively less intensity of susceptibility, and thus less pressures during the downturn of investment orders through its Phase 3.

Cutting back on future investment commitments is not adequate nor would it occur quickly enough to overcome the highly fragile situation described above. Current investment orders already committed need to be modified in order to bring about the necessary reduction in investment. The amount of such costly modifications depends on how fragile the current investment commitments are in terms of the level of susceptibility they create for the firm (and the industry). The more serious the time delays and the higher the supply prices in the traverse, the greater the intensity of susceptibility for highly fragile current investment orders. This requires immediate relief by mothballing projects, stalling construction of plant (even by creating intentional bad industrial relations to provoke a strike), and demanding government support on the basis of threats to cancel or delay partially implemented investment projects.

Postponement of investment strategies includes the shelving of endogenous innovations and possibly reducing R&D investment. This alleviates the pressure of high susceptibility, by concentrating on profit returns from old MOP which have a proven production track record, rather than the higher but more unpredictable returns from new MOP. As noted by Baran and Sweezy (see section 2.5), monopoly capitalists want to protect existing MOP, limiting potential innovation at investment cycle peaks. New innovations developed on the fringe of the corporate world tend to be ignored at this stage. Such innovation postponements tend to produce a mismatch of current investment to available new technology in the economy. Long contractions of the susceptibility cycle tend to inhibit structural change and create limitations on the current techno-economic structure of the economy. Only a recovery in investment strategies can overcome this technological mismatch.

The end of Phase 3 is identified by the peak of the investment activity cycle. Postponement of investment plans and modification downwards of current investment commitments lead, with a time lag, to the upper turning point in the investment activity curve of graph 3. The more the downturn in investment activity relies on modifications of previous investment orders compared to delaying future investment plans, the quicker the downturn in investment activity is realised.

Once investment activity falls in Phase 4, all the pressures on the three elements and the traverse begin to ease. Phase 4 starts with reductions in costs, with 'the marginal cost of funds' being the first to fall (Evans, 1969, pp. 86–95), followed by reductions in both raw material and stock maintenance costs as industry demand pressures ease. The capital goods and raw materials sectors suffer large overcapacity as demand pressures ease in a large number of sector 2 industries. This sends input prime costs down in final goods manufacturing industries.

In a sector 2 industry under price leadership, the dominant firm attempts to maintain the GPM, with prices only falling relative to prime costs. Such price-cutting aims to remove excess capacity in industry through the collapse of the uncompetitive fringe that developed over the boom and whose high costs prevent any more price cuts. Excess capacity is, thus, still a problem in Phase 4, with economic activity and industry demand falling. However, the rate of MOP coming on stream has been drastically reduced (flattening out the solid black line of capacity utilisation in graph 1). In industries where there are many high-cost producers, their continuing fear of overcapacity with falling demand induces much more competitive price-cutting in order to maintain production and capacity usage at higher levels than in low-cost oligopoly industries (see dotted line in graph 1).

Higher excess capacity in Phase 4 leads to large fixed (overhead) costs which need to be met when production and sales are falling. The need to hold on to salaried management staff, to pay contractual interest obligations and to depreciate capital stock, all loom as larger amounts to pay out of gross profits while low-cost producers maintain GPMs. With net profits being further squeezed, firms require the support of short-term finance to overcome liquidity problems (cash flow problems), which raises the debt levels further. Thus, gearing ratios in Phase 4 remain high, or even increase.

Phase 4 ends at the trough of excess capacity utilisation in graph 1. Disposal of old, less-efficient capital stock and the withdrawal of the uncompetitive fringe (sometimes taken over by the larger firms which may engage in asset stripping) results in excess capacity decreasing and moving back towards desired levels during Phase 5. The combination of reduced prime costs in Phase 4 and reduced excess capacity in Phase 5 significantly adds to the reduction of tension in investment ordering. This develops a lower susceptibility (or higher resilience) to investment commitments, with entrepreneurs finding that current investment orders in Phase 5 are being made without the attendant pressures of Phase 3. Of course, the level of investment orders in Phase 5 is low relative to Phase 3.

Financial concerns are the preoccupation of all capitalists in Phase 5 rather than fixed business investment. Rentiers disappear into speculative markets with their funds. Financial investment in the productive sector to support fixed business investment is no longer attractive. The high tension suffered in Phase 3 dissuades rentiers, who instead seek more short-term capital gains, which tends to induce a financial boom during Phase 5. This emerging financial boom is spurred on by entrepreneur-owners who move into speculative finance during periods of large excess capacity in an effort to overcome short-term cash flow problems through capital gains rather than short-term borrowings. Thus, the speculative financial boom in Phase 5 is the *result* of past real investment factors in Phases 3 and 4, rather than the *cause* of future boom activity in the real sector as is advocated by 'financial instability' oriented economists such as Vickers and Minsky (see section 2.3.3).

Entrepreneur-managers of diversely owned companies attempt to reduce gearing ratios by selling (disposing of) assets, reducing secondary (prime cost) labour force (unskilled and less-skilled workers), taking over smaller companies with good cash flows or good saleable assets, and reorganising plant and office management (disembodied technical change). All entrepreneurs of dominant firms are restructuring their balance sheets to improve cash flow, while entrepreneurs of smaller firms are busy trying to prevent bankruptcy by using the same financial tools. These actions quell the insecurity that entrepreneurs feel about inefficient and excessive capital stock, as well as putting their finances on a sounder footing. Phase 5 ends at the lowest point (trough) of the susceptibility cycle (graph 2), when entrepreneurs feel least susceptible to tensions of investment commitments because investment orderings are at their lowest, relative to the current cycle.

Graph 2 depicts an upturn in the susceptibility cycle at the end of Phase 5, with investment orders moving upwards to start another cycle. Investment activity (in graph 3) follows with an upturn after a Phase 6 time lag. Phase 1 starts again once investment activity turns up. Economists have great difficulty in explaining the lower turning point of investment cycles.[15] Given the traverse, excess capacity in sector 1 creates a severe barrier to any upturn in investment orders in this sector (see section 5.5). It means that an upturn needs to come from sector 2 or else the susceptibility cycle skids on the bottom of the trough. The nature of the upturn in the susceptibility cycle and the role of consumption goods industries in this upturn needs to be explained.

5.6.3 Recovery and Structural Change (Phase 6)

Lower turning points can be identified empirically through the same three self-generating elements used to track upper turning point disturbances. Tension from all three elements has reduced to such an extent by the end of Phase 5 that entrepreneurs are now highly prone to taking a competitive advantage. The costs of postponement in investment throughout the contractionary period have reached such very high levels that each entrepreneur expects the other competitor to seize a competitive advantage of the situation.

The increase in investment orders, however small, at the trough of the susceptibility cycle is crucial for the turnaround of the endogenous investment cycle after a time lag between orders and activity. The large excess capacity in existence at a time of generally depressed conditions makes any increase in investment orders a highly sensitive action, even a small modification upwards, given the uncertainty in the general economic climate at that time. This uncertainty carries a strong aversion to any new investment orders. A few points can be advanced in an attempt to explain the upturn in the susceptibility cycle under these conditions.

First is the nature of the susceptibility cycle itself that provides a clear indication about the turnaround. At the bottom of the susceptibility cycle with relatively few investment orders, entrepreneurs experience lower susceptibility than at any time since the previous trough. This provides a sense of relief from tension, but it is also the signal for more tension. No entrepreneur in a competitive oligopoly structure can afford to be complacent, and low susceptibility is seen by entrepreneurs themselves as complacency. Remaining complacent means that significantly high postponement costs are being ignored. Competitive entrepreneurs more accepting of innovation potentials induce endogenous innovations in this situation of low susceptibility and high postponement costs. Such innovations require new MOP which make some current (but old) MOP obsolete and, therefore, not part of the excess capacity calculation.

Endogenous product innovation is the platform for robust investment expansion (see section 4.5). Stimulation of needs in sector 2 using a certain technological paradigm is the basis of searching for profits. Success in product innovation is more strongly based on the back of a new paradigm (e.g. pocket calculators on the back of the microchip), rather than the old paradigm which has limited new product creations. Some firms modify their investment orders slightly upwards with minor product innovations to create a competitive advantage and obtain some positive marginal ΔP. These firms develop new tension and their susceptibility cycles begin to rise. Success in small innovations generate more widespread adoption of the new needs-based innovations, establishing what Schumpeter calls a 'swarm' effect. Process innovations aim to reduce production costs, thus becoming more relevant when profits are being squeezed as the susceptibility cycle moves strongly up towards its peak.

Induced (or endogenous) innovation comes out of the need to gain a competitive advantage by increasing market share and improving all three self-generating elements. Such innovation is rarely anything more than style changes, minor improvements or perhaps even new packaging. This contrasts with autonomous (or exogenous) innovation, a secular factor that relates to long-term development of major technological innovations and which leads to massive flow-on of new products and methods. Exogenous innovations occur rarely but create long-term secular paradigm shifts, which are the basis of swarming-induced innovatory behaviour in the cyclical process.

With the inclusion of the state, megacorps (and their industries) seek its assistance in reducing the social costs of production, at the time when these firms attempt to expand their market by utilising or decommissioning idle productive capacity. State support in this way, during recessions, is part of the 'stop–go' mechanism of the political business cycle that is endogenous to the model. Examples of state support are infrastructure spending (or subsidies) and tariff (or sales tax) cuts. Without competitive pressures for investment and innovation and government support for these pressures, secular stagnation of the type described by Steindl (1952) becomes a reality. In the next chapter, exogenous factors keeping these endogenous mechanisms from working are described.

The two different types of entrepreneurs also make a difference to the nature of susceptibility cycle upturns. Entrepreneur-owners have less aversion to the introduction of innovations than entrepreneur-managers. The former have a weaker preference for safety and place stronger weight on their own beliefs under uncertainty. With low susceptibility, entrepreneur-owners are induced by their competitive instincts and their drive for power to appropriate new markets, requiring new investment orders. Entrepreneur-managers in diversely owned companies are much more circumspect about making long-term investment commitments. The latter are more inclined to invest in slight modifications of existing markets or processes. Such activities do not create the same impetus to the investment cycle as do the commitments of the more tightly knit companies under entrepreneur-owners. Thus, the number of diversely owned compared to tightly owned companies determines how easy or difficult it is for the industry investment upturn to transpire. More tightly owned companies in the economy, with relatively less aversion to innovation, tends to make cyclical upturns easier to achieve.

It must be stressed that the lower turning point of the susceptibility cycle is no mirror image of the upper turning point for two reasons. First, the different preferences for safety between firms (and industries) have a large effect on the lower turning point, but very little effect on the upper turning point. At the peak, all firms have high susceptibility and thus the fragility of the situation induces a reversal in all investment orders. At the trough, tightly owned companies with their relatively lesser aversion to innovation lead investment orders out of the doldrums. If successful, this creates a snowball effect. How easily the lower turning point comes about depends on the institutional structure of the economy – the amount of low-aversion tightly owned companies compared to high-aversion diversely owned companies.

Secondly, the strength and timing of the lower turning point is much more problematical than the upper turning point. At the lower turning point, timing (and strength) of the upturn depends on how endogenously the new competitive improvements (induced innovations) are introduced, including taking out of mothballs previous stalled investments, and how endogenously the firms (and industries) lobby for government support to underwrite their projects. These endogenous forces relate to future expectations of profits and are not guaranteed to occur at any particular time. The extent to which such forces come into play is also uncertain. The downturn is timed much more tightly because pressures to contract affect all firms at the same time but to varying degrees. Pressures to contract investment orders come from too-high susceptibility across all firms. Pressures to expand investment orders, when susceptibility is low, depends on a more problematical issue of when a firm (or industry) does finally take the plunge and change to tension-enhancing from tension-relieving actions. The particular institutional framework within an economy influences how firms respond to low susceptibility and what it implies for the strength and timing of the upturn.

From the perspective of the traverse, initiating endogenous product innovations generally requires the supply of new types of equipment (process innovation) for the production of the new product. Sector 1 must respond to this new form of investment demand in order for product innovation to be successful. At the trough of the susceptibility cycle, co-ordination of product and process innovation ensures appropriate implementation. Such co-ordination is based on megacorps' ability to make their own required plant and equipment, or to buy up needed processes from failed firms or through close linkages to 'science-based' and 'information-intensive' firms (see Figure 3.1). High excess capacity in sector 1 induces co-operation with the needs of sector 2. If such linkages and methods break down or do not exist, tensions of the proposed new innovations *intensify*, making any innovation-induced rise in the susceptibility cycle more problematical.

As the susceptibility cycle rises with the broader adoption of some product innovations, sector 1 finds it more economic to supply greater levels of needed equipment. Only when the success of the innovation creates supply constraints towards the top of the susceptibility cycle does the intensification of susceptibility lead to reductions in investment orders (see Figure 5.3).

Technological change and its role under uncertainty in altering patterns of investment orders is an important institutional aspect of the economy. It depends on the entrepreneurs' degree of 'safety preference' *vis-à-vis* their belief in market growth with renewed investment orders (at the bottom of the susceptibility cycle), and their ability to withstand pressures to contract investment orders (at the top of the susceptibility cycle). These entrepreneurial dilemmas, based on the susceptibility cycle, recognise technological change as not simply an addition of a trend line to the investment cycle, but as a crucial factor affecting profit returns at the margin (new MOP versus old MOP). The amount of technological change affects productivity, profit returns and, thus, investment order patterns. In this way, the susceptibility cycle model incorporates technological change into cyclical investment behaviour while still embracing its growth effects. This approach puts into practice Kalecki's desire to integrate technological change (and long-term developments) much more closely with short-term cyclical behaviour.

5.7 TIMING OF THE SUSCEPTIBILITY CYCLE

The interaction of the three self-generating elements raises the possibility that the timing of these different elements may create conflicting signals, and this mitigates against the operation of the susceptibility cycle. Profit squeeze and increasing risk tend to coincide, since increases in profit rate generate larger retained earnings and reduce the need for more debt and share issue. Capacity utilisation may not always exactly relate to the other two elements at the same point on the susceptibility cycle as set out in Figure 5.4.[16]

Any deviations from the schematic representation in Figure 5.4 alters the timing and magnitude of the susceptibility cycle. For example, if the utilisation rate reaches a peak later, then Phase 1 would extend further over time before Phase 2 begins (since Phase 2 begins when the utilisation rate reaches 'normal'). If production stays at 'normal' utilisation rate longer, this extends Phase 2 longer, and so on. If at the same time profit squeeze occurs earlier, this reduces Phase 2 from the extension given to it by a longer normal utilisation rate. On the other hand, if all elements lead to squeezing the period of Phase 2 (quicker profit squeeze, shorter normal utilisation rate, higher increasing risk), then the strength of Phase 2 is greater. This leads to steeper expansion of the susceptibility cycle and a higher upward wave than the generalised version in graph 2. Such 'squeezing' tends to make the entrepreneurial reaction lag shorter, reducing the time covered by Phase 2.

The specific institutional structure of an economy and the specific industry being examined determine the length and magnitude of each phase of the susceptibility cycle. The three self-generating elements are crucial to determining their precise shape. Other factors can also affect timing; in particular, time lags in the investment decision-making process described in Figure 5.1 are crucial. The clearest example is the time lag between the decision to modify downwards investment commitments (start of Phase 3) and its realisation in the downturn of investment activity (start of Phase 4). The quicker the cancellations and modifications of current investment commitments are translated into a slow-down in the capital-goods-producing industries, the shorter is Phase 3. No time lag between the two means that Phase 3 disappears altogether, and the peaks of graphs 2 and 3 coincide. Phase 4 is not particularly affected by the lack of this time lag. If the industry and economy-wide institutional structures show short time lags, then the whole susceptibility cycle is shortened, while longer time lags lengthen the cycle.

The periodicity of investment cycles is an empirical question. Industry investment studies done in the 1960s for the USA show investment (activity) functions with cycles varying between four and ten years, depending on the nature of the industry, and with the larger capital-intensive industries exhibiting longer cycles (Evans, 1969, pp. 117–21).

The susceptibility cycle is the behavioural mechanism which drives the investment cycle. Periodicity of the susceptibility cycle is determined by the underlying institutional structures and the psychological attitudes of entrepreneurs to these structures. For this reason there is no *a priori* periodicity. Only observation of investment orders (or lag-adjusted investment activity) provides some empirical guide to the periodicity of susceptibility cycles. In Figure 5.4 the periodicity of the susceptibility and investment cycles is the same since the time lag is assumed to remain constant. Only the investment cycle is lagged. As indicated above, reducing the time lag would reduce the periodicity of susceptibility and investment activity cycles simultaneously.

5.8 SUMMARY

The susceptibility cycle model can be formally summarised in an investment order function which provides the objective reflection of susceptibility.

$$I_{t+1} = f(P_t, \Delta P, g_t, u_t) \tag{5.1}$$

where, I_{t+1} is the level of aggregate investment orders in the forthcoming period; P_t is the current level of profits (ability to invest such that $P'>0$); ΔP is the actual increment in profit levels (inducement to invest such that $\Delta P'>0$); g is the current gearing ration with a limit based on the minimum proportion 'h' of retained earnings 'RE' (such that $g \leq hRE$, and $g'>0$); u is the actual degree of utilisation ($u'<0$) and Peak of susceptibility is reached when I_{t+1} is at maximum value. This is the point where contradictory pull creates enough susceptibility tension for investment orders to downturn, reflecting falling susceptibility. The peak occurs under the following conditions: (a) when P is high with ΔP beginning to decrease; (b) when g> hRE as a result of change in g rising farther than RE in boom; and (c) when u falls below desired degree of utilisation.

Trough of susceptibility is reached when I_{t+1} is at minimum value. The trough occurs under the following conditions: (a) when P is low with increasing ΔP (this is the only completely symmetric contradictory pull mechanism, but as Stegman (1982) has shown, often this element is not enough to illicit a turnaround in investment cycles); (b) when g limit is reached (lowest gearing ratio limit); and (c) when u limit is reached (overcapacity limit). These limits are based on competitive pressures to increase market share after a period of investment order contraction.

A lag structure to the functional form of equation (5.1) allows for production lags (the traverse) and differing institutional structures.

Long-term developmental changes to the structure of equation (5.1) are based on the extent of change in P (or profit squeeze limits) needed to reach the turning point; the limits set on h and g for financing; and the limits of overcapacity and undercapacity acceptable to monopoly capitalism. All three endogenous elements have certain rules of thumb regarding these limits which can vary in the longer-term as economies and industries develop and alter (see details, based on empirical patterns identified, in Chapter 7).

NOTES

1. See discussion using the Levine approach in section 2.7.
2. See discussion on Goodwin in section 2.5.
3. See discussion on Baran and Sweezy in section 2.4.
4. Details on how this upturn develops and how it differs between differentiated and non-differentiated industries is presented in section 5.6.3 of this chapter.
5. Penrose (1959) is central to understanding firm dynamics of growth and maturity. These dynamics, of which commissioning problems are only one aspect, are used to develop a framework for the empirical patterns identified in the innovatory process (see Chapter 7).
6. See discussion in Salter (1960, pp. 58–65) of the problem of postponement in the use of new best practice techniques in the production process and delays in scrapping (and replacing) old MOP from a neoclassical perspective.
7. Salter (1960) is a very rare neoclassical study on investment and its implications for MOP increments at the margin. From its neoclassical framework Salter assumes that firms' investment is based on market responses. What Salter's analysis neglects is the high anxiety of entrepreneurs which can force them to ignore such market signals in preference for safety. In this behavioural Kaleckian approach, profits from marginal increments in MOP provide a guide to susceptibility.
8. Bhaduri (1986, p. 180) explains the upturn in the investment cycle in a similar way: 'a low level of investment generate[s] its own method of revitalisation through recreation of investment opportunities. With accumulating investment opportunities exerting a positive influence on the level of investment, the level of investment begins to rise gradually.' The advantage of this book's explanation of the upturn is that it relates the generation of 'revitalisation' to motivation of entrepreneurs in terms of incremental changes in profits.
9. Following Kalecki, borrower's risk and not lender's risk is generally the earlier limiting constraint on borrowing in the modified Kaleckian institutional framework of this model (see section 4.4).
10. Sylos Labini (1967) uses profits or liquidity variables to measure increasing risk (see section 2.3.3), instead of gearing ratios. Sylos Labini's approach is inappropriate for this analysis because it is impossible to show how susceptibility is brought about through increasing risk *on its own* without the intrusion of the first element – profits. Profits cannot be used as a guide to both susceptibility elements. Del Monte (1981) employs the interest rate as a proxy for liquidity instead of profits. This again is another measure used to monitor increasing risk which is inappropriate for this study. Any variable which is proxied by the interest rate makes the analysis a price-responsive mechanism. The Kaleckian approach presented in this book is based on quantity response mechanisms as primary sources of change with price responses as supplementary secondary sources of change. Further, if the interest rate is considered as a proxy for increasing risk, then it would be the long-term rate of interest which is relevant for investment in capital stock which lasts for a long time. Yet, the fact is 'that the long-term rate of interest does not show marked

cyclical fluctuations' (Kalecki, 1971, p. 113), which makes this variable inappropriate for an analysis of susceptibility inherent in a cyclical, unstable path of investment.

11. Whereas Steindl applies this fear concept to his long-term stagnation thesis (Steindl, 1981a, p. 46), in this study, 'fear of excess capacity' bolsters the susceptibility concept used to explain short-term investment instability.

12. This is in contrast to a neoclassical perfectly competitive industry where each firm's investment orders have minimal implication for potential capacity, and no firm is aware of what another firm is doing due to the large number of firms in the industry. In such a mythological industry structure, fear of excess capacity does not become an issue.

13. The wording of the phrase in quotations and the last sentence derive from Beresford and McFarlane (1980, p. 230): 'two key factors determine the *rate* of investment – the relative indebtedness of business and the degree of utilisation of capacity . . . The latter acts as a controller of investment, the increase in the level of excess capacity acting to inhibit new investment' (original emphasis).

14. Exogenous factors which have similar intensifying effect on susceptibility are discussed in Chapter 6.

15. For example, the accelerator, which empirically has some parallels to the model in the text, has been regarded favourably over a long period (see section 2.7). However, it has a poor explanatory value at the bottom of the investment cycle when excess capacity prevents the accelerator from working in reverse at the bottom of the cycle from how it does at the top of the cycle. Any attempt to make the accelerator more 'flexible' by taking excess capacity into account weakens any possibility of explaining the upturn itself.

16. Zarnowitz (1973, p. 71), in the time series data of chart 10-1 for the USA 1948–61, shows the peaks in business 'investment orders and contracts' occurring *after* the peaks in 'capacity utilization' for all four upper turning points. This is consistent with Figure 5.4. Comparative timing in the troughs of investment orders and capacity utilisation show the reverse to what is observed in the peaks for all five lower turning points presented. In all five cases, utilisation turns upwards very shortly (less than six months) after investment orders. This is inconsistent with Figure 5.4, but not with the general model. Given the more problematical nature of lower turning points, it is quite possible in the susceptibility cycle model for endogenous innovation to begin just *before* the trough in susceptibility. This induces an upturn in investment orders (and susceptibility) ahead of notional utilisation figures. The strong growth period under study by Zarnowitz, with its energy-based mass production technological paradigm still in the ascendancy, ensured much success with endogenous innovation (see Freeman and Perez, 1988, p. 52). This reinforces the susceptibility analysis which perceived that successful competitive advantage generates quick and strong investment upturns. In the more uncertain 1980s under massive structural change, it seems that utilisation troughs reverted to preceding, rather than following, investment troughs. This pattern is evident for 1980s' Australian business investment, as shown in chart 34 of Commonwealth of Australia (1993, p. 2.41). Finally, it should also be noted that capacity utilisation figures are highly unreliable. These are notional figures which are strongly affected by the extent of innovation and the timing of decisions to officially designate certain MOP as obsolete and marked for decommissioning (see section 4.5).

6. Exogenous Factors Affecting Susceptibility

In reality, of course, the economy is always influenced by outside factors (e.g. weather) so that a comprehensive explanation of its motion cannot be purely endogenous. (Zarnowitz, 1985, p. 544)

6.1 DISTINCTION BETWEEN EXOGENOUS AND ENDOGENOUS FACTORS

The opening quotation notes that no purely endogenous model can furnish a complete appreciation of cyclical forces in the economy. From a Kaleckian approach, exogenous factors enter the endogenous cyclical process as structural aspects that modify the cycle pattern, but never suppress the self-repeating sequential pattern.

Angell (1941, p. 5) identifies exogenous factors which affect business cycles as seasonal, secular or random. This chapter uses the same category of exogenous factors in looking at investment cycles. All three types of factors affect the nature of susceptibility tensions with regard to investment decisions. The aim of this chapter is to examine how the human agency of susceptibility mediates between these exogenous factors and the investment cycle. Changes brought about by these exogenous factors can alter the duration, amplitude and intra-cycle trend of the generalised susceptibility cycle presented in Figure 5.4. Some of the internal sequences of the way the three self-generating elements interact could also be altered.

The next section outlines a general technique by which exogenous factors affect susceptibility cycles. This technique is applied to specific examples of exogenous factors in the rest of the chapter, beginning with the three secular ('long-run development') factors that Kalecki (1954) identifies. Random and seasonal factors are then briefly examined. Finally, two structural aspects of modern capitalism are examined for their secular affects on susceptibility: the role of the state and the international economy. Examples of exogenous factors are infinite, thus an exhaustive account of exogeneity is impossible. Some important examples only are raised in this chapter.

The distinction between exogenous and endogenous factors used by Angell (1941) is applied here. Endogenous economic factors are induced by the business cycle to establish a self-repeating process. Many variables affect the three self-generating elements of the susceptibility cycle. All such variables are endogenous factors. This includes macroeconomic variables affecting the firm's investment decisions, such as overall effective demand growth (including export and import demand), general price rises, wage pressures, interest rates and levels of employment. The 'stop–go' mechanism of political business cycles is induced by the economic pressures of business cycles, and then influences effective demand growth in a self-repeating way that ensures its inclusion as an endogenous factor. There are also self-repeating endogenous microeconomic variables such as mark-ups, degree of concentration, market demand, desired rates of utilisation, inventory stock levels and costs of production. The industry investment cycle also induces variation in endogenous innovation, as outlined in the previous chapter.

Exogenous factors are all secular (or developmental), random and seasonal factors not specifically related to the short-term cyclical behaviour of the economy. Included is the broad political-sociological role of the state over the long-term. Specifically, this includes the military-industrial complex, the general protectionist stance, technological competition with alternative economic systems, and the broad expansionary–contractionary attitudes of political elites in western economies. Particular short-term state policy reactions to business cycles with regards to macro or micro policies are part of the endogenous story in the previous chapter. In this chapter, the other area of exogeneity discussed comes from shocks from the international economy: oil price rises, the capital flows and waves of speculation that come with them, and the related area of exchange rate changes.

The analytical dichotomy, arbitrary as it is, has the power to disentangle distinct roles that certain factors possess, which would otherwise remain obscure. This dichotomy allows for the separation of a factor into exogenous and endogenous aspects and the different behavioural implications that has for investment decision-making. For example, endogenous technological innovation allows for crucial investment-induced innovatory behaviour, while exogenous technological innovation allows for long-term secular developments in the innovatory process. In the same way, the dichotomy disentangles the short-term cyclical endogenous role of the state and the long-term political-sociological exogenous role of the state.

6.2 INTENSITY OF SUSCEPTIBILITY

Exogenous factors affect susceptibility by altering the intensity of tensions experienced by entrepreneurs at a given level of investment orders. An *ameliorating* effect on susceptibility occurs when an exogenous factor reduces the intensity of tension built up over a particular level of investment orders. The relation between investment orders and susceptibility changes such that any contraction phase of the susceptibility cycle is short and weak; short in duration, because the investment orders to susceptibility ratio moves from 1:1 to (say) 1:1.5. The exogenous factor thus increases the rate of reduction of susceptibility when investment orders are decreasing. The downturn is weaker, because the exogenous factor encourages early competitive reinvestment, making the upturn less problematical and more likely to occur before the susceptibility cycle gets too deep.

When this same exogenous factor has an ameliorating effect on susceptibility during the expansion phase of the susceptibility cycle, then the cycle is long and strong; long in duration, because the investment orders to susceptibility ratio moves from 1:1 to (say) 1:0.5. The exogenous factor thus decreases the rate of increase of susceptibility when investment orders are increasing. The expansion is stronger because the exogenous factor encourages further investment before the peak of the cycle is reached. The peak and downturn still occur for all the same endogenous reasons, but it is at a higher level of investment orders than if the exogenous factor did not exist.

An *intensifying* effect on susceptibility occurs when an exogenous factor increases the intensity of tension built up over a particular level of investment orders. The relation between investment orders and susceptibility alters such that any contraction phase of the susceptibility cycle is long and strong; long in duration, because the investment orders to susceptibility ratio moves from 1:1 to (say) 1:0.5. The exogenous factor thus decreases the rate of reduction of susceptibility when investment orders are decreasing. The downturn is stronger because the exogenous factor discourages early competitive reinvestment, making the upturn more problematical and sending the susceptibility cycle into a deeper trough.

When this same exogenous factor has an intensifying effect on susceptibility during the expansion phase of the susceptibility cycle, then the cycle is short and weak; short in duration, because the same ratio moves from 1:1 to (say) 1:1.5, with the exogenous factor increasing the rate of increase of susceptibility when investment orders are increasing. The expansion is weaker, because the exogenous factor does not encourage much new investment, thus reaching the peak of the susceptibility cycle at a reasonably low level. The peak and downturn occur much earlier due to all the endogenous reasons of the previous chapter being allowed to operate strongly due to the exogenous factor in existence.

The above technique of incorporating exogeneity into endogenously generated susceptibility cycles is general. Examples of how specific exogenous factors can be applied to this technique makes up the rest of the chapter. First, the three secular factors that Kalecki (1954, pp. 158–61) identifies as having the potential to alter the long-term trend of investment spending are examined. They are exogenous innovations, rentiers' savings and the growth in population.

6.3 EXOGENOUS INNOVATION

Kalecki views major (or 'semi-autonomous') innovations as exogenously adding to secular long-term development. For Kalecki, such major developments place a ceiling on the intensity of technical progress and thus the rate of growth in MOP. A change in exogenous innovation moves the ceiling – affecting the long-term path of economic development – *and* induces changes in the relative application of new and old MOP – affecting the path of short-term investment activity. That is why in the framework set out in section 4.5 this exogenous factor is described as a random shock (to the cycle) which then develops into a long-term secular force.

Much research by the evolutionary school into the economics of technical change has tried to explain such processes (see section 3.6). This research establishes a microeconomic *cause* of techno-economic paradigm shifts based on 'constellations' of incremental and radical technological innovations which cluster together, applying new basic scientific principles (Freeman and Perez, 1988, pp. 46–7). Aggregation of these microprocesses initiates a macroeconomic *effect* of technical change which impinges on all industries. The importance of this effect to each industry in different economies depends on the application of such major innovations to their own production. Refinement and further minor adaptations of this major innovation become incorporated endogenously over time.

All minor improvements (endogenous innovation) are squeezed out of the old paradigm by established 'monopoly capital' entrepreneurs who want to protect existing MOP and delay the new paradigm taking over. This limits growth and sets a path for secular stagnation. Ensuing depression is the trigger, induced by entrepreneurs' competitive stimulation of demand, which leads to more R&D effort. This effort aims to reduce the uncertainty of the new paradigm and consequently encourages more effort in applying it. A 'log jam' in endogenous innovations which are based on this new paradigm compounds the latter's slow initial adoption. This occurs when established powerful entrepreneurs, with much old MOP, cannot justify the entire shake-up of industries, since not enough interrelated clusters have been formed.[1]

A 'paradigm shift' leads to an exogenous innovation input affecting the susceptibility cycle. Introduction of a new paradigm produces a large exogenous boost to investment at low susceptibility points. This investment boom relates to paradigm changes in large important industries that adopt new technology systems (e.g. petro-chemical innovations), or in the whole economy (e.g. steam engine innovations). Either way, the investment boom is strong and resilient over a series of future cycles in susceptibility.

Exogenous innovation occurs in an industry generally at the low susceptibility point, where there exists the competitive pressure on entrepreneurs to introduce it. When investment activity is high and susceptibility is high, entrepreneurs are not receptive to major new developments, but rather continue squeezing profits from the old paradigm, given the already large commitments made to this old paradigm during the rise of investment from the trough. As susceptibility is falling with investment order downturn, the financial constraints of high gearing in the industry are eased as debts are paid off or receivers are appointed. At low susceptibility the industry is financially restructured and becomes conducive to new investment orders. However, at this point it is not clear if or when the lower turning point of investment orders will be based on the decreasing opportunities from the old paradigm (providing only a modest upturn) or on the uncertainty of the new paradigm.

The problematical aspect of when the lower turning point eventuates in the susceptibility cycle is reinforced by the implications of exogenous innovation. Breakdown of an old technological paradigm occurs only when established entrepreneurs see no new profit opportunities in readapting this old paradigm through minor innovations. Uncertainty of future profits reduces investment orders and susceptibility further. At this point even replacement investment is postponed, sending the susceptibility cycle even lower.

Adoption rates in the diffusion of new technological paradigms determine the speed and amplitude of the new investment cycle (see section 3.6). Many small endogenous innovations in new, relatively small industries are the basis of the new technological systems. Also, strong capital goods supply linkages are not yet established by such small industries with capital-goods-producing (sector 1) industries. These adoption and linkage developments at low susceptibility appear in only a few dispersed areas around a world economy dominated by an old paradigm. Nevertheless, such developments create even more uncertainty for entrepreneurs in the major dominant industries, as excess capacity mounts and profitability becomes harder to achieve. A particularly severe low trough in an investment cycle develops due to the breakdown of the old paradigm. A deep structural downturn emerges as there is an increasing mismatch between investment in dominant, but declining, industries and the new available technology.

As the institutional framework slowly adapts to the new technological system, entrepreneurs' reactions against the uncertainty of profits comes from competitive pressures and growing inefficiencies of old MOP. This induces adaptation (by industries) and imitation (within industries) to technological trajectories that are totally new, establishing at very low susceptibility, the new investment upturn. It is creating a new investment boom and at the same time 're-establishing the conditions for a new phase of steady development' (Vercelli, 1989, p. 135). A paradigm shift occurs when the new adapted technological systems pervade the whole economy. Many from the evolutionary school identify such a shift as the beginning of a long wave in the economy's development (see Kleinknecht, 1987).

Investment in the leading-edge industries that accept the new technology systems entails exogenous innovation that has an ameliorating effect on susceptibility.[2] These industries generate instability biased towards strong investment peaks. Even during the introduction of a major exogenous innovation, the three elements of the susceptibility cycle are still working to create high susceptibility, eventually leading to a downturn in investment activity. The successful nature of these new technological systems ensures that the susceptibility cycle has a short and weak contraction phase.

Competitive pressures and government support for this new exogenous innovation quickly leads to an upturn again in susceptibility as entrepreneurs have a low degree of 'safety preference' with such new innovations.

For the aggregate investment cycle, as more industries adopt the new technology systems, '[t]he boom is more pronounced than the slump and as a result, a new long-run position with a higher level of investment is attained' (Kalecki, 1954, p. 151). This investment growth is accompanied by endogenous innovation which incorporates these new technology systems. In this way, the argument by Kalecki that '[t]echnical progress keeps the inducement to invest higher than it would be otherwise' (Kalecki, 1940, p. 179), can be understood in relation to his other, seemingly contradictory, view that innovation is part and parcel of ordinary fluctuating investment.

There is an intensifying effect on susceptibility when investment in industries does not substantially incorporate the new technology systems, generating instability biased towards strong investment troughs. Powerful entrepreneurs' interests in the old technology systems delay the adoption of the new technology systems, which tend to be located in weaker sectors of the business community (e.g. the sailing ship example in section 3.6). Deep and long contractionary phases of the susceptibility cycle occur whenever minor endogenous innovations, based on the old technology system, become outdated and entrepreneurs have meagre new adaptations (when diffusion of the old technology slows down and imitators become scarce). An investment order downturn in the susceptibility cycle under these circumstances is deep and serious.

Delays in adopting the new exogenous innovation by the majority of dominant industries lengthens the downward bias in the aggregate investment trend. Only when 'monopoly capital' entrepreneurs begin seriously to incorporate the new technology systems in their own investment strategy, or when these very same oligopoly structures begin to collapse, is there a shift to the new systems and a long-term trend in aggregate investment that changes from contraction to expansion.

At the transition from one technology system to another, investment instability is at its greatest. Here leading-edge industries are on a new bandwagon supported by a growing but unstable demand which creates strong investment peaks and overcapacity situations. Here, also, established old technology-based industries have surplus capacity but the monopoly power to protect their existing capital stock structures through higher profit mark-ups. This creates strong investment troughs as new investment is kept to a minimum. The combination of these two forces produces aggregate investment instability that is particularly turbulent.

Upheaval within industries also occurs at this transition stage, as firms grapple with 'a painful and difficult process of adjustment' (Freeman and Perez, 1988, p. 62). This is specifically so for entrepreneurs who are locked into old systems but see the potential of the new systems (e.g. in the 1980s this applied to vehicle production, aluminium, printing, transport, insurance). Such industries have the susceptibility of investment intensified at the peak due to uncharted new demand and to uncharted new production systems as well.

A period of secular decline in economic development can now be associated with the limitations of scale production in oligopolistic competition, as the old technology systems are running out of possible new adaptations. Diffusion of the old systems through endogenous innovation slows down and imitators become considerably fewer. Large, powerful corporations attempt to protect existing MOP and ignore new technological systems being developed on the fringe of the corporate world. This tends to exacerbate the mismatch between new technologies and the powerful institutional framework based around monopoly capitalists.[3]

Non-differentiated oligopolies depend on endogenous process innovation as a barrier to entry of new or fringe firms (see section 4.5). For this reason the dominant firms in these homogeneous industries tend to have entrepreneurs who are not resistant to adopting new exogenous technology systems. Successful adoption ameliorates susceptibility and encourages endogenous innovation. Strong imitation within the industry occurs quickly to protect market shares, enabling the spread of the new systems by an effective diffusion process. This process produces strong and long expansion phases in the susceptibility cycle which develop momentum for effective diffusion of a paradigm shift. The same process produces weak and short contraction phases.

A historical and cultural background of successful early innovation and quick imitation exists in homogeneous industries. The only proviso to this tendency is the countertendency of firms to mature and of their entrepreneurs both to lose the taste for innovation and to become more susceptible when investing. Such increased susceptibility is ameliorated by entrepreneurs taking two strategies which have been used particularly strongly by non-differentiated oligopoly firms over a long period: (a) joint ventures (JV) with other large competitors or with specialised small firms to share the costs and risks (see section 3.5); (b) forming symbiotic links with small-based R&D science firms who continue to innovate strongly and provide the needed endogenous innovation to the large firm (see section 3.6).[4]

In differentiated oligopolies, strong successful market products tend to make entrepreneurs highly resistant to innovation. Imitation tends to be slow, as entrepreneurs are reluctant to change well-established differentiated products. Adopting product innovations is a gamble in uncharted demand functions, while process innovation requires altered production systems and product modifications. These factors intensify susceptibility of given investment orders, leading to contraction phases that are long and strong compared to the milder contraction in homogeneous industries, while expansion phases are short and weak. Strong contraction leads to high costs of postponement, serving to create the most effective spur to competition. Under such conditions, major exogenous innovations induce the removal of entrepreneurs' resistance to product innovation. Fringe firms, especially, are prepared to take the plunge first in order to gain a market share. Product imitation by the dominant firms follows to instigate an upturn in the susceptibility cycle.

Conditions which provide fertile ground for transition to new technology systems can be observed in economies with less-differentiated oligopolies that have mature products and strong inter-industry competition. This suggests that these same economies are prone to strong investment booms that build up susceptibility and cause instability during transition periods. In economies with strong differentiated oligopolies based on intra-industry competition (such as Japan), there is much endogenous innovation but limited exogenous innovation due to the powerful role of protecting existing MOP. This ameliorates susceptibility and provides a more stable investment environment, which is of great advantage during a long-term growth period in the world economy. However, it is a disadvantage during a long-term contraction in the world economy when there is a tendency to continue endogenous (often product-based) innovation on the back of an old technological system, and as a consequence intensifying susceptibility.

6.4 RENTIERS' SAVINGS

The second secular factor that Kalecki identifies is rentiers' savings (Kalecki, 1954, p. 159). This relates to the stock of funds available for investment from two types of rentiers, neither of whom controls investment decisions: 'bondholders' and 'stockholders' (see section 4.3). Together these agents form the financial sector. In all industrial countries, the post-World War II period has seen the financial sector gain in importance in relation to the industrial sector.[5]

Reasons for the strong growth in financial accumulation is a study of its own, but the micro-based susceptibility cycle analysis provides some clues. In the contraction phase of the cycle, investment orders decrease, with entrepreneurs themselves becoming rentier savers as they place their funds in financial assets or real estate (Sylos Labini, 1962, p. 162). In the next expansionary phase of the cycle it would be expected that these funds would be used again for investment. However, if the expansion phase is weak, then much of the stock of savings remains in the financial sphere. The reason they remain could be due to lack of a new technological paradigm, with the old paradigm relatively not inducing much investment.

Another clue is the international shift of financial resources. This occurred in the 1970s with the oil-producing countries obtaining huge financial funds as a result of the oil price rises (1974 and 1979). All these funds could not be invested in MOP for the oil producing nations, due to their low level of development. The funds were placed in the hands of international banking rentiers, who used them to support non-oil exporting third world nations in extravagant and non-productive investment projects (Nicolini, 1985, p. 135). The low level of effective consumption demand, due to high oil-based prices in industrialised economies, and the concomitant low investment demand made third world investment projects highly susceptible to failure.

The Mexican financial crisis of 1982 saw the end of this process. What followed was a boom in financial markets in industrial economies: merger movement, leverage buyouts and stock exchange booms (Brailovsky, 1989). These processes increased dramatically paper financial assets without any corresponding real production. The expectations-boosted boom cracked in October 1987 with the stock exchange collapse. This created massive indebtedness as paper assets crashed. Supported by loose monetary policies after the stock market crash to prevent a depression, much of rentier savings were placed in real estate as a way of escaping the paper asset fall.

This is not the place for an in depth analysis of these processes. The argument so far is that this stock of rentiers' savings, especially since the early 1970s, has increasingly been used by rentiers for financial activities rather than for investment. Two significant examples have been provided above which help to explain this trend. First is the growing lack of a paradigm shift into a new strong investment-based technological paradigm, and second, the sudden growth in 'petrodollars'. As financial activities become relatively more attractive, rentiers increasingly prefer financial assets to funding investment, and entrepreneurs increasingly prefer to become rentiers by diverting internal funds (retained earnings) into financial assets. These developments intensify susceptibility because of the increased tension of entrepreneurs (and rentiers) for any given level of investment orders, compared to the alternative speculative uses of savings.

The continuing financial accumulation in non-productive assets leads to two secular macro feedback effects from effective demand to susceptibility. First, the level of investment expenditure is relatively low on average, compared to earlier decades of the post-war period. In the short term, this reduces overall effective demand. For entrepreneurs, this intensifies susceptibility further and weakens the expansionary phase of the susceptibility cycle while strengthening the contractionary phase. As noted in the framework set out in section 4.4, rentier capitalists and their speculative Ponzi-style debt structure become relatively more important than investment during booms (as business investment only has a subdued expansion). In the long term, capacity of production is affected by pressure for debt deflation under Ponzi-style debt structure. This retards the trend of economic development.

The second secular effect is the relatively larger proportion of the increasing volume of debt going outside the surplus producing system. '[T]his implies a corresponding accumulation of debt on which interest has to be paid. This interest comes from various sources – from government, from abroad, from concerns who have bought out others, from consumers' (Steindl, 1990, p. 9). Due to their relative wealth differences, Steindl (1990, pp. 2–9) argues that receivers of interest tend to have a higher propensity to save than payers of interest. This severely limits long-term growth in consumption as financial accumulation grows. The increase in consumer debt together with the realised capital gains from the financial sector (negative saving) are the two mainstays keeping the level of consumption buoyant in the short term. In trade-deficit open economies, this situation adds to import demand without much incentive for increased investment commitments. For the longer term, effective demand is held up on the basis of continued borrowing and capital gains which add further to debt structure which is unstable.[6]

Both secular effects described above generate social tensions. There is resentment to paying interest (especially to banks), and the financial sector is unable to underwrite the strong debt-based consumption boom. As a result of these portfolio allocation processes, rentiers' savings and their affect on financial accumulation reduce incentives to invest in MOP. This has an intensifying effect on susceptibility, weakening the expansion and strengthening the contraction phases. This retards long-term economic development, with only further Ponzi-style debt build-up allowing a short-term stimulus to investment which may counteract these severe tendencies.

Financial accumulation of rentiers' savings has the feedback effect of intensifying susceptibility. This explains how rentiers' savings as a secular factor 'introduces a negative trend in the system in somewhat the same way that innovations inject a long-run upward tendency . . . If rentiers' savings are increasing in relation to capital the negative trend will be accelerated' (Kalecki, 1954, p. 159).

6.5 GROWTH IN POPULATION

The third secular factor that Kalecki identifies is growth in population. The effects of this factor on investment are more problematical. Kalecki noted that a 'growing population widens the *potentialities* of the long-run expansion in output' (Kalecki, 1954, p. 160, original emphasis). Whether such potential is realised depends on the impetuses that this growth provides. Kalecki identifies two: the first is through unemployment and the corresponding effect on money wages; the second is through effective demand.

In the first case, Kalecki assumes a given static level of output with a rising population which increases unemployment and weakens trade unions. Based on Kalecki's pricing model, such an exogenous influence causes a long-term fall in money wages, an increasing degree of monopoly, and shifting income shares from wages to profits. The alternative is for prices to fall in proportion to the wages fall, maintaining the same mark-up. This latter effect reduces the volume of transactions and interest rates, assuming constant money supply. Higher profits or lower interest rates due to this impetus reduce the intensity of tensions experienced by entrepreneurs at a given level of investment orders (i.e. ameliorating susceptibility).

If investment rises over the long-term due to one or other of these effects, then unemployment would disappear, pushing money wages back up to the former level and the ameliorating influence disappears. Kalecki doubts the possibility of lower interest rates being maintained over the longer term since the rentier-bankers tend to adjust their lending policies to ensure that interest rates do not fall. The higher profits effect is most likely, but it also means a lower propensity to consume overall. This leaves unemployment (and lower money wages) as a long-term intensifying effect on susceptibility.

The second mechanism through which growth in population affects investment is the purchasing power effect (output is not assumed constant in this mechanism). Kalecki (1954, p. 161) argues that an increase in the population does not automatically imply a 'broadening of the market' with many more goods being demanded, leading to a long-term ameliorating effect on susceptibility. This is because the increased population must have the ability to purchase goods. What matters is whether there is a long-term increase in effective demand, irrespective of population growth. A static population which increases its purchasing power can bring about the same ameliorating effect as a growing population with an unaltered per capita purchasing power.

Modern consumer credit facilities and social attitudes to spending as status-seeking (Scitovsky, 1976) qualify Kalecki's second mechanism. Advertising-based status-seeking ensures the universal acceptance of bank credit card facilities, enabling purchasing power to be brought forward. This creates 'consumer debt crisis' of financial overcommitment that exacerbates poverty and social stress (Renouf, 1988). Population growth in such a consumer credit society provides an increase in effective demand, producing for entrepreneurs an ameliorating effect on susceptibility. For the banks, any small economic downturn, especially a reduction in investment expenditure, forces them to call in this consumer debt. A sharp, violent reduction in effective demand results, intensifying the contraction phase of the susceptibility cycle.

Industrialised economies have seen birth rates fall (Clark and Tabah, 1982). Under these conditions, the 'broadening of the market' must occur from growth in consumerism (both in goods and services). Where immigration is important, the population issue receives an extra dimension. To the extent that immigrants become part of the consumer debt boom, effective demand impetus is important. If immigrants add to unemployment, then the first impetus described above applies. The two impetuses then work in opposite directions, tending roughly to cancel each other out in terms of their effects on susceptibility.

The ecological concerns of the 1990s (greenhouse effect, ozone, pollution) can in fact reverse the two impetuses discussed above. The ecological concerns of a 'population bomb' may lead to declines in population rather than growth. Such negative growth could create pressures on labour markets, forcing shifts from profits to wages.

However, together with the reduced population, the ecological movement could also reduce (or remove) the consumerist spending behaviour, thus not pressuring shortages in the labour markets. An ecological movement successful on both fronts would lead towards a 'steady-state economy' (Daly, 1977) where the population growth factor does not operate. Daly considers innovation as essential in this type of economy to improve the quality of society without adding to the stock of human artefacts (Daly, 1977, p. 17). Such an economy would reduce the influence of exogenous factors on the susceptibility cycle, making this cycle more strongly endogenous. Even a steady-state economy would experience the instability of investment as outlined in the previous chapter.

6.6 RANDOM FACTORS

Random factors have no pattern and are caused by complex natural and/or human forces that cannot be analysed in any sequential logical manner. The most common random factors are wars, floods, droughts, earthquakes and social unrest. The first and last of these factors are caused by human forces and must be left to sociologists and political scientists to analyse. There does not seem to be any secular or cyclical pattern to their appearance. In both cases economic variables impinge on the way these two factors develop, the military-industrial complex being a strong influence on both wars and social unrest. The other three factors listed are caused by natural forces, with human forces exacerbating floods and droughts. Again there appears to be no secular or cyclical pattern to their appearance.

All random factors have two mechanisms which affect investment behaviour and the susceptibility cycle. The first mechanism is negative to investment. All human and natural random disasters have the long-term effect of reducing the supply of inputs into the economy: the destruction of foodstuffs, raw materials, capital goods and human labour. Such an effect adds crucially to the costs of inputs for quite a long period. Whether mark-ups remain constant depends at what point on the susceptibility cycle the firm is when such a disaster occurs. In the dominant industrial sectors, only limited squeezes on mark-ups occur at high (Phase 2 of Figure 5.4) and low (Phase 5) susceptibility when there is already pressure for mark-ups to be squeezed. The extent to which price rises reduce revenues depends on demand elasticities. Such cost and price pressures intensify susceptibility, making the investment orders upturn even more problematical than usual. The long-term pressure of such supply shortages can keep investment subdued over a whole cycle.

The same random factors have a second mechanism which operates in the short term (for part of the cycle). All human and natural disasters have the short-run consequence of adding to demand for public infrastructure and public services – rescue services, military and civil defence operations, armament supplies, police anti-riot squads, police baton and 'paddy-wagon' supplies. This demand pressure can have either of two effects on entrepreneurs. The first is price rises, if the demand cannot be met easily due to shortages. Also, obtaining the equipment from overseas increases imports. Price rises and current account deficits induce restrictive government policies, intensifying susceptibility and weakening investment demand. The second effect is increased production if there is excess capacity available and such demands can be met quickly. This has a short-term ameliorating effect on susceptibility, directly inducing a higher level of investment orders than if the random factor had not occurred.

Demand pressure prompts an upturn at low susceptibility, as firms attempt to gain a larger market share of these services or a larger supply to these services. In this way, the excess capacity effect can counteract long-term supply constraints. The same effect may even stimulate effective demand through the multiplier to postpone susceptibility concerns for a while, further adding to a boom in the economy, or may encourage the turnaround at the bottom of the susceptibility cycle. Given the institutional framework where the manufacturing sector is in excess capacity over most of the cycle (see Figure 5.4), then out of the two possible short-term demand pressure effects, the second is more likely than the first.

If the random factor generates widespread disaster and destroys the majority of supply inputs of the economy, then the combination of supply constraints and demand shortage pressure overwhelms any demand stimulus. This leads to high inflation, low production and the importation of all supply inputs. A high current account deficit results, with little ability to obtain any capital goods quickly. This seriously intensifies susceptibility. Only massive foreign aid to finance new capital developments (e.g. the Marshall Plan after Germany and Japan were devastated in the Second World War) can overcome such massive dislocation.

From the above analysis, the extent of the disaster determines whether it leads to a stimulus to investment (localised random factor) or is a constraint on investment (generalised random factor without foreign aid). The randomness of such factors means that these events create irregularities to the endogenous investment cycle model.

6.7 SEASONAL FACTORS

Over the calendar year there are exogenous ameliorating and intensifying effects on susceptibility which occur about the same time year after year. These are seasonal factors. Such seasonality is due either to natural cycles (e.g. harvesting crops; the demand for warm clothes and blankets) or to human nature devising certain well-established traditional patterns (e.g. Easter and Christmas; the annual fiscal budget presentation). These factors can be analysed in relation to their demand, supply and expectations outcomes.

Most seasonal factors affect demand by adding a stimulus in a regular seasonal pattern (e.g. Christmas, Easter, winter clothing). Firms know this pattern and gear their production for this demand. Capital goods capacity to take account of this seasonal demand is planned well ahead, creating a regular effect which is incorporated into firms' investment and production strategies. Similarly, on the supply side, the harvesting of crops is a regular pattern incorporated into the agricultural economy. The supply of crops creates demand for agricultural services similar to the previous demand factors, but it also creates a supply of goods needing to be processed (especially if they are perishable, e.g. making wine, canning fruits). Processing requires capital goods capacity to be planned and ready for this supply. Expectations built up before and after budget presentations can generate exogenous changes to demand and supply, and can be better analysed under the role of the state in the next section.

The variation in intensity of all seasonal factors can have an impact on susceptibility. A warm winter reduces demand for warm clothes, creating high inventory stocks and large excess capacity which would tend to intensify susceptibility. This is the same with poor Christmas or Easter demand, although these tend to be related to the endogenous factor of economic conditions. There may be some exogenous influences (Christmas falling on a Monday after Sunday 'closed shops' day), but they are minor.

A bumper harvest or a poor harvest are related back to the random factor of weather. Such weather-related variations in seasonal factors are analysed in the same way as random factors, i.e. by looking at the short-term and long-term implications of such variation in seasonality and how it alters the intensity of susceptibility. The tendency would be for such variations to affect susceptibility only in a minor way, since it would be expected that the next year would be closer to 'normal'. Only if a series of seasons shows consistent above or below 'normal' levels of demand would the susceptibility cycle be affected in a major random way. For example, a series of poor winter sales (due, say, to the greenhouse effect and warming of the country) would see excess capacity rise very high, intensifying susceptibility and inducing lower investment spending. It would also make the rise up from the bottom of the susceptibility cycle even more problematical.

6.8 ROLE OF THE STATE

The exogenous influence of the state on the susceptibility cycle is based on the relative autonomy view of the state set out in section 4.6. This view of the state implies that state decision-making and implementation is to a large extent driven by the needs of the business community (the oligopolistic sector in particular) and to a lesser extent trade unions. In a long-term macrogrowth model, all these needs are endogenous to the economy. However, for this analysis, only the self-repeating cyclical monetary and fiscal policies related to Kalecki's political business cycle are endogenous. Direct support for one industry based on the position in the business cycle is also regarded as endogenous. General government structural policies (e.g. protection, deregulation, trade practices, defence expenditure) are considered exogenous to any particular firm and generally exogenous to particular industries.

Direct and indirect exogenous influences of the state on the susceptibility cycle can be identified. The direct influence is on susceptibility and the investment decision of an oligopolistic firm or industry. Four important direct influences are discussed below, but this is not an exhaustive list. The indirect influence is where state actions alter national output first and then this has a feedback into specific industries, their firms and their respective susceptibility cycles.[7] Most factors outlined below derive from Steindl (1979) in his analysis of secular stagnation policies for the 1970s of governments in advanced capitalist economies.

The most important direct influence on large powerful capitalist economies is the military-industrial complex emphasised by Kalecki (1972a) and developed further by Steindl (1979). Expansion in military spending directly stimulates expectations of future profits from a guaranteed source (the government) to all those industries related to military spending. Such industries extract 'monopoly profits' from government departments not vigilant enough to recognise 'extortion prices', or involved symbiotically in the inflation of prices for military goods.[8] This adds confidence and ameliorates the susceptibility of new investment decisions in these defence-based industries, stimulating strong investment booms. Increased investment orders add to susceptibility at a slower rate than without this relationship to the state and also allows susceptibility to rise much higher before it reaches the peak of investment orders.

As the state spends more on armaments, defence-related businesses spend more on capital goods. These firms then become increasingly concerned that someone in government will 'blow the whistle' on extortionate prices or the level of spending, and this could then snowball into a reduction in military spending. Decisions to decrease military spending undermine the symbiotic relationships. The end of the Cold War has also been a strong inducement to reduce military spending. These forces intensify the susceptibility of defence-related industries, weakening investment order expansion and making an upturn difficult at the trough of the investment cycle.

Historically, Steindl (1979, pp. 8–9) notes that US military spending increased to a large extent in the immediate post-war period and propped up their full-employment objective. This provides an output effect via the multiplier which also ameliorates susceptibility in other sectors. However, in the same period, European military spending 'overstrained their already fully employed economies' (Steindl, 1979, p. 10), which would have the effect of intensifying susceptibility and making investment cycles trend downwards. By the early 1970s, the phasing down of the Vietnam War resulted in cuts US military spending (Steindl, 1979, p. 9). In the early 1980s, with President Reagan and increased superpower tension, military spending again began to expand rapidly (Sawyer, 1989, p. 302), only to come up against extortion claims and reduced superpower tension by the start of the 1990s.[9] This exogenous cycle of military spending ameliorates (e.g. early 1980s) and intensifies (e.g. 1970s and start of 1990s) the endogenous susceptibility cycle.

A related direct influence on susceptibility, especially in high-tech industries, is state-sponsored technological competition.[10] Steindl (1979, p. 10) notes the 'intensive technological competition between East and West, having its strongest effects in the decade 1957–68 which opened with Sputnik and ended with student unrest'. A new technological competition related to SDI (or Star Wars), occurred in the early 1980s in the USA and USSR. Most technological research is based on the military and space, ameliorating susceptibility in industries related to these areas during these periods of state competition.

The third direct influence is protection of markets in the domestic economy from international competition by tariffs, quotas, embargoes and subsidies. Such state interventions are endogenous to the susceptibility cycle if they are part of the self-repeating political business cycle mechanism (see section 5.6.3). Such interventions are exogenous if they are part of structural adjustment policies (e.g. across-the-board tariff cuts). The exogenous influence ameliorates susceptibility when protection is increased and intensifies susceptibility when protection is decreased.

The final direct influence is on the growing ecological concerns related to conservation and protection of the environment. This includes science-based research, support for infant recycling industries, direct funding of conservation groups, energy-based measures like increased petrol prices, and incentives for alternative fuels. State support of pro-environmentally sound industries and state discouragement of industries seen as detrimental to the environment lead to the amelioration and intensification of susceptibility in these above industries respectively.

Indirect influences on susceptibility are now examined. They relate to the implications for entrepreneurs' investment decision-making of the general macroeconomic policy stance of the state and its effects on the aggregate economy. The extent of these indirect influences vary according to how closely each industry (and firm) has become integrated into the government's support mechanisms.

Steindl (1979, pp. 8–9) identifies a secular 'political trend' in macropolicies of most of the large capitalist nations. Such a trend builds on the 'persistent and lasting character' of either a growth period or a stagnation period. Similarly, O'Connor (1973) notes that a strong growth period increases the pressure for long-term fiscal stringency (see section 4.6). Such secular trends in 'stabilisation' policies impact on the intensity of susceptibility.

In Steindl's analysis there are two post-war secular trends in stabilisation policies. The first trend was a period of expansion based on the full employment objective to which all western governments became committed in some form during the early post-war period. The Keynesian economics solution could be seen as a new innovative paradigm which shifted capitalist economies on to a higher growth ('full employment as an innovation') trajectory. Throughout this first period, the political business cycle did operate but the intentional state-based recessionary periods were short (being afraid of losing office if unemployment increased for any length of time).

During this period there was also the related close economic co-operation between capitalist economies in response to post-war political East–West tensions. Under the leadership of the US, co-operation developed in relation to Bretton Woods, GATT trade agreements, the Marshall Plan and American lending, and OECD co-operative arrangements. All these actions aimed to stabilise the business cycle and provide the West with the leading edge in growth and employment over the East. Susceptibility throughout this period was ameliorated, allowing a large investment boom to eventuate (with periodical small downturns coinciding with political business cycles).

The second trend was a period of stagnation or 'stunted growth' (Steindl, 1979, p. 10) based on removing inflation and growing public debt which built up during the expansion phase. The capitalist world saw the decay of US economic leadership with the dismantling of Bretton Woods in 1971. Yet despite the rise to economic power of Japan and West Germany at the same time, they were both too introspective to be willing to take over world economic leadership. This is similar to the circumstances when the UK saw its economic leadership decay after the Great Depression (see Kindleberger, 1973). In both cases the capitalist financial system favoured the 'old' leader, even though changes in trade and financial flows were generating growing current account surpluses for the emerging economic powers. This created a deflationary bias in the system as the reserve currency of the old economic leader became threatened. Keynes, along with Kalecki and Schumacher (1943), predicted this problem of a reserve currency based on one country. No new co-operative system developed after 1971.

In this 'restrictive climate' there emerges opposition by big business to returning to full employment policies because this would increase inflation, 'crowd out' private investment and increase public debt. Low economic activity damps business confidence and increases uncertainty. Susceptibility is intensified. Firms concentrate on cost-cutting, keeping low investment levels and holding on longer to capital stock. Increased protectionism and speculative use of funds develop in this climate as a countertendency to restrictive secular policies. Both have their own 'dangers' in association with trade or financial collapse (Steindl, 1979, p. 11). The only relief from these tensions are mild expansionary polices which end up being short-lived in such a long-term restrictive climate. Some other exogenous factor is needed which is much longer-term and able to ameliorate susceptibility is needed.[11]

6.9 THE INTERNATIONAL ECONOMY

In this section we examine how exogenous factors related to the international economy affect the domestic susceptibility cycle. Three issues serve as case studies: the OPEC oil price shocks; foreign investment; and exchange rate changes. In the first two issues, it is assumed that the exchange rate is fixed (with state policies that ensure accommodation of trade and capital flows occur so that there is no pressure for the fixed rate to alter). The effects of exchange rate changes are examined on their own after analysing the first two issues.

The most conspicuous exogenous shock to the international economy came from the OPEC oil price rises of 1974 and 1979, which could be considered a special case of 'random factors'. Nicolini (1985) examines the effects of these shocks in a Kaleckian framework, noting first the higher prime costs in oil-importing developed economies. Nicolini assumes no changes to the concentration of industry or the general elasticity of demand due to these price shocks. This results in a fall in the degree of monopoly reflected in a lower mark-up. Any attempt to regain the mark-up creates a further inflationary rise, adding to input prices and further squeezing mark-ups.

Entrepreneurs' susceptibility intensifies by the 'negative impact on expectations' that occurs from the decline in demand and increase in costs as a consequence of the inflationary OPEC shock (Nicolini, 1985, p. 135). The susceptibility cycle peak is attained at a lower level of investment orders than if there was no OPEC shock, and any upturn is harder to achieve. If the oil shock does not cause the actual turndown, then a small after-effect (e.g. the next wage rise or when finance for a new project falls through) can send the susceptibility cycle down. The cumulation of susceptibility from the oil shock and attempts to maintain the mark-up results in such intense susceptibility to an investment turndown that any small added tension is enough for investment orders to collapse.

Nicolini goes on to examine governments that adopt compensatory, expansionary or even restrictive macropolicies in the face of an investment collapse. To be successful, both compensatory and expansionary policies need to be internationally co-ordinated.[12] At a theoretical level, such policies have to be financed by foreign capital inflows (e.g. OPEC funds), exacerbating the capital account deficit in countries where such policies are adopted and an equivalent rise in the current account surplus in lending countries. In countries adopting these policies, foreign debts rise greatly with lower trade surpluses to pay for them. The only possible benefit must come from structural change, and this depends on some new technological innovation (endogenous-minor or exogenous-major) or government microeconomic reforms (see Chapter 8).

On the other hand, a recessionary policy reduces oil imports and places pressure back on the OPEC oil producers (and the laid-off workers in the domestic economy too). Reducing wages and the oil bill, also increasing excess capacity, can have an effect only if (a) enough countries do the same, and (b) the short-term recession is not further deepened by killing off long-term business expectations just when low susceptibility needs some competitive kick-start to get the investment by entrepreneurs going again. These are big risks, but they are the very state policies adopted in some co-ordinated manner world-wide in the 1980s and 1990s. For a while, a deep recession can be delayed by the appearance of a consumerist boom (see section 6.4), a technological paradigm shift to information technology and, coinciding with both, a speculative financial boom keeping investment spending relatively low. The inevitable collapse of both booms (as ensued in the early 1990s) brings on the policy-induced recession, with unemployment remaining very high as the new technology secures high productivity.

The secular pattern of foreign investment is an exogenous factor whose macroeconomic effects have implications for susceptibility. In this case there is a need to distinguish between net capital inflow countries and net capital outflow countries. In the former, the effects depend on whether this inflow is placed in hoarding (the financial capital gains sector) or in demand for goods and services. If it goes in hoarding, then this adds to a speculative financial boom and the ensuing financial collapse with large private foreign debt which needs to be met. It intensifies the susceptibility cycle, especially during the contraction phase as entrepreneurs concentrate on removing their firms' serious high debt levels, delaying any possible upturn. If it goes in consumption or investment spending, it adds to effective demand, building up expectations and profits, while reducing financing concerns and excess capacity. Susceptibility in this case is ameliorated.

In all cases foreign investment creates foreign liabilities which have to be met through future large interest and dividend repayments in the current account. A large export surplus in goods and services is needed to pay for such large income payable overseas, otherwise even more capital inflow is required, leading to even larger foreign liabilities. Given that structural change is slow, governments resort to secular recessionary policies to restrict imports. This has the effect of intensifying susceptibility.

A net capital outflow surplus economy (such as Japan), demands interest and dividends irrespective of the lending purpose. The income received needs a complementary deficit in goods and services trade to balance the current account, otherwise even more capital outflow is required, causing an even larger problem in the future. However, income receivers tend to have high marginal propensities to save (see section 6.4), making the possibility of an import surplus difficult. The government can implement an expansionary policy to encourage the purchasing of imports. This macropolicy ameliorates susceptibility. The only problems are (a) the reluctance of the domestic population to buy imports, and (b) the increasing government debt which is built up due to expansionary policy. Both are not inconsequential issues to be faced by entrepreneurs in a net capital outflow economy, and both can weaken the ameliorating effect on the susceptibility of the import trade surplus.

Over 90 per cent of all capital flows in the international economy are purely financial, leading to the term 'casino capitalism' for modern capitalist economies (Strange, 1985). This secular development is instrumental in causing variations of exchange rates, which is the final exogenous factor analysed in this chapter. Biasco (1987) on 'currency cycles' is adapted, in the remainder of this section, to understand the influence of exchange rates on entrepreneurs' susceptibility. The Biasco analysis is based on the primacy of capital movements in explaining exchange rate changes, with compensating trade flows very slow and uncertain.[13]

An exchange rate appreciation occurs when the views of currency market operators are altered due to political developments, anticipated behaviour on the part of exchange rate authorities, perceptions of other agents' reactions to specific major events (e.g. Gulf crisis) or sudden interest-rate differentials (Biasco, 1987, p. 38). This establishes an *ex ante* disequilibrium in the currency market as 'private capital movements will not (or only with difficulty) be offset by a compensating net flow of goods and service payments . . . The expectations that triggered the movement of capital continue' in the short-term, with the appreciating country benefiting from the slowness of change in trade contracts, and experiencing a drop in inflation and an improvement in the terms of trade (Biasco, 1987, p. 43). This further widens the variation in exchange rates between appreciating and depreciating countries.

Interventions by central bank authorities to such currency appreciation can be restrictive (as in West Germany in the early 1970s and 1990s) or expansionary (as in the US after the 1982 recession). In the former case, this delays any correction as interest rate differentials further support the original expectations of currency operators. In the latter case, expansion of income attracts more funds as capital gains are made in that country's financial asset markets. Both interventions support the widening of currency variations rather than narrowing them.

The real sector of an appreciating economy experiences an outflow of funds for investment in depreciating economies. Widening of currency markets thus intensifies susceptibility in the appreciating economy and ameliorates susceptibility in the depreciating economy. This is the 'compensating mechanism' which reduces currency variation, but it is a much lengthier process than the conventional one and it does not stop at 'equilibrium' (the original exchange rate price). Instead, it inverts the situation, with the depreciating economy becoming the appreciating one with all its attendant problems stated above. The perceptions of what is a 'weak' and a 'strong' currency are inverted eventually due to the slow process of real investment changes or, more likely, some attendant exogenous factor that comes with it.

All inversions are not symmetrical. A country that suffers the collapse of weak industries during currency appreciation will not see them reappear during the depreciating period. Restructuring requires new technologies, switching markets, strongly differentiating products or forcing fundamental cost economies. All such actions require investment. This only occurs once susceptibility has been ameliorated, and depends on the expectations of both currency operators and entrepreneurs that the situation has changed. This takes a significant length of time. Meanwhile, concentrating on areas of production least sensitive to international price variations leads to surplus capacity in these sectors and increased susceptibility.

6.10 CONCLUSION

At the beginning of the chapter, a general approach to incorporating exogeneity into the susceptibility cycle model was outlined. This approach involves both the amelioration and the intensification of susceptibility. The former tends to augment expansions of investment orders, thus adding strength to secular growth in investment orders. The latter tends to exacerbate contractions of investment orders, thus weakening this secular growth. Crucial to this analysis is that all such exogenous factors do not alter the basic endogenous mechanism set out in the previous chapter but only modify the duration, amplitude or inter-cycle trends within the susceptibility cycle. The chapter then examined the impact on susceptibility cycles of some important general exogenous factors.

The susceptibility cycle model, as a stylised story of causal relationships, has now been told. However, the model itself is not complete, nor can such behavioural analysis ever be complete. The model is sequential and analytical, based on a specific monopoly capitalist framework. It aims to understand the tensions that affect entrepreneurs' investment behaviour over time, creating widespread fluctuations which are called susceptibility cycles. In true Kaldorian (and Salter) tradition, the next chapter examines empirical patterns of industries and discerns how their history of investment behaviour fits the 'stylised sequence'. Then, this susceptibility hypothesis becomes a plausible story.

NOTES

1. For example, separate innovations in different aspects of a lightweight solar car have been developed, but a strong enough cluster has not been formed to push the steel petrol engine into the museum.

2. New major discoveries of raw materials have the same ameliorating effect as exogenous innovation. New fields of discovery, divorced from previous fields, provide strong investment expansions and weak investment contractions in the resource-based non-differentiated industries. Kalecki (1954, p. 158) broadens his definition of innovation to incorporate raw material discoveries as part of the long-term development process. An economy which is strongly resource-based has many industries investing strongly on the basis of major new discoveries, leading to investment cycles with strong and long investment expansions, and with short and weak investment contractions. Sylos Labini (1984a, p. 83) shows how major rises in relative prices of raw materials, such as oil, 'stimulate the invention of new products or the development of substitutes', which can bring about strong exogenous innovation and strong investment growth.

3. Steindl, back in 1952, recognised this secular decline as surplus capacity which reduces the incentive to invest in established monopoly capital sectors. In his introduction to the 1976 reprint of his 1952 work, Steindl stated that he was 'ready to admit a possibility which I denied in my book: that it might be the result of exhaustion of a long technological wave' (1976, p. xv).

4. For examples of these developments in non-differentiated industries, see case studies in Courvisanos (1994b) on the Australian steel and aluminium industries. Such developments also occurred in some differentiated industries recently. IBM, the strong leader in computers, saw its market share falling dramatically during the mid-1980s. The firm had fallen into a 'safe' strategy of only looking within its own firm for innovations. When IBM changed its strategy in 1988, this decline was stemmed as it looked to its clients and small competitors for innovation through joint R&D projects, something that its Japanese competitors had been doing for a long time (interview with

IBM's North-West US Computer Marketing Manager, Rome, 2 September 1990).

5.   Steindl (1990, p. 7) explained how 'the accumulation of wealth, power and prestige of finance has far outstripped the general pace of advance. Industry in the sense of material production could not keep pace with finance, because its share in the national product declined, but more important perhaps, because the industrial firms have more and more turned to financial activities, they have invested more and more of their gains in financial assets or real estate rather than in equipment and factories'.

6.   Debt based on expectations of a continual rise in asset prices creates Ponzi-style macroeconomic financial instability (Minsky, 1982); see section 2.3.3.

7.   This taxonomy of direct and indirect *influences* on susceptibility of the state's actions is completely separate from the more commonly perceived taxonomy of direct and indirect *means* by which the state influences the economy (or parts of the economy).

8.   Investigations into the US Reagan administration's defence purchases at inflated prices has been ongoing for a long time because of the intricate nature of these defence contracts.

9.   In a 1989 report on the deliberations of the US Congress on the 1990–91 Department of Defense (DoD) Appropriations Bills, concerns over extortionate prices were reflected in debates to cut spending in the new bill, and having 'a provision which directs DoD's Inspector General to ensure that contractor and DoD audit recommendations are being implemented' (Morrow, 1989, p. 12). Also, 'diminished East–West tensions make voting for level or even reduced defense spending a new political option' (Morrow, 1989, p. 8).

10.   It is related to the previous influence because: 'There is hardly an activity in our society which is as thoroughly based on science as warfare' (Steindl, 1979, p. 10).

11.   Looking at all those discussed up until now, the only hope is a technological shift to a new paradigm which would alter business confidence. Some writers in this field argue that such a paradigm shift has already occurred in relation to the area of information technology (see section 3.6).

12.   Nicolini (1985, p. 138) regards internationally co-ordinated expansionist policies (as in the early post-war period) as doubtful, and, based on Steindl's analysis described in the previous section, impossible in the stagnation mode of the 1970s and 1980s, economic summits on severe recessions by heads of governments notwithstanding.

13.   This position is also adopted by the neoclassical asset market approach to exchange rates (e.g. Krueger, 1983).

7. Long-Run Empirical Patterns of Cyclical Investment

> the evidence available in company histories suggests that, in general, firms do not grow at steady rates. Of course, this is partly the result of macroeconomic instability, or of an inability of managers to think of new uses for investment funds. But only partly. Most companies also exhibit cyclical behaviour that results from mistaken decisions. (Earl, 1984, p. 19)

7.1 SUSCEPTIBILITY AND MISTAKES

The investment process takes into account the first two aspects of the firm's growth potential mentioned in the opening quotation by Earl, namely the macroeconomic conditions and the investment options available to managers (or 'entrepreneurs' in this framework). Such strategies, once they are turned into investment commitments, create a psychological tension to the possibility of failure, given all the risks and uncertainties of the unknown future.

Susceptibility focuses on tension as it builds up in terms of profit squeeze, increasing financial risk and overcapacity. Once these elements have reached certain threshold levels, in relation to the general macroeconomic conditions identified by firms, entrepreneurs begin to recognise past investment commitments as (in Earl's words) 'mistaken decisions' which create tensions of 'panic-stricken' proportions. Firms modify downwards current investment projects and postpone the implementation of many investment strategies in order to release tensions. The turndown in investment activity is based on this perceived mistaken overinvestment. Where investment decisions are made *a priori*, perceived mistakes in investment decisions are recognised only *a posteriori*.

Seen in these terms, firms make investment commitment mistakes periodically. The periodic collapse of investment activity by industries is based on how such mistakes are made by the majority, if not all, the firms in the industry. This is particularly the case for monopoly capitalism where decisions of one leading firm influence the other firms (see section 4.2).

Similarly, the upturn in investment activity by an industry exposes the mistakes in underinvestment as a result of cautious investment commitments during the contraction phase of the business cycle. Susceptibility at the trough of the investment cycle is very low due to postponement of many investment projects, making it relatively easy for firms to 'fix up mistakes' by increasing investment commitments. Once one firm decides to expand investment orders, due to its relatively high resilience to uncertainty, other firms in the industry follow; this creates an upturn in investment orders.

In this chapter a suggestive correlation is established between the theoretical susceptibility cycle model and the post-World War II investment histories of industries in capitalist economies. It involves identifying patterns of susceptibility in the company histories of the leading firms of each industry being studied. The corporate history of mistakes, along with their profits, gearing and capacity utilisation, leads to an appreciation of how susceptible these firms are and how it affects their investment strategies and decisions.

Major case studies in the post-war corporate histories of three Australian manufacturing industries provide the basis for the investment patterns identified in the following sections. The appendix presents a set of three summary tables which compare investment cycles, and the major variables that influence these cycles, for the three industries: motor vehicles, steel and aluminium. Each table concentrates on a different period within the postwar era. In this format these case studies were first used to recognise pattern-matching explanations in Courvisanos (1994a).[1] Correlation across these three industries provided general patterns which supported the behavioural model established in theory over the previous chapters. In putting together this chapter, many publications of firm investment behaviour in other capitalist economies were consulted. These publications are independent of the susceptibility hypothesis, yet they have in total identified similar investment patterns to those coming out of the tables in the appendix.[2]

In corporate histories, two exogenous factors – technical change (exogenous innovation) and government structural policies (role of the state) – have tended to shift the susceptibility cycle most frequently and most significantly. The shifts lead to structural changes in the relevant firms and industries, setting certain secular trends within the cyclical process. These two exogenous factors are the only ones which are examined systematically in this chapter, although other diverse exogenous factors often appear in specific histories.

Interdependence of the three endogenous elements and the two exogenous factors provides the major determinants of a firm's susceptibility cycle and, with a time lag, the investment (activity) cycle. For this reason the analysis below does not look at each factor separately but in terms of the historical situation. General pattern-matching explanations are formed from these histories. These patterns provide the suggestive correlation between theory and practice.

7.2 DECISION-MAKING FRAMEWORKS

Two decision-making frameworks are identified by Bromiley (1986) in the investment process (see section 3.5). One is the marketing strategy (or product management), in which a set of executives examine investment decisions from the perspective of new products or better service which the MOP can provide in achieving long-term market dominance. The other is the financial planning strategy, in which another set of executives examines investment decisions from the perspective of rates of return over a prescribed period in relation to an acceptable gearing position. Entrepreneurs who look at both assessments often need to decide between (say) a risky business market strategy and a much more conservative financial planning strategy. The example of Japanese penetration of the US car market was not based on any good return on investment over a specific short time horizon (financial planning), but on a long-term marketing strategy (Thomsen, 1984).

How susceptible a firm is to a particular level of investment orders is based on the resolution between the two investment decision frameworks. This resolution is conducted by the firms' entrepreneurs in terms of the desired capital stock level and the nature of the MOP to reach that optimal stock level. An entrepreneur with an accounting or engineering background, by strongly supporting a conservative financial strategy (despite a sanguine marketing strategy), ensures that susceptibility will not rise quickly or strongly. *Subdued* susceptibility cycles are more apparent when both frameworks present conservative approaches.

If an entrepreneur is swept along by an optimistic climate and follows risky marketing strategies on investment (despite a conservative financial strategy), then susceptibility will be prone to a sizeable downturn as the strong contradictory pulls of high investment come into effect (see section 5.4). This produces susceptibility cycles that can be described as *pronounced*. When both frameworks present sanguine approaches, susceptibility cycles become *severe* as contradictory pulls lead to quicker and deeper contractions. Greater amplitudes result from this severe susceptibility condition. Note that all strategies refer to investment in MOP and not to financial speculation. Under specific conditions (see section 4.4), short-term speculative behaviour may starve investment in MOP of funds, exacerbating an investment orders downturn.

Resolution of the two frameworks differs over time. The same two assessments can be resolved very differently at different historical periods. This chapter examines empirical patterns in the whole postwar era. During such a long period of time, settlement of the particular approach to investment decision-making tends to vary with the general climate of investment. The willingness to invest at a time with (say) high gearing contrasts with the unwillingness to make the same investment at another time unless there is a much lower gearing ratio. Each specific environment creates a climate of investment which allows clear appreciation of how different investment project assessments are settled. Exogenous factors can alter the environment and thus the investment climate as well.

Analysis is presented in three historical periods which can be recognised as being different environments in terms of their general attitudes to investment. The periods are identified statistically from aggregate private sector capital expenditures in capitalist economies. They are: (a) *Period One*: the early post-war high-investment growth period; (b) *Period Two*: the 1970s decade, with declining and low investment as a proportion of GDP; and (c) *Period Three*: the 1980s and early 1990s instability, with the greatest post-war variability in investment as a proportion of GDP.[3]

The general post-war investment climate, divided into three distinct periods, provides the broad economic background (or environment) to the study of corporate investment behaviour. Each period provides a different perspective on the relative strengths, in general terms, of the various approaches (conservative or risky) to the two investment decision-making frameworks. Understanding the investment climate for each period in these terms permits an appreciation of how the magnitudes of the three endogenous elements can achieve certain levels of investment commitments. For example, in an investment climate that tends to support conservative financial strategies, high gearing ratios would be a hindrance to new investment commitments, whereas in a more risk-accepting investment climate, the same gearing ratios would not be a hindrance.

A general investment climate contributes the secular framework within which the susceptibility cycle operates. A company, or even a whole industry, may be operating during a particular period totally in opposition to this climate. Such a contrary attitude to the general secular trend needs to be explained, and it may help to understand better the nature of susceptibility (and thus instability) in that company or industry.

7.3 STRUCTURAL PATTERNS OF THE ENDOGENOUS ELEMENTS

Profit is the basic endogenous element in the susceptibility cycle model. While changing profit rates act as inducement, profit levels determine the ability to invest. Since the majority of investment is financed from retained earnings, Kaleckian pricing theory has the behavioural assumption that profits must be large enough to finance the purchase of MOP. In the context of the empirical studies, this is taken to mean that net profit is the variable which gauges entrepreneurs' primary degree of susceptibility.[4] High net profit means a strong rate of investment orders, reflecting growing susceptibility such that any small decrease in net profit is liable to induce a downturn of investment orders. While at low net profit, the weak rate of investment orders reflects low susceptibility (or strong resilience to uncertainty), such that any small increment in profits is liable to induce stronger competitive positions in markets by starting to increase investment orders and creating an upturn (see section 5.4.1).

The tension of changing profit levels and its impact on investment commitments provides the foundations of susceptibility levels. Period One had strong profit levels in the established energy-based industries with only minor decreases. This produced subdued susceptibility cycles with very strong capital stock growth rates. Weak profits in Period Two for these industries were the basis of more pronounced contractions in susceptibility cycles, with very little profit-based impetus for strong investment growth. Then, strong prices and profits at the beginning of Period Three conferred very large expansion in investment activity through the 1980s, with correspondingly large susceptibility rises of investment orders. A precarious position was reached by the late 1980s when financial and property markets collapsed. The early 1990s deep recession diminished profits, exposing severe susceptibility and leading to prolonged weak investment activity.

This overall historical pattern of profits and investment in capitalist economies conforms with the basic duality of interdependence between susceptibility and investment commitments (see section 5.2). Positive profitability signals the increase of investment commitments, generating increased susceptibility to reversing investment commitments in order to reduce risk and uncertainty exposure. With such a build-up of tension, only relatively minor negative alterations to profitability are needed to create a structural break by reducing investment commitments and thus releasing the tensions of susceptibility.

Profits alone provide a base load to the degree of susceptibility in any particular level of investment commitment. However, the susceptibility cycle turning points and amplitude cannot be explained by profitability alone. When capacity utilisation is very high and increasing risk is very low, susceptibility exposure depends largely on profitability-related investment decisions. This was generally the case in Period One. In Period Two, the depth and length of the investment activity contraction was not adequately handled by profits, since rising profits did not generate any strong competitive pressures towards reinvestment. Period Three's severity of fluctuations in susceptibility can be only partly explained by profit variability, since high profitability during the period did not result in any significant investment expansion.

Capacity utilisation is the endogenous element that is crucial in terms of the marketing strategy for investment planning. Attempts at long-term market dominance require new products (and related new processes) which can only be provided by a level of capital stock that would ensure a level of production capable of acting as a barrier to (either) entry or effective competition (see section 2.3.1). All the large energy-based industries consisted of major firms with significant degrees of monopoly power, which they strove to maintain by over-accumulation. During the strong demand growth of Period One, this was generally a successful strategy, which they continued into Period Two, despite the slow down in demand, and new technology which enabled smaller firms to produce at competitive costs. The excess capacity that resulted, together with reduced profit levels, ensured serious susceptibility problems that tended to extend the contraction phases of the investment cycles.

Two difficulties with analysing the excess capacity problem that arose in Period Two bore out concerns raised in the literature. One was the tendency for monopolised industries officially to underestimate the level of overcapacity. The other was the power of innovation to introduce new capacity by firms outside the strong cartels (e.g. mini-steel millers, independent smelter producers; see section 2.5). Both difficulties exacerbated the measured excess capacity of major firms, making the susceptibility concerns of excess capacity even more deep-seated.

By Period Three, serious overaccumulation required major rationalisation on a global scale. Older MOP were decommissioned quickly, while efficiency-based process innovation was the focus of all new MOP throughout the period. This was more successful in some industries than others. Major firms in the world aluminium industry attempted to make aluminium more product-differentiated, so as to reduce the impact of the excess capacity problem on susceptibility. This action reduced the homogeneity of the industry and weakened its process innovation.

In the meantime, the third endogenous element of increasing risk became of central concern to susceptibility in Period Three after relative unimportance during the previous two periods. Major firms did not come up against the limitations to external funding until after the large gearing rises during Period Three. Easy credit in the early part of Period Three built up large but acceptable gearing ratios in a climate of worldwide financial deregulation. This further encouraged investment in new MOP, developing very strong susceptibility which eventually led to deep investment contraction when the large gearing was no longer acceptable to the financial community. The prolonged time needed to return to lower acceptable ratios of gearing with susceptibility being sufficiently reduced, delayed the rise of manufacturing investment after the 1990–91 recession (see section 5.4.2).

To hasten the drawing down of 'increasing risk'-based susceptibility tensions, major firms became involved in spreading increasing risk across a wider business community. This was achieved by joint ventures (e.g. co-operative JV in aluminium; transitional JV in motor vehicles), equity-sharing (motor vehicles) and government industry support. All these arrangements were aimed at stabilising increasing risk at more acceptable levels. They have also tended to usher in major structural changes to these industries, resulting in extended contraction phases before major new technology-based investment expansions are committed (see section 6.3).

The nature of this increasing risk element is to add some minor susceptibility concerns during periods of stable and strong growth and periods of weak demand (where capacity utilisation is of central concern). Increasing risk becomes a major element of susceptibility when financial constraints are loosened under conditions of 'financial leverage'. Throughout Period Three, reduced regulatory conditions and the corresponding rise of market competition led to over-optimistic assessments of expected future yields and under-assessments of increasing risk. This was at a time of weakening monopoly power. Under such conditions, many debt-based investments failed, eventually leading to a crisis of confidence as susceptibility tensions rose inexorably. The subsequent investment contraction in the early 1990s was long, as structural change developed with the reestablishment of new strong monopoly power.

Historical patterns of the last two elements show that, under specific conditions, profit improvements may not be adequate to encourage investment growth. This is because susceptibility is not low (or resilient) enough to generate competition for new markets until the capacity utilisation and increasing risk characteristics have reached more acceptable levels: levels that are more appropriate for another strong investment expansion. No amount of profit improvement and support from governments along this profit-based path (e.g. tax concessions and accelerated investment allowances) can succeed without the other two elements being at more acceptable positions in terms of susceptibility.

7.4 CHANGING TIME LAGS IN THE INVESTMENT PROCESS

Time lags in the investment processes of major industries provide empirical micro-dimensions to the traverse. Identifying these lags and relating how they affect the susceptibility and investment cycle patterns enables an explanatory hypothesis to emerge which supports the theory of the traverse and susceptibility outlined in section 5.5.

Two areas of concern for susceptibility are based on the traverse. One is the length of the gestation period which is made up of the entrepreneurial reaction lag and the production lag. The other is rising costs of new MOP due to capacity shortages in the capital-goods-producing industries. Long time delays in both areas intensify susceptibility. At the margin, this intensification increases the likelihood of investment downturns and adds to the strength of the following contraction. It also increases the difficulties of initiating any investment upturns, tending to keep investment 'skidding' at the bottom of the investment trough with only minor inventory-stock-induced rises.

The case studies in small open capitalist economies like Australia (see Courvisanos, 1994b) show that their major manufacturing industries suffer particularly strongly from long time delays in both areas, intensifying susceptibility compared to the major OECD nations. The basic reason discerned from the studies is the relatively small scale of capital goods production. This leads to the need for imports of capital goods and all the problems of extra time and costs that importation involves, as well as their variability.

Overcoming these long time delay problems depends on the 'shiftability of capital goods' options available to the manufacturer (see section 2.6). Transnational corporations have the best options since they are able to import quickly from their own large-scale global sources of technology and staff for setting up new MOP. Often the MOP required are the same as in other manufacturing plants in other countries. This represents a growing post-war trend towards globalisation of production, which means that MOP can be produced on a large scale for all plants of the transnational firms. Technical assistance to locally based capital-goods-producing firms can also be provided to reduce time delays if there are 'local content' type trade restrictions in place by governments. All these shiftability options, while reducing length and variability of time delays, tend to keep R&D capacity relatively low in the countries with smaller foreign-based subsidiaries.

Cross-case industry tables developed by Courvisanos (1994a) across three Australian manufacturing industries (see Appendix) show the motor vehicle industry's investment cycles generally peaking before the basic metals (steel and aluminium) industries. The length of investment contractions were, however, not comparably shorter. This supports the explanation that the specific nature of MOP in the consumption goods sector 2 induces fewer shifting options and results in higher intensification of susceptibility (see section 5.5). Higher intensity was reflected in the motor vehicle industry through its earlier investment downturns than the two basic metals producers. Both steel and aluminium were strong vertically integrated industries, allowing for options of moving relative concentrations of investment upstream or downstream to avoid extended time delays which spawn this higher intensity. As part of a global structure, the transnational aluminium firms also had options to shift resources for production between different localities; while the domestic monopoly steel producer (BHP) diversified strongly to open its own options.

Recognising differences between various industries' time lags provides further emerging patterns of susceptibility. The Australian motor vehicle industry had a short entrepreneurial reaction lag, since investment decisions were based on global investment strategies developed at the headquarters of each transnational firm. The locally based firms did not have any added conflicts at the domestic level which would delay implementation of the global decisions.

Conflicts arose in the Australian basic metals industries to lengthen, often vitally, the entrepreneurial reaction lag. In the aluminium industry, the strong risky marketing strategy input of local partners was at odds with the more conservative global financial strategy of the transnational partner. In the steel industry, there were perennial conflicts between the more adventurous marketing strategies of the entrepreneur-managers and the very conservative financial strategies of most BHP board members. All three industries experienced lengthening of this lag through the three periods as greater structural changes and deregulation produced more uncertainty and required significant changes to investment strategies.

The entrepreneurial reaction lag is internal to the firm. The continued lengthening of this lag over the three periods indicates increased internal decision-making uncertainties in a more unstable and less-regulated manufacturing environment. Susceptibility is intensified as this lag is lengthened, tending to exacerbate the investment cycle amplitude.

The Australian motor vehicle industry's production lag was long and variable with high import capital costs, capacity constraints in small-scale local tooling firms and variable construction delays. Both basic metal industries had relatively short production lags as they had their own construction teams and direct links with overseas sources of capital goods to minimise the typically long construction stage. The aluminium firms attained MOP in relation to a global timetable of when capital goods and construction teams were available. BHP's strong links with overseas engineering firms provided similar benefits, but with less certainty and more variability. BHP had their production lag extended when sometimes they suffered shortages of construction inputs (early Period One) and commissioning problems from new technology (Period Three). Modern computer-based technology introduced in Period Three reduced cost and length of production lags in all three industries, because the nature of capital goods in these industries was no longer as large or as heavy to install.

The production lag generally involves factors external to the control of the firm. Long periods of weak investment activity (e.g. Period Two) diminish existing MOP producers, magnifying supply constraint problems in the new investment expansion and intensifying susceptibility. State-induced local MOP suppliers in a small import replacement market (especially motor vehicle tooling) are highly prone to folding. The resulting lack of local MOP production, together with increasing globalisation of technical advances and production, lead to low R&D capacity and more imported MOP. Technical advances tend to reduce the production lag, but with increased variability in the operational (or commissioning) part of the lag. Imported MOP with little local back-up support cause the most operational problems. So whereas susceptibility is ameliorated by cheaper and lighter computer-based

MOP, supply constraints (after long investment contractions) and commissioning problems (with mainly imported MOP) work the other way and intensify susceptibility.

Modern technology does not allow producers to have the Period One comfort of long delays in entrepreneurial and production lags with associated high capital costs. This poor traverse can exist only behind high tariff walls and primarily a domestic import-substitution market. In the globalised markets of the 1990s, such a traverse is unacceptable. Thus, firms' growing intensification of susceptibility comes from adapting to deregulated and globalised MOP sources. This can be minimised by close global links (e.g. via equity/model sharing, joint ventures, being a subsidiary of a transnational) which provide relatively less uncertainty with the traverse, ameliorating some of the susceptibility of time delays in investment decision-making.

7.5 EMPIRICAL PATTERNS OF INNOVATION

An empirical pattern emerges in capitalist economies of technological innovation and its relationship to investment. The basic institutional framework which is set up in section 4.5 underlies this pattern. Innovation operates differently in separate stages of a firm's development. Table 7.1 summarises how innovation and investment relate to each stage. The stages of development identified in the table are a taxonomic representation based on the study by Penrose (1959) of dynamic growth and maturity in major firms of an industry.

At the infant stage, firms in the industry are generally small, or strongly labour-intensive (with a history of limited technologically based capital stock). In these industries there is a great deal of exogenous process innovation going on in an attempt to incorporate the new technology system. This is reflected by investment in new processes embodying the new technology of capital goods producers. Investment is in new capacity that produces either new goods or completely new methods of generating established goods or services (Stoneman, 1983, p. 212).

High gearing, substantial constraints on the traverse and uncertain demand for new products are common problems at the infant stage, creating strong susceptibility. Thus, exogenous innovation in infant stage industries raises susceptibility quickly and strongly. This can be overcome by success through full capacity utilisation and high profits, leading to relatively subdued susceptibility cycles. Failure to overcome exogenous innovation problems intensifies susceptibility and enhances contractionary biased investment instability, while success ameliorates susceptibility and enhances expansionary biased investment instability.

Table 7.1   Stages of development

	Type of Industry	Role of Innovation	Effect on Investment
Infant Stage	Leading-edge technologically sophisticated	Process innovation central role	Exogenous stimulation for investment to rise (upturn in investment with strong susceptibility)
Growth Stage	New technology-based mass market	Product innovation central role	Subdued susceptibility strong stimulation to increase market share (boom in investment)
Mature Stage	Dominant scale and information-intensive technology	Fears of overcapacity. Technological frugality	Concentrate on greater utilisation (low investment, high susceptibility)
Transition Stage	Old dominant technology-based, altering to new technology	Major product innovations Diversification Alter processes (based on major exogenous changes to new technology systems)	Loss of industry control by majors Joint ventures Structural change in firms' capital stock. (severe susceptibility cycles, greater investment instability)

In the growth stage, investment by firms expands strongly as endogenous product-based innovation stimulates strong demand growth. This can also stimulate investment growth in non-differentiated commodities whose output is the subject of successful downstream product innovation (e.g. aluminium). Competition for market share is the spur to growing investment orders and higher susceptibility (see section 5.6.3). Success came with product innovation based on the dominant post-war technology system of Fordist mass production (Freeman and Perez, 1988, p. 52). Minor incremental process innovation that was investment-induced (Steindl's 'shadow of investment') also occurred. Success ameliorates susceptibility, allowing strong investment booms and weak investment slumps (see section 6.3).

In the mature stage, high sustained investment susceptibility occurs due to gearing and overcapacity concerns. Fear of further excess capacity in a market where demand has slowed or even declined creates a technological frugality in relation to fundamental research. Instead, there is a concentration on cheaper, more cosmetic endogenous innovations which limit both demand growth and significant technology improvements. The more differentiated the industry, the stronger is this dependence on cosmetic innovation. In this stage firms have very limited product innovation and minor cost-saving process innovation using the standard (now old) technology system. Such limited innovation reduces investment to relatively low average levels with weak investment booms and much stronger investment slumps. Intraindustry competition is weak as market shares stabilise for the mature products that are produced.

In the transition stage, firms see the need to transform their companies by altering substantially their own mature product (i.e. from petrol to solar cars), developing new products entirely, or diversifying into industries that produce them. This requires adoption of new technology systems (exogenous innovation) which are applied to endogenous innovation. New products can only be achieved by associated process innovation in new production methods. Strong inter-industry competition stimulates this innovation which is incorporated in expensive investment programmes that intensify susceptibility.

Bound to mature products, non-differentiated oligopolies (or monopolies) are keen to diversify. In Australia, BHP did this in Period Two, as it diversified strongly away from steel and concentrated on oil production after the huge OPEC price rises. Differentiated oligopolies in transition try major adaptations to their products and processes. Major firms in the global motor vehicle industry during Period Three began to adopt the lean production system with strategic alliances in model and equity sharing to ameliorate susceptibility. The global aluminium firms in Period Three began to lose control of their homogeneous product. So, with strong product innovation to differentiate alumina, these firms have attempted to stabilise their market decline. Innovation at the transition stage creates strong investment commitments which intensify susceptibility of major structural change.

From this historical analysis, an investment pattern emerges of susceptibility cycles interacting with technological innovation. Low susceptibility with war-established process innovations in the early post-war period produced subdued and upward-biased investment cycles. Much higher susceptibility due to excess capacity produced a downward bias with slightly more instability in the 1970s. High gearing in the 1980s together with powerful exogenous innovations based around shifts from energy-based oil input to electronic-based information input produced very sensitive susceptibility conditions, with manufacturing industries in a transition stage and information technology service industries (e.g. telecommunications, banks and finance) in a growth stage. This combination created strong booms and slumps in investment. Manufacturing had shown signs of investment growth in emerging technologically sophisticated industries (Wood *et al.*, 1991), but the early 1990s recession heightened the exogenous innovation problems, intensifying susceptibility and sending investment activity into a deep, extended trough.

Susceptibility of investment is intensified by paradigm shifts in basic technologies. Leading-edge technologically sophisticated (infant) industries have unstable demand and high gearing. At the same time, old cheap energy-based industries (including mineral non-differentiated oligopolies) are determined to hold on to their diminishing power, resulting in severe excess capacity and thus weak investment. Such investment instability is a limitation to efficient and smooth structural change. Allowing the market to resolve this limitation is long and painful. Old MOP (e.g. the motor vehicle industry in Period Three) refuse to give their dominance away, yet they are still trying to make some transition to alter process innovation. New MOP find lack of market power and experience in new technology management major stumbling blocks to strong investment growth.

7.6 CHANGING ROLE OF THE STATE

The role of the state in capitalist economies is only at the margins of the investment cycle analysis. Entrepreneurs are 'masters of their fate' (Kalecki, 1971, p. 13), encapsulated in the three endogenous elements of the susceptibility hypothesis. The state plays two supporting roles within this investment process. One is as a supplement to the endogenous elements through the operation of the political business cycle. The other is as an exogenous element which alters susceptibility in line with longer-term strategies of the state, whether at the micro-industry policy level or the macro-effective demand level.

The state's supporting role has changed over the post-war period, while the direction of change has been roughly the same in all capitalist economies. In the immediate post-war period there was a strong strategic interventionist role for the state as part of the war reconstruction process. Slowly this altered towards a more deregulatory and market-guiding support from the state. These changes have affected the nature of susceptibility in the investment process.

At the macroeconomic level, the historical factors described in section 6.8 played significant roles in affecting the susceptibility of investment in industries of all capitalist economies. Of direct exogenous influences, war-induced and Cold War-supported military (and science-related) spending provided the basis for growth in industries such as aluminium (Peck, 1961), electronics (Charles, 1987) and commercial aircraft (Mowery and Rosenberg, 1989) on a worldwide basis during Period One. This lowered susceptibility and induced a strong upward trend in investment cycles. However, well into Period Three, and with the Cold War ending, added uncertainty was experienced by major heavy manufacturing industries about future demand growth, further intensifying susceptibility in a period of already strong overcapacity.

The major indirect exogenous influence is the role of stabilisation policies in national economies. Period One (and to a lesser extent Period Two) macroeconomies were predicated on the full-employment objective and close to full capacity utilisation. Long-term support for 'full employment stabilisation' gave firms strong positive expectations with a reasonable level of certainty. This enabled firms to invest strongly with reasonably low susceptibility, despite entrepreneurial conservativeness in the large 'growth stage' industries. Matthews (1968) showed that it was this high level of private investment which led to high employment levels. Despite this Period One growth phase, Kalecki's political business cycle ('stop–go') type of state intervention guaranteed that investment would still be subject to short-term instability.

Steindl's 'stunted growth' phenomenon since the mid-1970s is based on deflationary bias in macroeconomic policies. This leads to long-term effective demand deficiency (Matthews, 1968), which intensifies susceptibility, thus inducing increased investment contractions and reduced investment expansions. Stabilisation policies under this regime have tended to be much less stimulatory and to have less impact on investment, especially under the conditions of severe overcapacity and high increasing risk prevalent in Period Three.

At the micro-industry policy level, post-war political economic history provides evidence of two forms of state support. Capitalist economies began the post-war era under some state-sponsored reconstruction programme. This involved a risk-with-state amelioration approach to industry policy. Generally this was followed later in Period One, and more strongly in Period Two, with an *ad hoc* assistance stance in industry policy.

Reconstruction programmes were a crude 'socialisation of investment' policy which involved either the nationalisation of the war-induced growth-stage private enterprises (e.g. UK, Sweden, France, Italy) or obtaining the patronage and partnership of innovative business managers from the major private firms (e.g. US, Australia, New Zealand, Canada). The aim in both cases was for a strong investment drive to reconstruct and diversify the national economy. The role of the state was still contradictory, given the 'political business cycle' imperatives, but its industry planning was risk-oriented and coherent due to the input of senior business executives (of nationalised or state-supported private firms). These strategies incorporated market-based decisions with state support to ameliorate susceptibility.[5]

Early post-war conservative governments did not want to manage the development of manufacturing, but still wanted to ameliorate the susceptibility of investing. Philosophically opposed to investment planning, such governments in practice were prepared to provide *ad hoc* assistance to business on the basis of individual firm and industry lobbying.[6] This state approach to investment boosted the business interests which more closely supported conservative financially-based investment planning: boards of major highly concentrated family-controlled domestic firms (Lawriwsky, 1984, p. 235) and senior management at the headquarters of transnational firms (Tsokhas, 1986, pp. 237–47). Based on this strategy, susceptibility was easily aggravated. This led to weak process innovation, with regular (but only minor) product innovation, that did not provide per capita growth to match investment growth. Mature Kaleckian monopoly capitalist-type firms were able to consolidate economic power, to the detriment of innovative but risky infant-stage firms. Conservative industry policy provided an *ad hoc* way to increase the quantity of investment without managing its quality.

In this environment of *ad hoc* assistance, a long tradition of 'colonial development' was fostered in small open economies where foreign transnational corporations (TNCs) dominated the small national economy. These firms tended to centralise their R&D in their home countries (Dunning, 1985, p. 419). When such companies did locate R&D overseas, they did so in countries with already high levels of technical expertise (Lewis and Mangan, 1987, p. 382). In countries without such expertise, such as Australia, Canada and New Zealand, conservative business behaviour (led by the domestic management of TNCs) stifled labour and management skills, since there was limited new MOP and R&D from which the 'learning curve' method of skills formation could develop.

State support for protected manufacturing industries in economies with strong effective demand throughout Period One disguised the relatively poor quality of investment. Once effective demand faltered in Period Two, governments began to implement the deregulatory (free trade) approach to industry policy, but with much backsliding to *ad hoc* assistance. In such an uncertain environment through the early 1970s, conservative entrepreneurs reduced drastically their investment commitments and capital expenditure in capitalist economies declined severely (see Hillinger and Reiter, 1992).

From the case study industries summarised in Table A.2, two problems can be perceived with the deregulatory approach to industry policy when it was first applied in Period Two.[7] The first was the retention of markets and economic power by mature monopoly capitalist firms. The second was the lack of learning-curve skills formation.[8] In concert with weakening world economic growth and domestic over-accumulation, susceptibility greatly increased, which prevented restructuring and created an inflexible structure. During the 1970s, a return to ad hocery occurred regularly when crises arose in specific areas of manufacturing. This ensured that firm's agents with conservative financial planning strategies remained dominant, protecting existing MOP in mature industries.

Regular returns to ad hocery were based on policies of tax concessions and investment allowances, which improved profitability in the second half of Period Two. They did not address the problem of excess capacity which was keeping susceptibility at levels that prevented competitive pressures from surfacing. Investment in Australian manufacturing remained low since, with large overcapacity, there was no impetus for a significant upturn in the susceptibility cycle, despite continued state support. As TNCs consolidated their economic power in their home economies, countries like Germany and the US showed a stronger late-1970s investment upturn, with excess capacity being removed quickly after the mid-Period Two investment trough (Hillinger and Reiter, 1992).

The 'credit binge' of the 1980s was set off by the higher lender's risk exposure due to financial deregulation coming on top of a higher inflation-based borrower's risk regime that developed in the late 1970s. Risky marketing strategies for investment dominated in this Period Three 'increasing risk' climate. Company boards and overseas headquarters allowed more risk-oriented domestic managers to develop major restructuring programmes. The deregulatory approach, which increasingly came to dominate industry policy in all major capitalist economies, intensified susceptibility already made more sensitive by risk-oriented business. This was in contradistinction to the late 1940s, when strategic industry policy was ameliorating the susceptibility of risk-oriented entrepreneurs.

Under these conditions, when deregulation threatened a segment of the economy (e.g. tariff reductions on textiles), there was withdrawal of investment rather than restructuring. Funds were diverted to financial speculative strategies which were less susceptible than investment in new technologies and all the essential related skill training, management and marketing techniques. To counter this, social democratic elected governments in countries like France and Australia introduced a variety of *ad hoc* interventionist policies to stimulate innovation (e.g. tax concession for R&D, specific industry plans, such as for cars and steel, support for small science-based firms). These measures were fairly limited in ameliorating susceptibility (for Australia, see Dunkley and Kulkarni, 1990).

The steel and motor vehicle industry plans in Australia come within the purview of the appendix case studies. These plans aimed at efficiency through reducing intervention, particularly tariffs. In this form, these plans did not conform to traditional notions of planning, even though they succeeded (to varying degrees) in ameliorating susceptibility and encouraging, through rewards and penalties, the adoption of new efficient MOP.[9] The investment downturn of 1990–91 happened just as these plans were being phased out and the full deregulatory arrangements were coming in. This tended to magnify the vulnerability of these industries and delay their investment recovery out of the early 1990s recession.

With the collapse of high financial leverage in the early 1990s' recession, business became severely limited by the much lower risk exposure of both borrowers and lenders. This reduced the capacity of business, especially smaller innovative firms, to restructure in line with the new technology systems (Mills *et al.*, 1993, p. 22). With the strong negative aspects of the endogenous elements keeping investment from reviving in this deep recession, the deregulatory approach exposed this weak manufacturing investment position further. The explanatory generalisation is that uncertainty and increased mistakes under deregulation intensifies the level of susceptibility. What results is much larger amplitude in investment cycles and longer investment trough periods with possibly only short weak stock-induced investment upturns.[10]

Freeman and Perez (1988, p. 60) argue that the new long wave of technological innovation appearing in Period Three and based on the electronic information technology paradigm is causing 'deep structural problems . . . in all parts of the world'. The analysis in this book implies that the 'structural crises of adjustment' (in the words of Freeman and Perez) has increased susceptibility to the extent that investment is highly unstable. This instability makes a crisis long and painful unless susceptibility is ameliorated. Allowing market power to determine the resolution of this crisis produces severe susceptibility cycles, increasing investment instability which looks positive for restructuring during investment upswings, only to be severely thwarted by strong investment downswings.

7.7 OTHER LONG-RUN EXOGENOUS FACTORS

No systematic exploration of other exogenous factors was conducted in the case study analysis. During the chronological review of any industry, various external factors may appear as part of the susceptibility-building behaviour of investment decision-makers. With often only one-off examples of particular factors, any general conclusions of their impact on investment behaviour are conjectural. Support for the factor tendencies outlined briefly below come from the theoretical literature referred to in Chapter 6. The patterns identified here 'are by-products of the main inquiry and, for this reason alone deserve to be treated with considerable reserve' (Salter, 1960, p. 144).

In terms of 'rentier savings' (see section 6.4), only in Period Three was there a secular trend to increased finance accumulation. This trend seemed to coincide with a lack of a 'paradigm shift' in innovation, such that there were weak incentives for investment in the old technology systems. The financial sector developed on the basis of rapidly growing financial speculation. The information needs of this finance accumulation were the foundations of the nascent information-based technology system which, by the late 1980s, was flowing generally into all industries. However, from its start in the late 1970s to the asset market crash of 1989–90, the financial accumulation trend intensified susceptibility by increasing the acceptable level of increasing risk (financial leverage) and reducing the effective demand effects of strong investment. The effects described by Steindl in section 6.4 seem to be supported by higher gearing and unstable investment during Period Three. The resulting debt deflation and increased differential in propensities to save by rich and poor have deepened and lengthened the investment trough of the early 1990s.

Population-related factors (see section 6.5) have been of major concern in recently European-settled economies (e.g. Australia, Canada, New Zealand, South Africa) due to the shortage of labour that has constantly plagued their development. At the end of World War II, this problem was heightened by a lack of skilled and unskilled labour required for major reconstruction programmes (Dyster and Meredith, 1990, p. 193). Immigration added to effective demand and productive capacity, which ameliorated susceptibility concerns in Fordist mass production manufacturing industries. The post-war 'baby boom' and growth of consumerism in all capitalist economies 'broadened the market' during Period One, adding to effective demand, especially for motor vehicles and the 'consumerism' of aluminium (after its mainly strategic use during the war). By the end of Period Two, immigration was a very minor influence and unemployment became significant and permanent. Both forces weakened consumerism, affecting particularly the motor vehicle industry. These forces added to the intensification of susceptibility in Period Three which have already been considered.

Most problematical within a pattern-matching approach are random factors (see section 6.6). Wars overseas caused short-term demand impetus (rather than supply reducing long-term effects for domestic-based wars), which ameliorated susceptibility. Skills built up during World War II added a further positive impetus to mass production manufacturing as in the motor vehicle industry. Poor industrial relations during Periods One and Two often led to 'random' strikes and serious production difficulties (as well as extending the production lag). This factor encouraged a shifting of resources away from such industrial based activities (e.g. Australia's BHP steel diversified into oil). Finally, severe droughts deepened the investment slump, but the end of droughts had strong and rapid positive susceptibility effects without being limited by supply constraints. This intensified investment expansion very quickly after recession (e.g. the 1982 end of the severe Australian drought added strong impetus to the nascent investment expansion which was lacking after the early 1990s trough).

Small open economies (SOEs) are strongly affected by changes in the international economy, each of which adds to or subtracts from the total sum of susceptibility already established by all the other factors discussed. Full employment in world capitalism during Period One (due to many factors previously examined) enabled manufacturing industries in SOEs to have relatively low susceptibility despite strong (often above average OECD) capital stock growth rates. The inflationary OPEC oil shocks in Period Two intensified susceptibility as TNCs attempted to maintain mark-ups (see section 6.9). The effect was to help turn strong investment expansions less than two years later into very deep investment contractions. Restrictive macropolicies in Period Three to overcome these inflationary pressures were applied in a coordinated manner worldwide. This created speculative booms and made it more difficult for investment to rise out of deep troughs.

The other two international economic factors raised in section 6.9 were foreign investment and exchange rates. SOEs historically depended on large capital inflows, seen by the very high levels of equity and loan foreign liabilities in manufacturing industries. Although in the short-term they ameliorated susceptibility, the long-term commitments they engendered and speculative borrowings for takeovers all contributed to intensifying susceptibility in SOEs' investment cycles.

Exchange rate movements can be examined using a Kaleckian pricing model developed by Bloch (1991). Based on the Australian experience, Bloch concludes that 'movements in the value of the Australian dollar serve to insulate the balance of trade from the external influence of the world business cycle' (Bloch, 1991, p. 114). Bloch then goes on to explain that this allowed the world business cycle to affect the domestic economy. Differences in two large depreciating periods show the possibilities. The mid-1970s depreciation led to a wages explosion, intensifying susceptibility and then assisting the deep contraction that followed. The mid-1980s depreciation saw discounting of wages under the Accord social contract, ameliorating susceptibility and adding to the investment boom in the late 1980s.

Given that exchange rate instability is not equilibrating and central bank interventions widen currency variations (Biasco, 1987), the examples above on wage formation indicate that domestic management of exchange rate movements impact on susceptibility and investment. Attraction of large capital inflows into depreciating currencies makes it imperative that domestic management leads investment into new technology-based industries. Inflow into mature-stage industries or into finance accumulation make adjustments to 'currency inversions' much slower, with intensified susceptibility leading to more contractionary biased investment cycles (see section 6.9).

7.8 'BUNCHING' OF INDUSTRY INVESTMENT CYCLES

The final pattern that emerges from industry studies is a synchronism of industry investment cycles and their joint synchronised impact on both total manufacturing investment (MI) and gross domestic product (GDP). This section outlines this pattern and provides an explanatory hypothesis drawing upon the susceptibility cycle model.

A perusal of the investment peak dates in the three cross-case summary tables in the Appendix suggests a synchronism which increases over time. In Period One, two out of the four peaks in the three industries are within one year of each other, and all contractions are relatively short. All three industries in Period Two experienced the one investment peak around 1972, followed by similar long contractions. In Period Three, all three peaks of each industry are very closely synchronised. This 'bunching' pattern of investment by industry groups is also noted in two empirical studies of US investment from different periods: Evans (1969, pp. 114–21) in his statistical study of early post-war investment by 13 manufacturing industries; and Fazzari and Mott (1986–7) in their econometric analysis of 835 firms in 20 manufacturing groups over the period 1970–82. Both studies identify this bunching as crucial to the cycle pattern of aggregate investment and business cycles.[11]

Empirical research suggests that there is bunching of innovations by large groups of firms which leads to long waves of investment (see Freeman *et al.*, 1982). A theoretical basis to such empirics can be found in the shifting from an old to a new technology system. The dearth of investment as the old system is maturing (see section 7.5) creates low susceptibility which allows for innovation bunching and new long waves of investment (see Dosi *et al.*, 1988). Further, inter-industry competition stimulates groups of industries to adopt the new technology systems at around the same time, when susceptibility is relatively low, reducing the inherent uncertainties that come with new technology investment (see Shapiro, 1988).

Figure 7.1 shows the close cyclical pattern between real gross investment of the three case study industries added together (three industries) and MI, for the period 1954–5 to 1987–8.[12] This pattern supports the capital stock share data which notes that these three industries contributed virtually all the total capital stock growth in manufacturing over this period (Lattimore, 1989, pp. 26–7). The figure is divided into the three periods, showing the three industries' 'bunched' investment pattern period-by-period. Each period is based on the different stages of firm development and their associated susceptibility (see Table 7.1). Bunching of the three industries helps significantly to provide MI with a pattern of investment which displays generally positive investment growth in Period One, followed by the relatively weak investment of Period Two, and highly unstable investment in Period Three.

The susceptibility cycle model can explain the relationship between the combined investment cycle of a group of major industries and the MI cycle. Short-term investment cycles vary in their amplitudes depending on the stage of development that groups of industries are located in. Long-term trend (or long-wave) investment expansions – with strong booms and weak slumps – occur when susceptibility is ameliorated in industries with new technology systems. This can be related to the early post-war Period One with its spread of the Fordist mass production system across all manufacturing industries.

Long wave investment contractions – with weak booms and strong slumps – occur when susceptibility is intensified in the major industries where the technology systems have grown old but are maintained in oligopoly structures as in Period Two. Inter-industry competition stimulates the adoption of new technology systems by some industries while others attempt to strengthen their oligopolistic control on old systems. The intensified nature of susceptibility that results during this transition stage makes investment highly unstable. Period Three represents such heightened investment instability.

Figure 7.1 Investment in the Australian manufacturing sector from 1954–5 to 1987–8: combined three case study industries and total manufacturing (1984–5, $A millions)

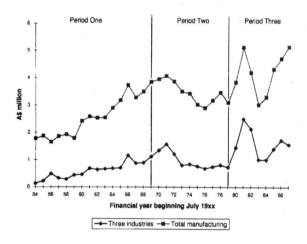

Source: Courvisanos (1994a, Table 7.3, p. 261)

In standard Keynesian theory, investment is a component of effective demand that contributes to the determination of GDP. Further, in the short-term, the changing level of investment is by 'virtually universal agreement . . . one of the main sources of cyclical fluctuations in the economy' (Freeman and Perez, 1988, p. 39). Both these theoretical points have been strongly supported by empirical investigations conducted by Hillinger and his colleagues at SEMECON, University of Munich. Their research, based on a study of 15 OECD economies, has shown that gross fixed capital formation (GFCF) is 'dominated by a deterministic pattern' and that the long cycles detected in the GDP 'seem to come from the GFCF' (Hillinger and Sebold–Bender, 1992, p. 106). Thus, there is a strong influence from aggregate investment to GDP and business cycles. Although the Australian MI's share of private business investment was between 25.2 and 28.5 per cent in the 1980s (BIE, 1990b, p. 9), the investment to output ratio in manufacturing was over 70 per cent more variable than in non-manufacturing (BIE, 1990a, p. 30, fn. 2). Thus, MI plays a notable role in short-term fluctuations of GDP.

From a longer-term perspective, the assertion that MI is an important influence on aggregate economic activity is based on the 'first growth law' set out by Kaldor (1966). The law states that 'there is a strong relationship between the rate of growth of GDP and the rate of growth of manufacturing production' (Reynolds, 1987, p. 200). This is the central component to the principle of 'cumulative causation' which sees that economic growth, 'centered on the 'self-reinforcing dynamics' internal to manufacturing, is a circular process of cumulative causation governed by the growth of demand' (Ricoy, 1987, p. 733).

Borrowing from Keynesian analysis, investment is the fundamental, but unstable, independent variable in effective demand. Linking this to cumulative causation implies that MI is the crucial determinant in manufacturing production. Then, using Kaldor's law to relate manufacturing to economy-wide output, the link from MI to GDP is rationalised. The corollary to this relationship is that changes in MI cause GDP to change and this is what causes business cycles.

An examination of deviations from MI and GDP trend lines for Australia over the period 1954–5 to 1987–8 lends support to the above corollary.[13] Figure 7.2 shows that after the large early 1950s Korean War boom, deviations from GDP growth decrease without much fluctuation. This pattern correlates with the same period of low amplitude investment cycle deviations around zero. When investment deviates strongly upwards from 1966 through to 1972, this leads to positive growth over trend in GDP. The collapse of investment deviations that followed in Period Two is reflected in a similar GDP deviation downturn two years later. Huge positive investment deviation in the 'resources boom' 1981–3 is followed by a strong GDP positive deviation after the 1982 drought. The large capital stock built up in metals enabled the economy to grow strongly when domestic and world demand for industrial materials expanded through to the early 1990s' recession. A more broader-based, but subdued investment upturn from late 1985 to the 1986–7 peak supported GDP growth. Off this graph, total business investment growth peaked in 1988–9, with GDP peaking one year later and reaching a deep trough in 1990–1.

Figure 7.2 Deviations from trend in manufacturing investment and GDP: Australia, 1954–5 to 1987–8 (1984–5 $A millions)

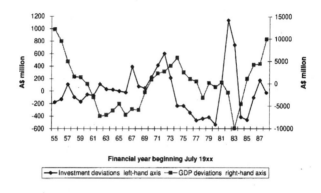

Sources: Courvisanos (1994a, Table 7.3, p. 261) for investment; Foster and Stewart (1991, Table 5.2a, p. 189) for GDP

On the basis of the 'bunching' patterns of investment, a blueprint can be devised which links manufacturing investment behaviour with business cycles. Groups of industries dominated by large firms adopt similar technologies and go through the four stages of firm development, with their associated susceptibility effects on investment, at around the same time. The resulting 'bunched' effect influences fluctuations in MI, and through MI's influence on aggregate investment, business cycles also. Thus, the synchronised investment patterns identified help significantly to generate an aggregate investment cycle pattern that strongly affects business cycles.

NOTES

1. See Yin (1989) for an exposition of how the case study approach to research can be used to develop general pattern-matching explanations that can either support or reject a model established in theory.

2. In chronological order of publication, the following international studies were consulted
    in supporting the empirical investment patterns discussed in this chapter. These patterns
    were initially identified in the Australian primary case study research summarised in the
    Appendix. Square brackets accompanying the reference indicate the specific area of
    investment behaviour studied. The references are:

    Andrews and Brunner (1951) [UK steel industry and endogenous elements];

    Hastay (1954) [manufacturing investment cycles];

    Penrose (1959) [time lags and growth paths];

    Richardson (1960) [information on endogenous elements and its uncertainty];

    Chandler (1962) [strategic planning and concentration];

    Eisner (1978) [endogenous elements, time lags];

    Hendriksen (1978) [US steel industry];

    Kay (1979) [research and development];

    Porter (1980) [excess capacity expansion];

    Sahal (1981) [patterns of innovation];

    Maxcy (1981) [global motor vehicle industry];

    Boswell (1983) [comparative study of steel companies];

    Stuckey (1983) [global aluminium industry];

    Bromiley (1986) [decision-making, endogenous elements];

    Coombs *et al.* (1987) [patterns of innovation];

    Chapman and Humphrys (1987) [innovation in various industries across different
    economies];

    Freeman and Perez (1988) [structural change and investment cycles];

    Dosi (1988a) [innovation process];

    Dertouzas *et al.* (1989) [decision-making, innovation];

    Mowery and Rosenberg (1989) [innovation and role of the state];

    Deiaco *et al.* (1990) [technology and the state in investment];

    Earl (1992) [UK and Australian motor vehicle industries];

    Granstrand (1994) [innovation in various sized industries].

3. Courvisanos (1994a, pp. 250–62) initially identified these three periods of investment
    cycles for Australia (see Figure 7.1). This same investment cycle pattern is supported by
    Hillinger and Sebold-Bender (1992) in their empirical study of Germany's gross fixed
    capital formation (GFCF) which shows that '[a]fter the 1970s the trend flattens, while the
    amplitudes of the cycles strongly increase' (p. 67). Further investigation of GFCF in
    another 14 OECD countries confirmed the same cyclical pattern, although some countries
    such as Australia and UK had a separate 12- to 13-year building investment cycle and a
    4.5–6-year equipment investment cycle, where Germany and surrounding European
    countries only had one 7–10-year investment cycle (Table 3.5, pp. 103–5).

4. Net profit is gross profit minus depreciation and income taxes. Empirically, depreciation
    tends not to vary over the business cycle, as it relates to technical conditions in the total
    capital stock. Income tax rates also do not vary with the business cycle. Net profit, as the
    variable that provides the wherewithal, highlights the *ability* and *incentive* to invest. In
    terms of the modified Kaleckian institutional framework, net profit relates to target mark-up
    policies of firms (see section 4.4).

5. Based on Table A.1 in the appendix, all three Australian case study industries show this
    investment planning for the period up to the end of the Chifley Labor (social democrat)
    Government in 1949 (see also Catley and McFarlane, 1981, pp. 65–72).

6. John McEwen was the minister who controlled Australian industry policy in the Menzies
    Coalition (conservative) Government from 1949 to 1971 on the basis that, in his own
    words, 'manufacturing is the only wealth-producing sector with the potential to increase
    jobs in sufficient numbers' (as quoted in Walsh, 1993).

7. This began in Australia with a 1973 across-the-board tariff cut of 25 per cent by the newly
    elected Whitlam Labor Government. For details, see the case study reports in Courvisanos
    (1994b).

8.   These two problems are consistent with the 'monopoly capital' modified Kaleckian framework set out in Chapter 4.

9.   Steel was successful in reducing chronic overcapacity (with old MOP) as BHP was a monopoly without fear of expansion from domestic competition. Motor vehicles was unsuccessful under similar plans for reducing capacity as the domestic competition of five producers induced continued overcapacity, with a fear of capacity-type and efficiency-type investment adding more capacity. The result was that product-related investment dominated, with a low level of automation (AIA, 1990, pp. 35, 64). From the debt angle, both industries experienced strong increasing risk in the investment expansion phase up to 1987–8, despite the industry plans. The strong tensions from overcapacity and debt by steel, and even more by motor vehicles, made them highly susceptible to a downturn. A sharp collapse of investment during the 1990–91 recession occurred in both industries.

10.   Inventory cycles, which 'are strongly affected by noise', have short (about 2.5–4 years) duration with only minor impact on investment and business cycles (Hillinger and Sebold-Bender, 1992).

11.   As noted in section 2.7, Goodwin (1990, p. 86) uses Schumpeter's innovative 'swarms' by different industries to produce this 'bunching' effect in a mathematical model of aggregate investment cycles.

12.   The three industries are motor vehicle, steel and non-ferrous metal (of which aluminium makes up around 50 per cent on average, but with a wide deviation over this long period). These three industries' investment figures are derived from the Australian Bureau of Statistics (ABS) census data of manufacturing establishments arranged in ASIC industry classification. This census source has provided no investment information after 1984–5. Lattimore (1989) takes ABS quarterly survey data on private sector capital expenditure to form a ratio and converts these survey data into ASIC classified investment data for the period 1985–6 to 1987–8. Figure 7.1 ends its 'three industries' investment depiction when Lattimore's conversion data cease. The complete series is at 1984–5 constant prices.

13.   GDP data is 'expenditure on GDP at constant prices' in million dollars at average 1984–5 prices, as presented in table 5.2a of Foster and Stewart (1991, p. 189). Note that the real gross manufacturing investment data are also set out in million dollars and based on constant 1984–5 prices. Both time series are fitted with a smooth trend function, then Figure 7.2 plots deviations (or residuals) off this trend line for each year of observable data.

8. Policy Implications and Future Directions

the chances of private investment 'regularising' itself without a supporting public policy are limited. (Lowe, 1954, p. 318)

8.1 INVESTMENT INSTABILITY AND HUMAN AGENCY

The need for greater business cycle stabilisation has been reasserted by the occurrence of greater business fluctuations since the early 1980s' recession. These stronger cycles have tended to create more dislocation and economic stress to a broader section of advanced capitalist economies. The previous chapter identified that business cycles exhibit patterns which are strongly dominated by the fluctuations in investment. Thus, any attempts to bring about greater stability to business cycles need to address the issue of investment instability.

The striking feature of the empirical analysis of private investment behaviour is the changing nature of susceptibility over time. This was recognised in the post-war investment cycle patterns in which susceptibility cycles went through a sequence from subdued to pronounced and finally to severe cyclical activity. The result was an increasing level of investment instability from the end of World War II to the early 1990s, which relates to a similar pattern in business cycles over the same period. This provides a strong argument for reducing investment instability.

Policies to reduce business investment instability, while maintaining an appropriate rate of capital stock growth comprise the basis of the policy perspective adopted in this chapter. Such policies were called 'regularisation' of investment in the 1950s when concerns over the level of instability in business cycles were also high as a result of the still vivid experiences of the 1930s' Great Depression. There are two forms of 'regularisation' of investment. One is by improving the private sector's investment decision-making through entrepreneurs themselves discovering ways of more efficiently managing susceptibility so that the investment cycles become more stabilised. The other is through the state establishing some form of market co-ordination of investment decisions that ensures stabilisation of cycles. The opening quotation by Lowe suggests that the former form of regularisation cannot be successful without crucial supporting efforts from the latter form.

The fundamental implication of the susceptibility model is that entrepreneurs cope with the dynamics of uncertainty by altering their investment commitments. It is 'capitalism's unwillingness to tolerate an effective system of compensatory or direct governmental planning' (Rousseas, 1989, p. 390) that creates inherent investment instability. Firms attempt to 'tame' uncertainty by the accrual of monopoly power through integration, takcovers, mergers and product differentiation. Success at this can mitigate susceptibility in the short-term, but by amassing this power, major monopoly capitalist firms (or 'megacorps') tend to concentrate on protecting existing MOP. This limits entrepreneurs' willingness to introduce new MOP based on new technological systems and paradigms, which in the long term restricts megacorps' adaptation to structural changes, thus intensifying susceptibility. Only detailed historical explication of susceptibility at the industry level, as evidenced in the Appendix, can supply specific implications for investment activity of such intransigent power.

With subdued susceptibility cycles, industry structures become, as Salter (1960, p. 154) puts it, 'fossilised in the capital stock'. He then explains that the 'rate at which structural change can proceed is accordingly limited by the rate of gross investment, for this determines the rate at which equipment appropriate to new industries comes into existence'. When megacorps reach the mature stage of development, fears of overcapacity lead to high susceptibility. This in turn leads to technological frugality and low rates of investment as these firms concentrate on increasing capacity utilisation and decommissioning old MOP. The infant firms in new industries, stimulated by major new exogenous innovations, are still too small and hampered by too high susceptibility for them to impact significantly on the general economic environment. The result is a strong impediment to structural change and intensified susceptibility where the investment cycle troughs are deep and the peaks are shallow. Generally this investment pattern emerged in capitalist economies during the 1970s (Period Two), with a lowering of the trend in investment growth.[1]

Ameliorating susceptibility from long-term over-accumulation requires major restructuring of management and operations. Established firms in major industries, after a long period of excess capacity, eventually recognise that the maturity of their products means that transition is imperative. This involves diversification, joint venture projects, major product innovations and, finally, the most significant: adoption of new technology systems. Rising effective demand and removal of industry protection stimulate this transition. Deregulated financial systems support transition programmes by financial leverage, in which much higher gearing ratios become acceptable. The result is risky marketing type investment strategies in competition with the new 'leading-edge' growth industries that are based on the new technology systems. In terms of Salter's analysis, this process 'de-fossilises' the capital stock and leads to significant structural change *if* that investment expansion is sustained for a long period. In this situation, however, the high level of investment is accompanied by large increasing risk, continued undesired excess capacity and highly variable profitability. All these elements work against such a sustained expansion.

Risky investment strategy is pursued in an environment of greater uncertainty. Firms find they have to 'cope' with rather than being able to 'tame' this uncertainty. This means that cycles of severe susceptibility develop, where investment booms are exacerbated by acceptance of high risks that create more uncertainty and intensified susceptibility. Once the susceptibility cycle's upper turning point has been realised by investing firms, the contraction of susceptibility is also exacerbated by the need to restructure the balance sheets of highly geared companies which have large excess capacity levels. The lower turning point of the susceptibility cycle is based on new innovation-induced competition, again within the context of structural change already broadly planned. Investment cycles of exacerbated peaks and troughs are the consequences of this susceptibility pattern. Generally this investment pattern has emerged in capitalist economies since the late 1970s (Period Three), with a flattening of trend growth but with greater fluctuation.[2]

This historically situated susceptibility cycle is best understood in terms of entrepreneurs' relative proportions between spontaneity and constraints on human action (Oakley, 1993b, pp. 12–15). The former refers to the chaotic responses of free human actions (or Keynes's 'animal spirits'), while the latter refers to the 'rules of the game' in Keynes's 'entrepreneur economy' that constrain action. In periods of strongly established technological systems and a state responsive to planning and stabilisation, relative proportions lean towards 'rules'. In periods of declining relevance of established technological systems and a state that is market-forces-oriented, relative proportions lean towards 'animal spirits'.

The susceptibility cycle model, in this re-stated form, takes the basic theoretical model and incorporates the historical structural changes that accompany various stages of firm development. Endogenously based increasing and decreasing susceptibility merges with exogenously based intensifying and ameliorating susceptibility to produce, in specific historical situations, susceptibility cycles that are subdued, pronounced or severe. In this way, historical explication has enriched purely theoretical formulation. Empirical analysis enhances the theoretical propositions, developing a closer approximation to understanding behaviour which is not directly observed.

The next two sections outline briefly the policy implications of this susceptibility cycle analysis in terms of, first, improving private investment decision-making; and secondly, introducing public policies. Possible directions for further research based on this book's analysis are presented in the final section of the chapter.

8.2 IMPROVING PRIVATE INVESTMENT DECISION-MAKING

Better methods of revising investment plans and commitments would ensure improved ability to cope with uncertainty and result in more stable susceptibility cycles. Rapid resolution of conflicts and revision of conventions require efficient evaluation of the three endogenous elements that are central to the endogenous susceptibility cycle process. This analysis alerts entrepreneurs to the nature of these three elements and the most appropriate way of handling mistakes of poorly anticipated profitability, unsustainable increasing risk and over-accumulation. Also, this analysis can help us to appreciate better the role of exogenous factors in the instability of investment, so that next time similar factors occur the entrepreneur's competence in coping with the unexpected improves. All these aspects are briefly highlighted below.

The profits-based contradictory pull mechanism (see section 5.4.1) is used to explain how the nature of profitability can affect the pattern of susceptibility cycles. Newly installed MOP add to internal funds more quickly than old MOP, improving the ability to fund larger investment orders. At the same time, greater tension occurs as larger investment commitments are adding to susceptibility at such a rate that firms slow down their investment orders, leading to more stable profit rates inherent in the large stock of old MOP. From theoretical and empirical analysis, retained earnings of old MOP as a source of investment funds has the least impact on the level of susceptibility. Reasonably stable profit rates with no external funding ensures a dampened susceptibility cycle. Jacoby and Weston (1954, p. 401) support this view that 'firm's preference for internal financing tends to stabilize investment by restraining the rate of asset expansion during upswings'. These authors were writing in the early post-war period, which reflected such moderate cycle behaviour. Entrepreneurs can 'regularise' investment cycles, by concentrating on retained earnings for funding investment.

Profitability has become more internationalised and variable as monopoly capitalists have developed global networks and alliances in less-regulated economies. Under these conditions, the profit element shows susceptibility cycles with increased amplitude. High profitability from new MOP with short payback periods in unstable conditions exacerbates susceptibility. As an inducement to invest, such a condition only provides short investment booms before the contradictory pull mechanism takes effect. Short bursts of profit growth lead to strongly fluctuating susceptibility, despite growing trend profit levels which are based on limited or no negative percentage annual changes.[3] The result is a lack of sustained investment commitments, so necessary for structural change in manufacturing. With no sustained investment expansion, the structural change needed in manufacturing in order to shift to the new technology systems is difficult to realise. While manufacturing investment continues to be unstable, structural change remains strongly inhibited.

Increasing risk involves borrower's, lender's and share issue risk. To protect itself from the risk of forced bankruptcy or loss of effective control to creditors (borrower's risk), a firm sets gearing (debt to equity) ratio limits for borrowing. Low gearing limits reflect an aversion to debt, so that share issue risk becomes the only significant external funding source of susceptibility. Early post-war studies showed that this aversion to debt tended to locate external funding tensions and consequent investment instability in share issue risk only (Jacoby and Weston, 1954, p. 389). High risk-exposure regimes lift gearing limits and produce strongly rising corporate gearing, and with it greater susceptibility cycle instability. Booming share market values overstate the asset cover available for higher gearing and also encourage increasing share issue risk. Compounding these risks is the higher proportion of cash flow devoted to the accumulation of non-physical (or speculative) assets under a high risk regime.

A deep and long period of low investment activity follows the collapse of increasing risk: first, in order that firms can restructure their balance sheets to overcome the high external funding commitments; second, so that lenders and financial investors can reduce their own level of risk by severely limiting lending and share issues while at the same time attempting to salvage as many of previous doubtful debts as possible.[4] The early 1990s' deep investment contraction represents such financial restructuring (Mills *et al.*, 1993). In the meantime, the pace of capital accumulation is so slow, with little competitive pressures to innovate, that very little structural change can be realised. A long downturn in the investment cycle for financial reconstruction is needed before physical reconstruction can be considered. Entrepreneurs can contribute to 'regularising' investment by ensuring that risk exposure is tightly controlled and unrealised speculative financial gains are not used as a basis for investment commitments.

Inherent under-estimation of excess capacity utilisation in monopoly capitalism is central to Kaleckian investment determination (see section 2.3.1). Empirical studies strongly support this 'tendency to overcapacity' position by showing that lengthy time lags on large investment commitments in capital-intensive industries combine with the slowing down of demand in a boom to increase strongly susceptibility to investment plans. This leads to a 'fear of overcapacity' in oligopoly industries as each firm's major investment decisions are known to add substantially to industry capacity, yet must also be countered with more capacity from competitors (see section 5.4.3). Competitive capacity enhancement establishes both the lower turning point and the renewed pressures in the susceptibility cycle. Without strong and reliable demand, such strategy leads to long-term over-accumulation and a heightened level of susceptibility. Entrepreneurs in 'regularising' investment need to guard against competitive pressures to over-accumulation.

The production lag, if it becomes longer than anticipated, intensifies susceptibility and may lead to downward modification of orders. A major shortening of the lag would ameliorate susceptibility. Long gestation periods by firms in mineral processing (e.g. steel and aluminium) and elaborately transformed manufactures (e.g. motor vehicles) create large overcapacity when MOP come onstream well after demand falls off. Downward modification of these large 'lumpy' current investment orders are costly and time consuming. This makes these firms highly susceptible and hesitant in future commitment of funds to long-term investment projects. Such difficulties magnify the problem of realising strong investment commitments from these firms at the trough of investment cycles.

Service industries (e.g. tourism and finance), in contrast, have much shorter time lags and can be quicker to modify investment orders in order to overcome overcapacity threats. For example, tourism was 'exceptionally rapid' in capital formation during the mid-1980s in Australia (Shann, 1989, p. 38). This is due to tourism having a large proportion of construction-type investment in relatively small 'lumps' with very little high-technology capital goods inputs. In such industries, situations of high susceptibility can be removed in short time periods, which is essential given the more income-elastic nature of their demand. These more market-responsive industries finish up having relatively more unstable investment cycles, many small business failures and much 'reinventing the wheel' by new entrants.[5]

The traverse analysis developed in section 5.5 argues that susceptibility is intensified if, when supply constraints arise, there are no 'options for shiftability'. Halevi (1983, p. 350) recognises that consumer goods producers (e.g. motor vehicles) have much greater difficulty in shifting MOP purchases than capital goods producers (e.g. steel) due to the 'lock-in' of the former to specific brand technology. This means that when there is an investment boom, delay and price effects due to supply constraints intensify susceptibility in consumer goods industries, tending to weaken investment booms and extend investment slumps. This is particularly of concern in deep investment troughs (e.g. early 1990s) and when capital goods industries such as steel and aluminium are becoming increasingly 'commodified' through product innovation (see section 7.5). Entrepreneurs can 'regularise' investment by ensuring adequate and timely supply of capital goods with strong shifting options in case of supply constraints.

The final susceptibility implications for private investment decision-making relate to innovation. The introduction of major innovations initially depends on finance for R&D and the ability to develop a cluster of successful innovations which are applicable in a particular industry.[6] Financing this process towards innovation and marketing requires patience and 'deep pockets' of funds. Sahal (1985, p. 60) notes that large oligopolistic TNCs have both these attributes, yet their attempts 'to routinize the course of research and development activity is doomed to failure'. As mature-stage firms, their technological frugality identified in the empirical studies reinforces this 'routinisation' of innovation.

Sahal (1985, p. 60) argues that small businesses (often at an infant stage) have greater creative diversity than large firms and thus are able to pursue multiple approaches to problems of innovation. Small firms borrow because they lack sufficient retained earnings or a strong equity base. Borrowing quickly increases their susceptibility and makes them highly prone to unstable investment cycles with threats of illiquidity and bankruptcies.[7] Empirical analysis supports the weak R&D position, based on large firms' failure in action and small firms' difficulty in survival. Attempts at transition to new technology systems by mature industries result in closer supporting links with smaller firms that are strongly R&D-oriented (see section 3.6). Such links aim to 'regularise' investment by ameliorating the susceptibility arising out of the respective weaknesses of both types of business organisations.

Successful introduction of major innovations through new technology systems 'make the economy less vulnerable to depression' (Schmidt, 1954, p. 342) due to the amelioration of susceptibility. The traverse to this new path of economic growth can be blocked by a sense of security among management when old MOP are used for production. This acts as a strong disincentive to introducing new techniques. Firms with relatively newer MOP, embodying better technology, suffer considerably more in increased susceptibility as investment orders increase, compared to other firms who have relatively older MOP when they start investing. This is due to Kalecki's analysis (see section 2.2) of the ability of old MOP to retain the markets (and profits) of older, more stable products and methods. The large oligopolies concentrate on what they do best, taking advantage of established stable markets and buying into research when it seems it may become a competitive threat (Sylos Labini, 1990a).

Once introduced, innovations face the further problem of developing the new labour skills needed. Case studies show that firms generally allow management and labour to develop their skills with the new equipment as they simultaneously attempt to become world competitive. This is the 'learning curve' method, which intensifies susceptibility.[8]

Fragility created by low stable custom and lack of experience leads to greater susceptibility for firms with relatively more new MOP. There is the tendency for such firms which are involved in new technology to be the first to reduce investment orders and to suffer large costs during the downturn. This reduces the impact of structural change as the most dynamic firms tend to be the most fragile and susceptible to large reductions in investment. Also, there is the lack of strategic importance to large firms of investing capital in 'intangibles' which assist the necessary technical change – R&D, skill training, management and marketing techniques. All these intangibles are not part of the corporate growth plan as are purchases of MOP, takeovers and offshore investments (BIE, 1990b, p. 28). Again, this limits severely the ability of the economy to succeed in structurally changing towards the new technology systems. Entrepreneurs need to incorporate strategies on intangibles into their efforts to introduce new technology, in order to counter 'the shock of the new' and generate a strong growth path of innovative capital accumulation with subdued investment cycles.

8.3 PUBLIC POLICIES

Three types of public policies can be used to overcome problems with business investment that have been identified by the susceptibility cycle analysis: indirect and direct policies aimed at stabilising investment cycles and encouraging innovation into the dominant techno-economic paradigm; and 'socialisation of investment'. All three policy types, if properly designed, provide guidelines and support and a macroeconomic environment conducive to subduing susceptibility cycles. This should permit confidence for innovative capital accumulation to occur. Each of the three policy types is examined below.

Indirect public policies aim to stabilise investment cycles, not by directly affecting susceptibility, but by providing macroeconomic stability through effective demand management. This stabilises the cyclical patterns of private entrepreneurs' susceptibility by mitigating the contradictory pull mechanism in all three endogenous elements. The early post-war period (Period One) of macroeconomic stability exhibited such a phase of subdued susceptibility cycles. Public policies as a whole must be steady and consistent in line with clear government objectives. Uncertain or contradictory macroeconomic policies intensify susceptibility and produce investment cycles which have deep contractions and short expansions. Such cycles were experienced in many industries during the 1970s (Period Two) as governments made dramatic macropolicy changes regularly and/or were uncertain on future directions.

Offsetting fluctuations in private investment activity by public investment is a specific indirect public policy approach advocated in Kalecki (1945, pp. 89–90). Kearney and Chowdhury (1991) show that when the long-run multiplier between public and private investment is unity, public investment can be very effective in producing upper and lower turning points for total investment cycles. Stabilising total investment would have the macroeconomic effect of inducing private investment to follow and contribute a substantial impetus in the same direction as public investment. Private investment's susceptibility cycles become more subdued as a result. In this environment, entrepreneurs are induced to support the direction(s) of the state's public investment initiatives (e.g. urban and environmental planning) and produce a high level of investment with minimal instability.

Direct public policies are aimed at altering directly private investment decisions. Industry policy has a central influence in directly affecting private investment decision-making. This is achieved by giving entrepreneurs direction as to where and how much to invest. This is done in two ways. One is by increasing relevant information, which reduces the 'fear of overcapacity' and the uncertainty of future profit returns and debt commitments. When investment orders are increasing, advice and guidelines from the state can mitigate rising susceptibility by reducing risk and uncertainty related to the endogenous elements. When investment orders are decreasing, the same information can encourage a shift in quantity and direction in investment so as to bring forward the investment upturn.

The other way in which industry policy works is by offering direct relief from susceptibility by reducing competitive threats (e.g. tariffs, quotas) or increasing financial support (e.g. bounties, tax incentives and allowances). Such policies do not increase information but reduce the costs of making investment commitments in the present (e.g. increasing net profit and reducing debt). The consequence of this is to slow down rising susceptibility or to elicit an investment turnaround into innovative areas when susceptibility is falling.

Ad hoc interventionist industry policy concentrates on direct relief on demand from industry rather than any strategic guidelines on structural change. This policy ameliorates susceptibility and stabilises investment cycles if it is implemented well. When the major industries are in the growth stage, this relief provides a very strong rate of investment. However, such stability tends to 'fossilise the capital stock' when these major firms become mature and technologically frugal. Low rates of investment result in these industries, while the infant industries do not have the political or economic power to gain industrial policy support in order to break into a growth phase with a high rate of investment. Stable investment cycles with limited investment growth for structural change results.

Since the early 1980s, diffusion of the new electronic-based information technology paradigm throughout world capitalism has made structural change essential (Freeman and Perez, 1988, pp. 60–2). It has induced a switch to the deregulatory industrial policy approach in many capitalist economies after the stagnation of the 1970s' during which the *ad hoc* interventionist approach had 'fossilised the capital stock'.

The deregulatory approach is based on fostering a responsive private investment strategy which enables a restructuring away from regulated and protected mature industries towards higher value-added growth industries. This strategy is dependent on the neoclassical view of investment, in which firms calculate rates of return from costs of capital (see section 1.3). The concentration is on the efficient flow of market information to provide the guidelines on rates of return, while removing interventionist public policies that distort this market information and intensify susceptibility. Once removal of interventionist industrial policies creates 'a level playing field', then investment no longer flows to high-cost inefficient mature industries but, instead, to efficient information technology export-based growth industries.

The analysis in this book argues that if deregulatory industrial policy succeeds along neoclassical lines, susceptibility becomes severe as firms attempt to cope with the new risky investment strategies. The deregulatory approach increases uncertainty in all three endogenous elements, adding to the already severe susceptibility. Further enhancement of susceptibility occurs during the implementation of investment projects if there is high capital import dependence, long time lags in the realisation of high-technology commitments, and a lack of access to the best technical processes.

When deregulation heightens susceptibility, there is a tendency for funds to move into areas seen as less susceptible to long-run risk and uncertainty. Concentration is on short-run risk with reduced levels of uncertainty. This involves using the new information technology to reduce short-run risk in speculative ventures, or taking short-run high returns in commodity-based booms. Neither strategy produces outcomes intended by deregulation. Instead, both strategies generate an investment pattern of long contractions with acute short booms based on quick returns.[9] A low long-run trend rate of gross investment results. Such a pattern of investment strongly limits structural change in the economy.[10]

Agents' susceptibility as it relates to investment exists as long as the future remains uncertain. Unstable investment with short booms results from a high level of susceptibility. Amelioration of this high level by strategic government industry policies can provide a more stable investment pattern at an overall higher level of gross investment. Such a pattern yields a flexible structure of production so necessary for developing a more export-oriented economy. A flexible structure of production, as Salter (1960, p. 154) notes, requires a high level of gross investment over a long period in order that large, time-consuming investment projects can be realised. This includes having an efficient capital-goods-producing sector that can quickly meet the requirements of these investment projects. All capitalist economies which are successful at exporting depend on certain crucial socio-political institutions and regulations to ameliorate susceptibility down to a level which can provide a high and stable gross investment over reasonably long periods (Department of Trade, 1987; Fitzgerald, 1990).

More than market information is needed. Direct public policies in the form of indicative government planning of business investment (involving both information-cum-guidelines and direct relief) to match corporate investment planning is essential for ameliorating susceptibility and alerting entrepreneurial minds to export orientation. Kalecki, in many articles on economic planning, argued for a transformation of organisations to provide a perspective planning approach. This involves a long planning horizon of 15 to 20 years within which medium-term investment plans of five years are altered as developments change the overall perspective. A combination of grass-roots workers' councils and central planning would yield the new social project (Kalecki, 1986). Applying this to market economies requires entrepreneurs in megacorps to continue correcting for disequilibrium by quantity, not price, adjustments in order to ameliorate susceptibility. The adjustments in this case would be based on socially determined guidelines. How to ensure that such guidelines are met by globally based megacorps which operate outside national jurisdictions would be an enormous challenge.

A restructuring of the process of investment planning, by incorporating a diverse social milieu in participatory mechanisms, is necessary to achieve an export-oriented restructured economy with a much less susceptible investment programme for entrepreneurs. Such a managed (or strategically planned) approach to industry policy aims to develop a flexible structure of production in stages, as the perspective of past developments is taken into account in the state planning guidelines. This would incorporate a planned integrated method to develop skills in all the areas of best practice that can be adopted in market economies, introducing technical change in a co-ordinated fashion only after skills are learnt.

Tax concessions and reduced profit tax liability to encourage firms to undertake investment are specific direct policy measures used regularly by governments to stimulate investment out of a trough. They may be part of broader industrial policy or simply anti-cyclical macroeconomic policy. Such measures directly influence the profits element of susceptibility cycle analysis. Improved profits increase the ability to invest only if these concessions are not used to reduce an unsustainable gearing ratio. Improved profits do not enhance the expectational aspect of the profits element, which depends strongly on effective demand for the firm's output. Further, over-accumulation in a trough sustains susceptibility at a level which is a strong impediment to large investment expansion, regardless of the profits element. Empirical studies have shown that such measures have very limited value, and are only useful at the margin when the other two elements are not in a highly susceptible position (Courvisanos, 1994b; see also Higgins, 1954; McIntyre and Tipps, 1985).

The third type of public policy is 'a somewhat comprehensive socialisation of investment' (Keynes, 1936, p. 378). Keynes argues that this proposal should only be implemented if the other two policy types do not succeed because 'the long-run behaviour of businessmen proved intractable and irresponsible in the face of government attempts to achieve different objectives' (McFarlane, 1982, p. 84). This impels the state to organise investment directly by calculating 'the marginal efficiency of capital-goods on long views and on the basis of the general social advantage' (Keynes, 1936, p. 164). Kalecki concentrated much of his latter years' research on how the state could technically accomplish this.[11] He regarded central planning of investment as having 'the biggest role to play in delineating the economic patterns to be pursued' (McFarlane, 1971, p. 104).

In essence, state organisation of investment would aim to prevent over-accumulation and financial leverage. This should strongly ameliorate endogenously based susceptibility, but not overcome instability from exogenous factors. Whereas Keynes believed that such planning could be done by the state as an impartial 'referee', Kalecki saw the capitalist state's priority as protecting capitalist interests through the political business cycle, which would exacerbate the endogenous susceptibility elements. For this reason Kalecki's central planning of investment is conducted under a broad perspective plan within a socialist political structure. This structure is based on new democratic participatory mechanisms which help to develop investment plans based on rules of feasibility given available resources and technology.[12]

8.4 WHERE DO WE GO FROM HERE?

Five suggested paths of further research are nominated below. The first is in the econometrics field. A formal simulation model describing the susceptibility cycle analysis could be developed by the use of non-linear dynamics in the form of Goodwin's repellers, attractors and stochastic (exogenous) shocks on investment (see section 2.7).[13] Further econometrics could involve vector autoregression (VAR) analysis for policy response questions (see Kearney, 1990). By constructing impulse response functions based on regressions of investment expenditure, the behaviour of a system prior to, and after, the implementation of a specific type of industry policy can be compared.

Secondly, further detailed research on explanation-building chronological case studies is needed. Industries studied over long time periods (including the 1991–2 deep recession) in many different capitalist economies can generalise the manufacturing-based susceptibility cycle model by further re-statements. Studies are especially needed in the growing information-technology and human services industries. Patterns of investment instability, and behind them firms' motivations, in these further industry studies can then be used for more insightful pattern-matching of explanations. Then, cross-country comparisons of specific sectors and industries between capitalist economies would show how different institutional frameworks impact on the analysis.

Thirdly, a deeper behavioural examination of the corporate imagination (*à la* Shackle and Simon) can be made with the help of the susceptibility cycle analysis as a framework. Qualitative survey analysis of the type conducted by Bromiley (1986) can help to explain how entrepreneurs feel about their investment commitments and the mistakes that they make. Such in-depth qualitative surveys could supplement the case study approach by providing a more complete motivational picture of investment decision-making at the firm level and its implications for the instability of the industry. Such research could enable business to plan its own investment strategies better and, by so doing, reduce susceptibility and stabilise the investment cycle at a high growth trend. The answers for business will probably differ depending on the sorts of investments, business activities and circumstances involved. Research must be able to identify these differences before it can be applied.

Fourthly, the susceptibility cycle model is the starting point for conducting 'instrumental analysis' (*à la* Lowe). This study supports Lowe's premise that, despite research alluded to in the above paragraph on the mistake-ridden private sector, there is not sufficient order and coherence in monopoly capitalism. This book derives links from the motivational and structural patterns of firms' investment orders (the traverse) which explain that businesses are not able to stabilise investment and remain flexible enough to restructure effectively in terms of new-technology systems. The first step in Lowe's instrumental analysis is the traverse, which this book examines in terms of instability. The second step is to develop direct controls.[14] These controls, based on an understanding of human agency, would seek the co-operation of entrepreneurs and other agents (e.g. workers and rentiers) to alter investment behaviour towards a more stable, but dynamic, path of diffusion of new technology systems which would expedite reaching generally accepted economic goals. Such goals could be set up through the Kaleckian perspective planning approach.

Finally and most importantly, research needs to be conducted on the sociology of corporate behaviour and its implications for investment. This is the 'raw material' of all the previous research paths. Study of investment behaviour requires proper development, from first principles, of ethological theory in entrepreneurial decision-making processes. Ethology is 'the science of the situational determination of the developing character and conduct of human agents' (Oakley, 1993a, p. 30). The susceptibility cycle analysis began as an explanation of observed aggregate investment instability. In the conduct of this study, it was necessary to delve into the perceptions and expectations of entrepreneurs who make these decisions. However, the study only went as far as explaining instability; there is still much more study needed on understanding the basic moral and situational conditions that influence the interaction between the character and conduct of investment decision-making by entrepreneurs.

The above list of possible projects stemming from the concept of susceptibility indicates the breadth and depth of research that is still required. The approach in this book of building a behavioural base to an existing, more abstract Kaleckian analysis is only at the beginning of a new path for economics. Other economists are also on this same path, as exemplified in Pheby (1989). This type of research will give economics a more holistic approach to understanding the human behaviour of commerce. The result should be a more effective force for policy action, taking account of the interaction between the social, moral and economic climate.

NOTES

1. For Australia, see Figure 7.1 in previous chapter; and for more details, see Courvisanos (1994a, pp. 250–62). For Germany, see Hillinger and Sebold-Bender (1992, pp. 76–7). For US, see Hillinger and Reiter (1992, pp. 129–30).
2.   For statistical evidence, see references in note 1 above.
3. This is supported by statistical evidence produced by Hillinger *et al.* (1992) that shows that investment cycle behaviour 'is more pronounced if firms discount the future strongly (short foresight), whereas longer foresight attenuates cyclical behaviour' (p. 179).
4. After the 'credit binge' of the 1980s, all banks are required to meet new, tighter international capital adequacy regulations which reduce the capital base, make fewer loans available and increase bank margins (Walsh, 1991a). Significantly, at that time, when banks needed to concentrate on this balance sheet rectitude and there was reluctance to examine new investment potential, Australian banks were forced to take control of vast areas in retail, media, food processing, construction, resources, and textiles either through 'receiverships or involved in work-out situations where the banks have effective veto power' (Walsh, 1991a). There is no way in which major strategic investment plans can be developed under such circumstances.
5. Early post-war evidence in the US shows that 'there is a much wider fluctuation of capital investment among small than among large organisations' (Boatwright, 1954, pp. 109–10). The susceptibility-based analysis presented in the text explains, in behavioural terms, why this differential exists.
6. For example, changing over to a solar-based car or an all-aluminium recyclable car depends on a 'log jam' of innovations all practical in their implementation. One innovation on its own is not worth the automotive or the aluminium industry's effort to fit it into an existing structure.
7. Still based on survival, there is some evidence that smaller firms tend to sacrifice their R&D staff and facilities to current sales development in boom times, while deferring commercial exploitation in the face of weakening markets. This further exacerbates the small firms' procyclical impact on investment cycles (see Schmidt, 1954, pp. 342–3).
8. This method was also adopted by the banks when they were deregulated and massive new information technology was introduced. It was an approach which continued for a decade, with consequences of massive speculative investments followed by bad debts, high profit margins and risk-averse policies towards high-technology investments (Reinecke, 1988, p. 191; Light *et al.*, 1991).

9. See note 3 above for reference to supporting statistical evidence. It reinforces the argument that only longer-run perspectives ameliorate the amplitude of susceptibility cycles.

10. To argue, as Brian Loton (Chairman of BHP) does, that an accelerated pace of deregulation will lead to an accelerated pace of structural change (Ellis, 1991) is not to appreciate the uncertainty in investment planning that such acceleration brings about. As well as the implementation problems of importing capital, time delays and access to the needed technology all intensify susceptibility.

11. See many of the articles in Kalecki (1972b and 1986). In section 2.6, two of Kalecki's articles in this area of research are discussed. Kalecki (1963) sets out the structure of investment in terms of decision-making with constraints from the capital-goods-producing industries. Kalecki (1957) concentrates on problems in the construction period of investment. Nuti (1986) provides an excellent modern reinterpretation of Kalecki's theory and practice of planning with social control of investment as its central focus. US commentator Alexander Cockburn revives this approach in a 1991 issue of *New Statesman*: 'the Left has to argue a case it has virtually let go by default for 20 years: the social control of investment, the "socialisation" of the market, in which democratic investment planning represents the popular will, as against the corporate drive for profitability' (as quoted by Walsh, 1991b). Cockburn believes that this new socialism should be based around the ecological concerns of the public, or what he calls eco-socialism.

12. Kalecki's approach is not the soviet-style command planning. In fact, Kalecki was a trenchant critic of 'planners overstepping the limits of people's forebearance in their trading off of current for future consumption, [and] . . . the (related) limits of the planners' own ability to deliver the consumption goods promised' (Nuti, 1986, p. 341).

13. Correspondence from Peter Earl suggests setting up on a computer a multisector model, with a limited number of firms in each sector and probabilities of succumbing to shocks, to chart investment cycles and the three endogenous elements through time in a way which would also demonstrate the nature of the traverse. By use of a lottery system to see which firms would succumb if the probabilities were right, it would also be possible to explore the path-dependent nature of the overall development of the system, with different combinations of spillover impacts and traverse paths arising according to which numbers came up in each simulation round.

14. Lowe calls these 'secondary controls', which are 'dynamic controls that operate more directly on motivations and consequent market behaviours' (Oakley, 1987, p. 18). Such controls are successful only if expectations are constrained by the generally accepted choice of macro-goals. Micro-goals and action directives consistent with the macro-goals would reduce business uncertainty and susceptibility of investment, enabling efficient dynamic economic development. Richardson (1960), on investment co-ordination by information agreements and industrial concentration, would assist such micro-goals in policy-oriented research.

Appendix: Case Study Summaries of Three Australian Manufacturing Industries

Table A.1: Cross-case industry conclusions on Period One (1945–70)

	Motor vehicle	Steel	Aluminium
Competition type	Strong intra-industry, product based	Strong inter-industry from aluminium and copper – homogeneous commodity	Strong inter-industry based on new products
Investment strategy	Conservative financial	Conservative financial	Risky marketing (of local partners) vs. conservative financial (of majors)
Expansion: contraction (yrs) for 1944–5 to 1969–70	17:8	17:8	10:6 (for 1953–4 to 1969–70)
Investment cycle peaks (P)	1952–3 1956–7 1959–60 1964–5	1948–9 1956–7 1961–2 1967–8	Non-ferrous cycles 1955–6 1963–4 1966–7
Contribution to trough (%) (real terms)	12.5 25 25 40	14 40 30 56	37 64 75
Period of contraction to trough (yrs)	2 2 2 2	1 1 2 1	3 1 1
Real increase from peak to peak (%)	P 89 P -19 P 87 P 29	P 195 P 53 P 19 P	P 288 P 233 P
Susceptibility cycles	Subdued	Subdued	Pronounced
Time lags	Short ent. reaction/long and variable production	Long ent. reaction/relatively short and variable production	Long and variable ent. reaction/stable, relatively short production

	GM-H	BHP	Alcoa
Profits	GM-H av. return assets 1948–70: 14.6% high retained earnings	BHP av. net profit as prop. of share equity 1954–70: 8% Low retained earnings	Alcoa (Aust.) small losses 1961–6. Average return on assets 1967–70: 2.8% virtually no retained earnings available
Increasing risk	Low gearing ratios (except Chrysler), cheap loans and no equity raising	Low average gearing ratio 1954–70: 0.15 Funds: internal 1940s, shares 1950s, debt 1960s.	Lack of domestic finance, reliance of parent Alcoa for borrowings Joint ventures to reduce risk
Capacity utilisation	Very high, due to 'over demand'	1946–55: Severe excess capacity 1956–70: Limited excess capacity (often 'over-full' capacity)	Low, due to 'over-investment' strategy
Exogenous innovation	Cheap energy-based product basically unchanged War-induced minor modifications in process innovation	War-induced modification in process innovation Only one new major process innovation (BOS)	Public sector innovation • discoveries of bauxite • R&D on processing to alumina
Endogenous innovation	Product innovation regular from parent company Regular model cycles with minor process innovation (cycle length reduced from 5 to 1.25 years)	Lack of product innovation Technological frugality (R&D imported on contract).	Slow and incremental process innovation up to ingot stage (investment-induced) Strong inter-industry competitive product innovation: aluminium products
Government intervention	1. Cheap loans to GM-H (1940s) 2. Import restrictions and tariffs (1950s) 3. Local content plans (1960s) 4. Road and urban development	Tariffs and import restrictions Public infrastructure (ports, housing)	Public infrastructure (ports, housing power, access to mining areas) Pressure to establish refineries and smelters in return for mining leases
Source (from Courvisanos, 1994b)	Appendix A (Section A.3)	Appendix B (Section B.3)	Appendix C (Section C.3)

Table A.2 Cross-case industry conclusions on Period Two (1971–80)

	Motor vehicle	Steel	Aluminium
Competition type	Continued strong intra-industry, product based	Weaker inter-industry; rise of low cost mini-mill producers	Rise of independent and state-sponsored primary producers
Investment strategy	Conservative financial: 'world Sourcing'	Conservative financial	Conservative financial: joint ventures
Expansion: contraction (yrs) for 1969–70 to 1979–80	6:4	5:5	6:4
Investment cycle peaks (P)	From previous period 1971–2 (P) 23 1978–9	From previous period 1972–3 (small rise 1974–5) (1981–2)	From previous period 1971–2 (small rise 1975–6) (1981–2)
Contribution to trough (%) (real terms)	32 60	71	92
Period of contraction to trough (yrs)	4 2	7	5
Real increase from peak to peak (%)	29 P 23 P	17 P -27 P	7 P 164 P
Susceptibility cycles	Pronounced: excess capacity	Pronounced: excess capacity	Pronounced: world excess capacity
Time lags	Short ent. reaction/long and variable production	Extra long ent. reaction with large capital stock replacement decisions	Long and variable ent. reaction/short production

Profits	GM-H av. return assets 1971–9: 2.5% Ford av. return on assets 1971–9: 4.1%. Low retained earnings	BHP av. net profit as prop. of share equity FAVA 1971–80: 6% NON-FAVA 1974–80: 10.8%	Alcoa (Aust.) av. return on assets 1971–80: 5.1% Late 1970s: 50% of net profits as retained earnings
Increasing risk	Low (or nil) gearing ratios (except Chrysler)	BHP av. gearing ratio 1971–80: 0.22 Very low debt structure, rising strongly to 1977	Alcoa (Aust) Av. gearing ratios 1972–80: 0.53. Reliance on bank loans and equity issues. Significantly reduced 1977 to 1979.
Capacity utilisation	Serious excess capacity via marketing strategy of fragmentation, capacity investment and import growth	Overaccumulation, serious after strong 1960s expansion. BHP av. cap. util. rate 1971–80: 85.6%	Significant world excess capacity until late 1970s Alcoa (Aust.) av. cap. util. rate 1974–80: 86.6%
Exogenous innovation	Very limited product innovation Concentrate on cost-saving process innovation Emphasis on small cars	High energy cost; minor energy-based process innovations Minimal R&D, mini-steel mill development	High energy costs: restructuring location of smelting Weak R&D innovation
Endogenous innovation	Longer model cycles Fragmented production process — world sourcing of cost-saving	Diversification away from steel by BHP Minor process innovation: less-polluting better steel grade	Limited to making quick construction operations and process innovations to reduce energy costs
Government intervention	Uncertainty over industry plans Incentives for local 4-cylinder manufacture	Tariffs continued from period one Shift to resource boom infrastructure support and tax incentives in late 1970s	Dramatic change in policy in early 1970s • control foreign investment in resources • reduce tax concessions • national resources authority Late 1970s: return to period one policy
Source (from Courvisanos,1994b)	Appendix A (Section A.4)	Appendix B (Section B.4)	Appendix C (Section C.4)

Table A.3 Cross-case industry conclusions on Period Three (1981–92)

	Motor vehicle				Steel				Aluminium			
Competition type	Continued strong product-based, but with process-based co-operation				Rise of intra-industry, with BHP tightening its vertical integration (counter strategy)				Strong commodity based price variable structure, weakening of oligopoly			
Investment strategy	Conservative financial: equity link supply arrangements				Risky marketing: mini-mills and export orientation (technology based)				Risky marketing: low-cost commodity based export orientation			
Expansion: contraction (yrs) from 1979–80 to 1991–2	8:4				7:5				Non-ferrous cycles 4:4 (for 1979–80–87–8)	Alcoa (Aust.) cycles 3:9		
Investment cycle peaks (P)	1981–2	1987–8	1990–1		1981–2	1986–7	1990–1		1982–3	1981	1985	1991
Contribution to trough (%) (real terms)	48	42	?		78	48	?		82	85	55	?
Period of contraction to trough (yrs)	2	1	?		2	2	?		4	3	5	?
Real increase from peak to peak (%)	0.33 P	121 P	4.5 P	? P	-27 P	42 P	-11 P		161 P	-60 P	8 P	P
Susceptibility cycles	Pronounced: high gearing				Severe: high gearing				Severe (for Aust.); excess capacity and high gearing			
Time lags	Lengthening ent. reaction/shortening production				Long ent. reaction/lengthening production (commissioning problems)				Lengthening ent. reaction with increased uncertainty/short production			

Profits	GM-H average return on assets 1980–92: -2.4% Ford average return on assets 1980–92: 5.3% Losses suffered by all five producers during 1980s	BHP average net profit as prop. of share equity 1981–92: 11.7% Retained earnings approximately 50% of net profits.	Alcoa (Aust.) average return on share funds 1981–92: 15.8% Av. retained earnings by Alcoa (Aust.): 30% of net profits Alcan (Aust.) average return on share funds 1981–92:4.0%
Increasing risk	Early 1980s rising gearing (GM-H: 0.59 in 1983) Shift to high short term gearing in late 1980s Liquidity constraints at US parent companies	BHP average gearing ratio 1981–92: 0.29 Strongly rising debt structure from 1986 to peak in 1989 (0.47) – Bell takeover attempt.	Alcoa (Aust) Average gearing ratio 1981–92: 0.27 1980–7: 0.37 Alcan average gearing ratio 1981–92: 0.41: Reliance on 'money market' borrowings and joint ventures
Capacity utilisation	Around 50% excess capacity throughout period, serious weakness in market demand. Plant closures and 'rationalisation' of production facilities	Early 1980s extreme overcapacity due to 'illusory' resources boom – massive decommissioning of capacity in mid-1980s BHP average capacity util. rate 1981–92: 88.4%	Capacity shortage of concern: 1979–81 World overcapacity in mid-80s and early 1990s, as inventories built up (most Australian plants near full capacity, exceptions e.g. Alcan 1982:71%, 1st half 1983: 60%)
Exogenous innovation	Lean production process with regional network strategies (EEC, US, Asia) Model-sharing by strategic alliances	Efficiency based process innovation Computer-based continuous casting and direct reduction smelting	Strong product innovation and product differentiation upstream to alumina Failure of process innovation
Endogenous innovation	Minimum R&D: reduction 'in-house' R&D and componentary Very long basic model cycles and model range reductions	Product innovation in coated products and licensing at steel processing technology (export oriented strategy)	Minor process innovation from o/s parents: allowing smelters and refineries to run well below full utilisation with efficient energy use Low R&D intensity

241

Table A.3 continued

	Motor Vehicle	Steel	Aluminium
Government intervention	1979—83: indecision on industry policy 1984—92: Button Plan — rationalisation of plants and models, with reduced tariffs. Post-1988: market-based strategy with less planning	1979–83: Infrastructure and tax support (*ad hoc* policies with resources boom) 1984–9: Steel Plan – support for rationalisation of capacity and efficiency investment Post-1989: market-based (free trade) approach.	1979–83: Infrastructure and tax support (*ad hoc* policies with resources boom) 1984–9: Steel Plan – support for rationalisation of capacity and efficiency investment Post-1989: market-based (free trade) approach.
Source (from Courvisanos, 1994b)	Appendix A (Section A.5)	Appendix B (Section B.5)	Appendix C (Section C.5)

Bibliography

ABA (Australian Banker's Association) (1990), *Submission to the Parliamentary Inquiry into the Banking Industry*, Melbourne, December.

AIA (Automotive Industry Authority) (1990), *Report on the State of the Automotive Industry 1989*, Canberra: Australian Government Publishing Service, May.

Almon, S. (1968), 'Lags Between Investment Decisions and their Causes', *Review of Economics and Statistics*, **50**, May, 193–206.

Andrews, P.W.S. (1949), *Manufacturing Business*, London: Macmillan.

Andrews, P.W.S. and Brunner, E. (1951), *Capital Development in Iron and Steel*, Oxford: Basil Blackwell.

Angell, J.W. (1941), *Investment and Business Cycles*, New York: McGraw-Hill.

Ansoff, H.I. (1979), *Strategic Management*, London: Macmillan.

Arestis, P., Driver, C. and Rooney, J. (1985–6), 'The Real Segment of a UK post Keynesian Model', *Journal of Post Keynesian Economics*, **8** (2), Winter, 163–81.

Asimakopulos, A. (1975), 'A Kaleckian Theory of Income Distribution', *Canadian Journal of Economics*, **8** (3), 313–33.

Asimakopulos, A. (1977), 'Profits and Investment: a Kaleckian Approach', in G.C. Harcourt (ed.), *The Microeconomic Foundations of Macroeconomics*, Boulder, Col.: Westview Press; London: Macmillan, 328–42. Discussion of Paper 343–53.

Asimakopulos, A. (1983), 'Kalecki and Keynes on Finance, Investment and Saving', *Cambridge Journal of Economics*, **7** (3/4), September/December, 221–33.

Aubin, T. (1990), 'Rise in Elderly a Factor in Privatisation', *The Australian*, 20 July, 2.

Baran, P. and Sweezy, P. (1968), *Monopoly Capital*, Harmondsworth, Middx: Penguin. First US edition, Monthly Review Press, 1966.

Beresford, M. and McFarlane, B.J. (1980), 'Economic Theory as Ideology: a Kaleckian Analysis of the Australian Economic Crisis', in P. Boreham and

G. Dow (eds), *Work and Inequality*, Volume 1, South Melbourne: Macmillan, 215–234.

Bhaduri, A. (1986), *Macroeconomics: The Dynamics of Commodity Production*, London: Macmillan.

Bhaduri, A. and Steindl, J. (1983), 'The Rise of Monetarism as a Social Doctrine', *Thames Papers in Political Economy*, Autumn, 1–18.

Biasco, S. (1987), 'Currency Cycles and the International Economy', *Banca Nazionale del Lavoro Quarterly Review*, **160**, March, 31–60.

BIE (Bureau of Industry Economics) (1990a), *Manufacturing Investment*, Research Report No. 33, Canberra: Australian Government Publishing Service, February.

BIE (1990b), *Manufacturing Enterprises Investment and Other Strategies for Growth*, Discussion Paper No. 8, Canberra: Australian Government Publishing Service, May.

Bischoff, C.W. (1971), 'Business Investment in the 1970s: a Comparison of Models', *Brookings Papers on Economic Activity*, (1), 13–58.

Bloch, H. (1990), 'Price Leadership and the Degree of Monopoly', *Journal of Post Keynesian Economics*, **12** (3), Spring, 439–51.

Bloch, H. (1991), 'The Impact of World Manufacturing Growth on Australia's Trading Position', *International Review of Applied Economics*, **5** (1), 100–15.

Boatwright, J.W. (1954), 'Comment' on De Chazeau paper, in National Bureau of Economic Research, *Regularization of Business Investment*, Princeton, N.J.: Princeton University Press, 109–12.

Boswell, J. (1983), *Business Policies in the Making: Three Steel Companies Compared*, London/Boston: George Allen & Unwin.

Boulding, K.E. (1981), *Evolutionary Economics*, Beverly Hills/London: Sage.

Boyd, I. and Blatt, J.M. (1988), *Investment Confidence and Business Cycles*, Berlin: Springer-Verlag.

Brailovsky, V. (1989), 'The Macroeconomic Implications of Paying: Policy Responses to the Debt "Crisis" in Mexico, 1982–88', *Political Economy: Studies in the Surplus Approach*, **5** (1), 37–58.

Bromiley, P. (1986), *Corporate Capital Investment: A Behavioral Approach*, Cambridge: Cambridge University Press.

Burkett, P. and Wohar, M. (1987), 'Keynes on Investment and the Business Cycle', *Review of Radical Political Economics*, **19** (4), 39–54.

Caldwell, B.J. (1989), 'Post-Keynesian Methodology: An Assessment', *Review of Political Economy*, **1** (1), 43–64.

Carmichael, J. and Dews, N. (1987), *The Role and Consequences of Investment in the Recent Australian Economic Growth*, Reserve Bank of Australia Research Discussion Paper No. 8704, Sydney, April.

Carroll, V.J. (1990), 'Rambo Banks', *The Independent Monthly*, May, 12–15.

Carvalho, F. (1988), 'Keynes on Probability, Uncertainty, and Decision Making', *Journal of Post Keynesian Economics*, **11** (1), Fall, 66–81.

Casson, M. (1990), *Enterprise and Competitiveness: A Systems View of International Business*, Oxford: Clarendon Press.

Catley, R. and McFarlane, B.J. (1981), *Australian Capitalism in Boom and Depression*, Chippendale: Alternative Publishing Cooperative.

Caves, R.E. (1984), 'Scale, Openness and Productivity in Manufacturing Industries', in R.E. Caves and L.B. Krause (eds), *The Australian Economy: A View From the North*, Sydney: Allen & Unwin.

Caves, R.E., Ward, I., Williams, P. and Wright, C. (1987), *Australian Industry: Structure, Conduct, Performance*, 2nd edn, Sydney, Prentice-Hall, Australia.

Chamberlain, T.W. and Gordon, M.J. (1989), 'Liquidity, Profitability, and Long-run Survival: Theory and Evidence on Business Investment', *Journal of Post Keynesian Economics*, **11** (4), Summer, 589–610.

Chandler, A.D. (1962), *Strategy and Structure*, Cambridge, Mass.: MIT Press.

Chapman, K. and Humphrys, G. (eds) (1987), *Technical Change and Industrial Policy*, Oxford: Basil Blackwell.

Charles, D.R. (1987), 'Technical Change and the Decentralized Corporation in the Electronics Industry: Regional Policy Implications', in Chapman and Humphrys (eds) (1987), 176–98.

Chenery, H.B. (1952), 'Overcapacity and the Acceleration Principle', *Econometrica*, **20**, January, 1–28.

Chilosi, A. (1982), 'Breit, Kalecki and Hicks on the Term Structure of Interest Rates and the Theory of Investment', in M. Baranzini (ed.), *Advances in Economic Theory*, Oxford: Basil Blackwell, 80–9.

Clark, C. and Tabah, L. (1982), 'The Decline of World Fertility', *Quadrant*, **26**, June, 39–43.

Clark, P.K. (1979), 'Investment in the 1970s: Theory, Performance, and Prediction', *Brookings Papers on Economic Activity*, (1), 73–113.

Commonwealth of Australia (1993), *Budget Statements 1992–93*, Budget Paper No. 1, Canberra: Australian Government Publishing Service, August.

Coombs, R., Saviotti, P. and Walsh, V. (1987), *Economics and Technological Change*, London: Macmillan.

Cornwall, J. (1990), *The Theory of Economic Breakdown*, Cambridge, Mass.: Basil Blackwell.

Courvisanos, J. (1994a), *A Kaleckian Behavioural Theory of Investment Cycles,* Vol. 1, PhD dissertation, Department of Economics, University of Newcastle, N.S.W., Australia.

Courvisanos, J. (1994b), *A Kaleckian Behavioural Theory of Investment Cycles,* Vol. 2, PhD dissertation, Department of Economics, University of Newcastle, N.S.W., Australia.

Cowling, K. (1982), *Monopoly Capitalism*, London: Macmillan.

Crotty, J.R. (1990), 'Owner-Manager Conflict and Financial Theories of Investment Instability: a Critical Assessment of Keynes, Tobin and Minsky', *Journal of Post Keynesian Economics*, **12** (4), Summer, 519–542.

Crotty, J.R. (1992), 'Neoclassical and Keynesian Approaches to the Theory of Investment', *Journal of Post Keynesian Economics*, **14** (4), Summer, 483–96.

Cubbin, J. and Leech, D. (1983), 'The Effects of Shareholding Dispersion on the Degree of Control in British Companies: Theory and Measurement', *Economic Journal*, **93** (370), June, 351–69.

Cyert, R.M. and March, J.G. (1963), *A Behavioral Theory of the Firm*, Englewood Cliffs, N.J.: Prentice-Hall.

Daly, H.E. (1977), *Steady-State Economics*, San Francisco, Cal.: W.H. Freeman.

Deiaco, E., Hörnell, E. and Vickery, G. (eds) (1990), *Technology and Investment: Crucial Issues for the 1990s*, London: Pinter.

Del Monte, G. (1981), 'Review of MOSYL, 1967 to 1981', *Review of Economic Conditions in Italy*, (2), June, 323–8.

Demesetz, H. (1982), 'Barriers to Entry', *American Economic Review*, **72** (1), March, 47–57.

Department of Trade (1987), *Australia Reconstructed*, Canberra: Australian Government Publishing Service, July.

Dertouzos, M.L., Lester, R.K., Solow, R.M. and MIT Commission on Industrial Productivity (1989), *Made in America: Regaining the Productive Edge*, Cambridge, Mass.: MIT Press.

Dixon, R. (1986), 'Uncertainty, Unobstructedness, and Power', *Journal of Post Keynesian Economics*, **8** (4), Summer, 585–90.

Domberger, S. (1979), 'Price Adjustment and Market Structure', *Economic Journal*, **89**, March, 96–108.

Dornbusch, R. and Fischer, S. (1984), *Macroeconomics*, 3rd edn, New York: McGraw-Hill.

Dosi, G. (1982), 'Technological Paradigms and Technological Trajectories: a Suggested Interpretation of the Determinants and Directions of Technical Change', *Research Policy*, **2** (3), June, 147–62.

Dosi, G. (1988a), 'The Nature of the Innovative Process', in Dosi *et al.* (eds) (1988), 221–38.

Dosi, G. (1988b), 'Sources, Procedures, and Microeconomic Effects of Innovation', *Journal of Economic Literature*, **XXVI**, September, 1120–71.

Dosi, G. and Chiaromonte, F. (1990), 'The Microfoundations of Competitiveness and their Macroeconomic Implications', presented at the OECD Conference on Technology and Competitiveness, 24–27 June.

Dosi, G., Freeman, C., Nelson, R., Silverberg, G. and Soete, L. (eds) (1988), *Technical Change and Economic Theory*, London: Pinter.

Dougherty, C. (1980), *Interest and Profit*, London: Methuen.

Duesenberry, J.S. (1967), *Income, Saving and the Theory of Consumer Behaviour*, Oxford: Oxford University Press.

Dunkley, G. and Kulkarni, A. (1990), 'Structural Change and Industry Policy in Australia', *Regional Journal of Social Issues*, (24), 19–32.

Dunning, J.H. (ed.) (1985), *Multinational Enterprises, Economic Structure and International Competitiveness*, Chichester, Sussex: John Wiley.

Dyster, B. and Meredith, D. (1990), *Australia in the International Economy in the Twentieth Century*, Melbourne: Cambridge University Press.

Earl, P.E. (1983), 'A Behavioral Theory of Economists' Behavior', in A.S. Eichner (ed.), *Why Economics is Not Yet a Science*, London: Macmillan; Armonk, N.Y.: M.E. Sharpe, 90–125.

Earl, P.E. (1984), *The Corporate Imagination: How Big Companies Make Mistakes*, Brighton, Sussex: Wheatsheaf; Armonk; N.Y.: M.E. Sharpe.

Earl, P.E. (1988), 'Introduction', in P.E. Earl (ed.), *Behavioural Economics*, Vol. 2, Aldershot, Hants: Edward Elgar, 1–16.

Earl, P.E. (1992), 'The Evolution of Cooperative Strategies: Three Automotive Industry Case Studies', *Human Systems Management*, **11**, 89–100.

Earl, P.E. and Kay, N.M. (1985), 'How Economists Can Accept Shackle's Critique of Economic Doctrines Without Arguing Themselves Out of Their Jobs', *Journal of Economic Studies*, **12** (1/2), 34–48.

Eckard, E.W. (1982), 'Firm Market Share, Price Flexibility, and Imperfect Information', *Economic Inquiry*, **20**, July, 388–92.

Eichner, A.S. (1976), *The Megacorp and Oligopoly*, Cambridge: Cambridge University Press (reissued Armonk, N.Y.: M.E. Sharpe, 1980).

Eichner, A.S. (1987), *The Macrodynamics of Advanced Market Economies*, Armonk, N.Y.: M.E. Sharpe.

Eisner, R. (1978), *Factors in Business Investment*, Cambridge, Mass.: Ballinger.

Eisner, R. and Strotz, R.H. (1963), 'Determinants of Business Investment', in Commission on Money and Credit, *Impacts of Monetary Policy*, Englewood Cliffs, N.J.: Prentice-Hall, 60–337.

Ellis, S. (1991), 'BHP Steel to Struggle in Final Quarter', *Sydney Morning Herald*, 25 March, 25.

Evans, M.K. (1969), *Macroeconomic Activity*, New York: Harper & Row.

Fazzari, S.M., Glenn Hubbard, R. and Petersen, B.C. (1988), 'Financing Constraints and Corporate Investment', *Brookings Papers on Economic Activity*, (1), 141–95.

Fazzari, S.M. and Mott, T.L. (1986–7), 'The Investment Theories of Kalecki and Keynes: an Empirical Study of Firm Data, 1970–1982', *Journal of Post Keynesian Economics*, **9** (2), Winter, 171–87.

Feiwel, G.R. (1975), *The Intellectual Capital of Michal Kalecki: A Study in Economic Theory and Policy*, Knoxville, Tenn.: University of Tennessee Press.

Fitzgerald, T. (1990), *Between Life and Economics*, Crows Nest: ABC Books.

Fitzgibbons, A. (1988), *Keynes's Vision: A New Political Economy*, Oxford: Clarendon Press.

Forman, L. and Eichner, A.S. (1981), 'A Post Keynesian Short-period Model: Some Preliminary Econometric Results', *Journal of Post Keynesian Economics*, **4** (1), Fall, 117–135.

Foster, J.B. (1986), *The Theory of Monopoly Capitalism*, New York: Monthly Review Press.

Foster, R.A. and Stewart, S.E. (1991), *Australian Economic Statistics: 1949–50 to 1989–90*, Reserve Bank of Australia Occasional Paper No. 8, Sydney, February.

Freeman, C. (1982), *The Economics of Industrial Innovation*, 2nd edn, London: Frances Pinter.

Freeman, C. (1991), 'Innovation, Changes of Techno-Economic Paradigm and Biological Analogies in Economics', *Revue Economique*, **42**, 211–31.

Freeman, C. and Perez, C. (1988), 'Structural Crises of Adjustment, Business Cycles and Investment Behaviour', in Dosi *et al.* (eds) (1988), 38–66.

Freeman, C., Clark, J. and Soete, L. (1982), *Unemployment and Technical Innovation: A Study of Long Waves and Economic Development*, London: Frances Pinter.

Frisch, R. and Holme, H. (1935), 'The Characteristic Solutions of a Mixed Difference and Differential Equation Occurring in Economic Dynamics', *Econometrica*, **3** (2), 225–39.

Goldstein, J.P. (1982), *Mark-up Pricing and the Business Cycle: The Microfoundations of the Variable Mark-up*, PhD dissertation, Graduate School of the University of Massachusetts, US

Goldstein, J.P. (1985a), 'The Cyclical Profit Squeeze: a Marxian Microfoundation', *Review of Radical Political Economics*, **17** (1/2), 103–28.

Goldstein, J.P. (1985b), 'Pricing, Accumulation, and Crisis in Post Keynesian Theory', *Journal of Post Keynesian Economics*, **8** (1), Fall, 121–34.

Goldstein, J.P. (1986), 'Markup Variability and Flexibility: Theory and Empirical Evidence', *Journal of Business*, **59** (4), 599–621.

Goodwin, R.M. (1951), 'The Nonlinear Accelerator and the Persistence of Business Cycles', *Econometrica*, **19** (1), January, 1–17.

Goodwin, R.M. (1964), 'Econometrics in Business-Cycle Analysis', in Hansen (1964), 417–68.

Goodwin, R.M. (1982), *Essays in Economic Dynamics*, London: Macmillan.

Goodwin, R.M. (1986), 'The M-K-S System: the Functioning and Evolution of Capitalism', in H.-J. Wagener and J.W. Drukker (eds), *The Economic Law of Motion of Modern Society: A Marx–Keynes–Schumpeter Centennial*, Cambridge: Cambridge University Press.

Goodwin, R.M. (1987), 'Macrodynamics', in R.M. Goodwin and L.F. Punzo, *The Dynamics of a Capitalist Economy: A Multi-sectoral Approach*, Cambridge: Polity Press, 1–160.

Goodwin, R.M. (1989), 'Kalecki's Economic Dynamics: A Personal View', in Sebastiani (ed.) (1989), 249–51.

Goodwin, R.M. (1990), *Chaotic Economic Dynamics*, Oxford: Clarendon Press.

Gough, I. (1979), *The Political Economy of the Welfare State*, London: Macmillan.

Granstrand, O. (ed.) (1994), *Economics of Technology*, Amsterdam: North-Holland.

Halevi, J. (1981), 'The Composition of Investment under Conditions of Non Uniform Changes', *Banca Nazionale del Lavoro Quarterly Review*, **34** (137), June, 213–32.

Halevi, J. (1983), 'Employment and Planning', *Social Research*, **50** (2), Summer, 345–58.

Hall, R.E. (1977), 'Investment, Interest Rates, and the Effects of Stabilization Policies', *Brookings Papers on Economic Activity*, (1), 61–103.

Hall, T.E. (1990), *Business Cycles: The Nature and Causes of Economic Fluctuations*, New York: Praeger.

Hansen, A.H. (1964), *Business Cycles and National Income*, expanded edn, London: George Allen & Unwin.

Harcourt, G.C. and Kenyon, P. (1976), 'Pricing and the Investment Decision', *Kyklos*, **29** (3), 449–77.

Hastay, M. (1954), 'The Cyclical Behavior of Investment', in National Bureau of Economic Research, *Regularization of Business Investment*, Princeton, N.J.: Princeton University Press, 3–35.

Hawkins, R.G. (1979), 'Business Fixed Investment in the 1970s', in W.E. Norton (ed.), *Conference in Applied Economic Research*, Sydney: Reserve Bank of Australia, December, 193–231.

Hayes, S.E. and Stone, J.A. (1990), 'Political Models of the Business Cycle Should Be Revived', *Economic Inquiry*, **28** (3), July, 442–65.

Hendriksen, E.S. (1978), *Capital Expenditures in the Steel Industry 1900 to 1953*, New York: Arno Press.

Hicks, J.R. (1932), *A Theory of Wages*, London: Macmillan.

Hicks, J.R. (1973), *Capital and Time*, Oxford: Clarendon Press.

Higgins, B. (1954), 'Government Measures to Regularize Private Investment in Other Countries than the United States', in National Bureau of Economic Research, *Regularization of Business Investment*, Princeton, N.J.: Princeton University Press, 459–81.

Hilferding, R. (1981), *Finance Capital: A Study of the Latest Phase of Capitalist Development*, ed. with an intro. by Tom Bottomore, London: Routledge & Kegan Paul.

Hillinger, C. (ed.) (1992), *Cyclical Growth in Market and Planned Economies*, Oxford: Clarendon Press.

Hillinger, C. and Reiter, M. (1992), 'The Quantitative and Qualitative Explanation of Macroeconomic Investment and Production Cycles', in C. Hillinger (ed.) (1992), 111–40.

Hillinger, C. and Sebold-Bender, M. (1992), 'The Stylized Facts of Macroeconomic Fluctuations', in C. Hillinger (ed.) (1992), 63–110.

Hillinger, C., Reiter, M. and Weser, T. (1992), 'Micro Foundations of the Second-Order Accelerator and of Cyclical Behaviour', in C. Hillinger (ed.) (1992), 167–80.

Jacoby, N.H. and Weston, J.F. (1954), 'Financial Policies for Regularizing Business Investment', in National Bureau of Economic Research, *Regularization of Business Investment*, Princeton, N.J.: Princeton University Press, 369–449.

Jorgenson, D.W. (1963), 'Capital Theory and Investment Behavior', *American Economic Review*, **53** (2), May, 247–59.

Junankar, P.N. (1972), *Investment: Theories and Evidence*, London: Macmillan.

Kaldor, N. (1966), *Causes of the Slow Rate of Economic Growth in the United Kingdom*, Cambridge: Cambridge University Press.

Kalecki, M. (1933), *Próba teorii koniunktury*, Warsaw: Institute for the Study of Business Cycles and Prices, June (in Polish).

Kalecki, M. (1935), 'A Macrodynamic Theory of Business Cycles', *Econometrica*, **3** (3), July, 327–44.

Kalecki, M. (1937a), 'The Principle of Increasing Risk', *Economica* (New Series), **4** (16), November, 440–6.

Kalecki, M. (1937b), 'A Theory of the Business Cycle', *Review of Economic Studies*, **4** (2), February, 77–97.

Kalecki, M. (1940), 'A Theorem on Technical Progress', *Review of Economic Studies*, **8** (3), 178–84.

Kalecki, M. (1943a), 'Political Aspects of Full Employment', *Political Quarterly*, **14** (4), 322–31; abbreviated version in Kalecki (1971), 138–45.

Kalecki, M. (1943b), *Studies in Economic Dynamics*, London: George Allen & Unwin.

Kalecki, M. (1944), 'Three Ways to Full Employment', in Oxford University Institute of Statistics, *The Economics of Full Employment*, Oxford: Basil Blackwell, 39–58.

Kalecki, M. (1945), 'Full Employment by Stimulating Private Investment?', *Oxford Economic Papers* (Old Series), **7**, March, 83–92.

Kalecki, M. (1950), 'A New Approach to the Problem of Business Cycles', *Review of Economic Studies*, **16**, 57–64.

Kalecki, M. (1954), *Theory of Economic Dynamics*, London: George Allen & Unwin.

Kalecki, M. (1957), 'The Influence of the Construction Period on the Relationship between Investment and National Income', *Ekonomista*, (1), 3–13 (in Polish); English version in Kalecki (1986), 97–108.

Kalecki, M. (1963), 'The Structure of Investment', in *Introduction to the Theory of Growth in a Socialist Economy*, Warsaw: PWN; Oxford: Basil Blackwell, English translation (1969), Ch. 11; reprinted in Kalecki (1972b), 102–23.

Kalecki, M. (1967), 'The Problem of Effective Demand with Tugan-Baranovsky and Rosa Luxemburg', *Ekonomista*, (2), 241–9 (in Polish); English version in Kalecki (1971), 146–55.

Kalecki, M. (1968), 'Trend and Business Cycle Reconsidered', *Economic Journal*, **78** (2), 263–76; reprinted with minor changes in Kalecki (1971), 165–83.

Kalecki, M. (1970), 'Theories of Growth in Different Social Systems', *Scientia*, **105** (5/6), 311–16.

Kalecki, M. (1971), *Selected Essays on the Dynamics of the Capitalist Economy, 1933–1970*, Cambridge: Cambridge University Press.

Kalecki, M. (1972a), *The Last Phase in the Transformation of Capitalism*, New York: Monthly Review Press.

Kalecki, M. (1972b), *Selected Essays on the Economic Growth of the Socialist and the Mixed Economy*, Cambridge: Cambridge University Press.

Kalecki, M. (1982), 'Some Remarks on Keynes' Theory', *Australian Economic Papers*, **21**, December, 245–53.

Kalecki, M. (1986), *Selected Essays on Economic Planning*, Cambridge: Cambridge University Press.

Kalecki, M. (1991), 'The Marxian Equations of Reproduction and Modern Economics', rev. ed. in Osiatyński (1991), 459–66; originally published in *Social Sciences Information*, **6** (7), December 1968, 73–9.

Kalecki, M. and Schumacher, E.F. (1943), 'International Clearing and Long-term Lending', *Bulletin of the Oxford Institute of Statistics*, **5**, Supplement, August, 29–33.

Kalecki, M. and Szeworski, A. (1991), 'Economic Problems of Production Automation in Capitalist Countries', in Osiatyński (1991), 374–85; original Polish version in *Ekonomista*, (3), 1957, 105–15.

Katona, G. (1980), *Essays in Behavioral Economics*, Ann Arbor, Mich.: University of Michigan Institute for Social Research.

Kay, N.M. (1979), *The Innovating Firm*, London: Macmillan.

Kearney, C. (1990), *Fiscal Financing Decisions and the Exchange Rate: A Multi-Country Empirical Analysis*, School of Business & Technology Discussion Paper Series No. E9001, Sydney: University of Western Sydney Macarthur, October.

Kearney, C. and Chowdhury, K. (1991), 'Cointegration and Crowding Out: the Relationship Between Public and Private Investment in Australia', presented at the University of Tasmania, Hobart, October.

Kenway, P. (1980), 'Marx, Keynes and the Possibility of Crisis', *Cambridge Journal of Economics*, **4** (1), 23–36.

Keynes, J.M. (1936), *The General Theory of Employment, Interest and Money*, London: Macmillan.

Keynes, J.M. (1937), 'The General Theory of Employment', *Quarterly Journal of Economics*, **51** (2), February, 209–23.

Keynes, J.M. (1973), *The Collected Writings of John Maynard Keynes*, ed. D. Moggridge, vol. XIV, London: Macmillan.

Keynes, J.M. (1979), *The Collected Writings of John Maynard Keynes*, ed. D. Moggridge, vol. XXIX, London: Macmillan.

Khalil, E.L. (1987), 'The Process of Capitalist Accumulation: A Review Essay of David Levine's Contribution', *Review of Radical Political Economics*, **19** (4), 76–85.

Kindleberger, C.P. (1973), *The World in Depression, 1929–1939*, London: Allen Lane.

Kleinknecht, A. (1987), *Innovation Patterns in Crisis and Prosperity: Schumpeter's Long Cycle Reconsidered*, London: Macmillan.

Kregel, J.A. (1989), 'Savings, Investment and Finance in Kalecki's Theory', in Sebastiani (ed.) (1989), 193–205.

Kregel, J.A. (1989–90), 'Operational and Financial Leverage, the Firm, and the Cycle: Reflections on Vickers' Money Capital Constraint', *Journal of Post Keynesian Economics*, **12** (2), Winter, 224–36.

Kriesler, P. (1987), *Kalecki's Microanalysis: The Development of Kalecki's Analysis of Pricing and Distribution*, Cambridge: Cambridge University Press.

Kriesler, P. (1988), 'Kalecki's Pricing Theory Revisited', *Journal of Post Keynesian Economics*, **11** (1), Fall, 108–30.

Kriesler, P. (1989), *From Disequilibrium to the Traverse in Economic Theory*, School of Economics Discussion Paper No. 89/13, Sydney: University of New South Wales, October.

Kriesler, P. and McFarlane, B.J. (1991), *Michal Kalecki on Capitalism*, School of Economics Discussion Paper No. 91/13, Sydney: University of New South Wales, December.

Krueger, A.O. (1983), *Exchange Rate Determination*, Cambridge, Mass.: Harvard University Press.

Kuh, E. and Meyer, J.R. (1963), 'Investment, Liquidity, and Monetary Policy', in Commission on Money and Credit, *Impacts of Monetary Policy*, Englewood Cliffs, N.J.: Prentice-Hall, 339–474.

Lachmann, L.M. (1976), 'From Mises to Shackle: an Essay on Austrian Economics and the Kaleidic Society', *Journal of Economic Literature*, **14** (1), March, 54–62.

Lachmann, L.M. (1986), *The Market as an Economic Process*, Oxford: Basil Blackwell.

Lattimore, R. (1989), *Capital Formation in Australian Manufacturing, 1954–55 to 1987–88*, Bureau of Industry Economics Working Paper No. 54, Canberra, May.

Lawriwsky, M.L. (1984), *Corporate Structure and Performance: The Role of Owners, Managers and Markets*, London: Croom Helm.

Lawson, T. (1985), 'Uncertainty and Economic Analysis', *Economic Journal*, **95**, December, 909–27.

Lawson, T. (1990), 'Realism, Closed Systems and Expectations', presented at the Ninth International Summer School of Advanced Economic Studies, Centro Internazionale di Studi di Economica Politica, Trieste, Italy, 21–31 August.

Lee, F.S. (1985), 'Kalecki's Pricing Theory: Two Comments', *Journal of Post Keynesian Economics*, **8** (1), Fall, 145–8.

Levine, D.P. (1975), 'The Theory of the Growth of the Capitalist Economy', *Economy Development and Cultural Change*, **23**, October, 47–74.

Levine, D.P. (1981), *Economic Theory, vol. II: The System of Economic Relations as a Whole*, London: Routledge & Kegan Paul.

Levine, D.P. (1984), 'Long Period Expectations and Investment', *Social Concept*, **1** (3), March, 41–51.

Lewis, D.F. and Mangan, J. (1987), 'Research and Development in Australia: the Role of Multinational Corporations', *Prometheus*, **5** (2), 368–85.

Light, D., Maley, K. and Cleary, P. (1991), 'How Australia's Banks Fouled Their Nest', *Sydney Morning Herald*, 5 February, 11.

Loasby, B.J. (1967), 'Long Range Formal Planning in Perspective', *Journal of Management Studies*, **4**, 300–8.

Loasby, B.J. (1984), 'On Scientific Method', *Journal of Post Keynesian Economics*, **6** (3), Spring, 394–410.

Lowe, A. (1954), 'Comment' on Brozen paper, in National Bureau of Economic Research, *Regularization of Business Investment*, Princeton, N.J.: Princeton University Press, 318.

Lowe, A. (1955), 'Structural Analysis of Real Capital Formation', in M. Abramovitz (ed.), *Capital Formation and Economic Growth*, Princeton, N.J.: Princeton University Press and National Bureau of Economic Research.

Lowe, A. (1965), *On Economic Knowledge: Towards a Science of Political Economics*, New York: Harper & Row.

Lowe, A. (1976), *The Path of Economic Growth*, Cambridge: Cambridge University Press.

Marris, R. (1964), *The Economic Theory of 'Managerial' Capitalism*, London: Macmillan.

Martin, S.P. (Chairman) (1991), *A Pocket Full of Change: Banking and Deregulation*, House of Representatives Standing Committee on Finance and Public Administration, Canberra: Australian Government Publishing Service, November.

Marx, K. (1954), *Capital: A Critique of Political Economy,* vol. I, Moscow: Progress Publishers.

Matthews, R.C.O. (1959), *The Trade Cycle,* Digswell Place: James Nisbet and Cambridge University Press.

Matthews, R.C.O. (1968), 'Why Has Britain Had Full Employment Since the War?', *Economic Journal,* **78** (311), September, 555–69.

Maxcy, G. (1981), *The Multinational Motor Industry,* London: Croom Helm.

Mayer, M. (1990), *The Greatest-ever Bank Robbery: The Collapse of the Savings and Loan Industry,* New York: Charles Scribner's Sons.

Mayer, T. (1958), 'The Inflexibility of Monetary Policy', *Review of Economics and Statistics,* **40**, November, 358–74.

McFarlane, B.J. (1971), 'Michal Kalecki's Economics: An Appreciation', *Economic Record,* **47**, March, 93–105.

McFarlane, B.J. (1982), *Radical Economics,* London: Croom Helm.

McIntyre, R.S. and Tipps, D.C. (1985), 'Exploding the Investment-Incentive Myth', *Challenge,* **28** (3), May–June, 47–52.

McKibbin, W.J. and Siegloff, E.S. (1988), 'A Note on Aggregate Investment in Australia', *Economic Record,* **64** (186), September, 209–15.

Meacci, F. (1989), 'The Principle of Increasing Risk versus the Marginal Efficiency of Capital', in Sebastiani (ed.) (1989), 231–45.

Medio, A. (1987), 'Trade Cycle', in J. Eatwell, M. Milgate and P. Newman (eds), *The New Palgrave: A Dictionary of Economics,* vol. 4, London: Macmillan, 666–71.

Meyer, J.R. and Kuh, E. (1957), *The Investment Decision: An Empirical Study,* Cambridge, Mass.: Harvard University Press.

Mills, K., Morling, S. and Tease, W. (1993), *Balance Sheet Restructuring and Investment,* Reserve Bank of Australia Research Discussion Paper No. 9308, Sydney, June.

Minsky, H.P. (1982), *Can 'It' Happen Again?,* Armonk, N.Y.: M.E. Sharpe.

Mitchell, W.C. (1951), *What Happens During Business Cycles,* New York: National Bureau of Economic Research.

Modigliani, F. and Miller, M.H. (1958), 'The Cost of Capital, Corporation Finance and the Theory of Investment', *American Economic Review,* 48, 261–97.

Morrow, M.E. (1989), 'Congress Finds New Ways to Micromanage FY90 Budget', *Armed Forces Journal International,* November, 8–12.

Mott, T. (1982), *Kalecki's Principle of Increasing Risk: The Role of Finance in the Post-Keynesian Theory of Investment Fluctuations,* PhD dissertation, Stanford University, California, US.

Mott, T. (1985–6), 'Kalecki's Principle of Increasing Risk and the Relation Among Mark-up Pricing, Investment Fluctuations and Liquidity Preference', *Economic Forum,* **15** (2), 65–76.

Mowery, D.C. and Rosenberg, N. (1989), *Technology and the Pursuit of Economic Growth,* Cambridge: Cambridge University Press.

Nelson, R.R. (1990), 'Capitalism as an Engine of Progress', *Research Policy*, **19** (3), June, 193–214.

Nelson, R.R. and Winter, S.G. (1980), 'Firm and Industry Response to Changed Market Conditions: an Evolutionary Approach', *Economic Inquiry*, **18**, 179–202.

Nelson, R.R. and Winter, S.G. (1982), *An Evolutionary Theory of Economic Change*, Cambridge, Mass.: Harvard University Press.

Nickell, S.J. (1978), *The Investment Decisions of Firms*, Digswell Place: James Nisbet and Cambridge University Press.

Nicolini, J.L. (1985), 'The Degree of Monopoly, the Macroeconomic Balance and the International Current Account: the Adjustment to the Oil Shocks', *Cambridge Journal of Economics*, **9**, 127–40.

Nordhaus, W.D. (1975), 'The Political Business Cycle', *Review of Economic Studies*, **42** (2), April, 169–90.

Nuti, D.M. (1986), 'Michal Kalecki's Contribution to the Theory and Practice of Socialist Planning', *Cambridge Journal of Economics*, **10**, 333–53.

Oakley, A. (1987), 'Introduction: Adolph Lowe's Contribution to the Development of a Political Economics', in A. Lowe, *Essays in Political Economics: Public Control in a Democratic Society*, New York: New York University Press.

Oakley, A. (1993a), 'Human Agency and Methodology in Classical Political Economy', *History of Economics Review*, (20), Summer, 13–40.

Oakley, A. (1993b), *The Traverse as a Problem of Human Agency*, Department of Economics Research Reports or Occasional Paper No. 193, Newcastle: University of Newcastle, September.

O'Connor, J. (1973), *The Fiscal Crisis of the State*, New York: St Martin's Press.

O'Donnell, R.M. (1989), *Keynes: Philosophy, Economics and Politics*, London: Macmillan.

Ong, N.P. (1981), 'Target Pricing, Competition, and Growth', *Journal of Post Keynesian Economics*, **4** (1), Fall, 101–16.

Ong, N.P. and Levine, D.P. (1982), 'Corporate Investment Strategy and the Endogenous Business Cycle', revised version, January, University of Denver (mimeo).

Osiatyński, J. (ed.) (1990), *Collected Works of Michał Kalecki,* vol. I *Capitalism: Business Cycles and Full Employment*, Oxford: Clarendon Press.

Osiatyński, J. (ed.) (1991), *Collected Works of Michał Kalecki,* vol. II *Capitalism: Economic Dynamics*, Oxford: Clarendon Press.

Pavitt, K. (1984), 'Sectoral Patterns of Technical Change: Toward a Taxonomy and a Theory', *Research Policy*, **13**, 343–73.

Pavitt, K. (1990), 'Some Foundations for a Theory of the Large Innovating Firm', Brighton, Sussex: Science Policy Research Unit, University of Sussex, March (mimeo).

Peck, M.J. (1961), *Competition in the Aluminum Industry 1945–1958*, Cambridge, Mass.: Harvard University Press.

Penrose, E.T. (1959), *The Theory of the Growth of the Firm*, Oxford: Basil Blackwell.

Pheby, J. (ed.) (1989), *New Directions in Post-Keynesian Economics*, Aldershot, Hants.: Edward Elgar.

Pitelis, C.N. (1986), 'Corporate Control, Social Choice and Capital Accumulation: an Asymmetrical Choice Approach', *Review of Radical Political Economics*, **18** (3), 85–100.

Porter, M.E. (1980), *Competitive Strategy: Techniques for Analyzing Industries and Competitors*, New York: The Free Press; London: Collier Macmillan.

Poterba, J.M. (1988), 'Comments' on Fazzari, Glenn Hubbard and Petersen (1988), *Brookings Papers on Economic Activity*, (1), 200–4.

Pulling, K.A. (1978), 'Cyclical Behavior of Profit Margins', *Journal of Economic Issues*, **12** (2), June, 287–305.

Qualls, P.D. (1979), 'Market Structure and the Cyclical Flexibility of Price-cost Margins', *Journal of Business*, **52**, April, 305–25.

Qualls, P.D. (1981), 'Cyclical Wage Flexibility, Inflation, and Industrial Structure: an Alternative View and Some Empirical Evidence', *Journal of Industrial Economics*, **29**, June, 345–56.

Radosevic, S. (1991), 'In Search of an Alternative Theory: a Critique of Dosi *et al.*'s *Technical Change and Economic Theory*', *Review of Political Economy*, **3** (1), 93–111.

Reinecke, I. (1988), *The Money Masters*, Melbourne: William Heinemann Australia.

Renouf, G. (1988), 'Consumer Debt Crisis', *Impact*, May, 13.

Reynolds, P.J. (1983), 'Kalecki's Degree of Monopoly', *Journal of Post Keynesian Economics*, **5** (3), Spring, 493–503.

Reynolds, P.J. (1987), *Political Economy: A Synthesis of Kaleckian and Post Keynesian Economics*, Brighton, Sussex: Wheatsheaf.

Richardson, G.B. (1960), *Information and Investment: A Study in the Working of the Competitive Economy*, London: Oxford University Press.

Ricoy, C.J. (1987), 'Cumulative Causation', in J. Eatwell, M. Milgate and P. Newman (eds), *The New Palgrave: A Dictionary of Economics,* vol. 1, London: Macmillan, 730–5.

Robinson, J. (1973), *Collected Economic Papers,* vol. IV, Oxford: Basil Blackwell.

Rosenberg, N. (1976), *Perspectives on Technology*, Cambridge: Cambridge University Press.

Rousseas, S. (1989), 'Anti Systems', *Journal of Post Keynesian Economics*, **11** (3), Spring, 385–98.

Rowley, R. and Hamouda, O. (1987), 'Troublesome Probability and Economics', *Journal of Post Keynesian Economics*, **10** (1), Fall, 44–64.

Rowthorn, R. (1981), 'Demand, Real Wages and Growth', *Thames Papers in Political Economy*, Autumn, 1–39.

Runde, J. (1991), 'Keynesian Uncertainty and the Instability of Beliefs', *Review of Political Economy*, **3** (2), 125–45.

Sahal, D. (1981), *Patterns of Technological Innovation*, Cambridge, Mass.: Addison-Wesley.

Sahal, D. (1985), 'Invention, Innovation and Economic Evolution', in E. Rhodes and D. Wield (eds), *Implementing New Technologies*, Oxford: Basil Backwell, 50–62.

Salter, W.E.G. (1960), *Productivity and Technical Change*, Cambridge: Cambridge University Press.

Samuelson, P.A. (1980), *Economics*, 11th edn, New York: McGraw-Hill.

Sardoni, C. (1987), *Marx and Keynes on Economic Recession*, Brighton, Sussex: Wheatsheaf.

Sawyer, M.C. (1982), *Macro-economics in Question: The Keynesian–Monetarist Orthodoxies and the Kaleckian Alternative*, Armonk, N.Y.: M.E. Sharpe.

Sawyer, M.C. (1985), *The Economics of Michal Kalecki*, London: Macmillan.

Sawyer, M.C. (1989), *The Challenge of Radical Political Economy*, Hemel Hempstead, Herts: Harvester Wheatsheaf.

Schmidt, E.P. (1954), 'Promoting Steadier Output and Sales', in National Bureau of Economic Research, *Regularization of Business Investment*, Princeton, N.J.: Princeton University Press, 319–68.

Schmookler, J. (1966), *Invention and Economic Growth*, Cambridge, Mass.: Harvard University Press.

Schumpeter, J.A. (1939), *Business Cycles: A Theoretical, Historical and Statistical Analysis of the Capitalist Process*, 2 Vols, New York: McGraw-Hill.

Scitovsky, T. (1976), *The Joyless Economy*, Oxford: Oxford University Press.

Sebastiani, M. (ed.) (1989), *Kalecki's Relevance Today*, London: Macmillan.

Shackle, G.L.S. (1969), *Order and Time in Human Affairs*, 2nd edn, Cambridge: Cambridge University Press.

Shackle, G.L.S. (1970), *Expectation, Enterprise and Profit: The Theory of the Firm*, London: George Allen & Unwin.

Shackle, G.L.S. (1972), *Epistemics and Economics: A Critique of Economic Doctrines*, Cambridge: Cambridge University Press.

Shann, E. (1989), 'Recipe for an Export Boom', *Sydney Morning Herald*, 19 October, 38–9.

Shapiro, N. (1981), 'Pricing and the Growth of the Firm', *Journal of Post Keynesian Economics*, **4** (1), Fall, 85–100.

Shapiro, N. (1988), 'Market Structure and Economic Growth: Steindl's Contribution', *Social Concept*, **4** (2), June, 72–83.

Simon, H.A. (1976), *Administrative Behavior*, 3rd edn, New York: The Free Press.

Simon, H.A. (1986), 'Foreword', in Bromiley (1986), ix–x.

Sordi, S. (1989), 'Some Notes on the Second Version of Kalecki's Business-Cycle Theory', in Sebastiani (ed.) (1989), 252–74.

Spence, A.M. (1977), 'Entry, Capacity, Investment and Oligopolistic Pricing', *Bell Journal of Economics*, **8** (2), Autumn, 534–44.

Stegman, T. (1982), 'The Estimation of an Accelerator-type Investment Function with a Profitability Constraint, by the Technique of Switching Regressions', *Australian Economic Papers*, **21**, December, 379–91.

Steindl, J. (1941), 'On Risk', *Oxford Economic Papers*, (5), June, 43–53.

Steindl, J. (1952), *Maturity and Stagnation in American Capitalism*, Oxford: Basil Blackwell.

Steindl, J. (1964), 'On Maturity in Capitalist Economies', in *Problems of Economic Dynamics and Planning: Essays in Honour of Michał Kalecki*, Warsaw: PWN – Polish Scientific Publishers, 423–32.

Steindl, J. (1969), 'Capitalism, Science and Technology', in C.H. Feinstein (ed.), *Socialism, Capitalism and Economic Growth*, Cambridge: Cambridge University Press, 198–205.

Steindl, J. (1976), 'Introduction' to reprint of Steindl (1952), New York: Monthly Review Press, ix–xvii.

Steindl, J. (1979), 'Stagnation Theory and Stagnation Policy', *Cambridge Journal of Economics*, **3** (1), March, 1–14.

Steindl, J. (1981a), 'Ideas and Concepts of Long Run Growth', *Banca Nazionale del Lavoro Quarterly Review*, **34** (136), March, 35–47.

Steindl, J. (1981b), 'Some Comments on the Three Versions of Kalecki's Theory of the Trade Cycle', in N. Assorodobraj-Kula, C. Bobrowski, H. Hagemejer, W. Kula and J. Łoś (eds), *Studies in Economic Theory and Practice: Essays in Honor of Edward Lipiński*, Amsterdam: North-Holland, 125–33.

Steindl, J. (1984), 'Reflections on the Present State of Economics', *Banca Nazionale del Lavoro Quarterly Review*, (148), March, 3–14.

Steindl, J. (1989), 'Reflections on Kalecki's Dynamics', in Sebastiani (ed.) (1989), 309–13.

Steindl, J. (1990), 'Effective Demand in the Short and in the Long Run', presented at the Ninth International Summer School of Advanced Economic Studies, Centro Internazionale di Studi di Economica Politica, Trieste, Italy, 21–31 August.

Stoneman, P. (1983), *The Economic Analysis of Technological Change*, Oxford: Oxford University Press.

Strange, S. (1988), *Casino Capitalism*, London: Basil Blackwell.

Streever, D. (1960), *Capacity Utilisation and Business Investment*, Bureau of Economic and Business Research, Bulletin No. 86, University of Illinois.

Stuckey, J.A. (1983), *Vertical Integration and Joint Ventures in the Aluminium Industry*, Cambridge, Mass.: Harvard University Press.

Summons, M. (1990), 'Aluminium Industry Report', *Australian Business*, 11 April, 35–42.

Sylos Labini, P. (1962), *Oligopoly and Technical Progress*, Cambridge, Mass.: Harvard University Press.

Sylos Labini, P. (1967), 'Prices, Distribution and Investment in Italy, 1951–1966: an Interpretation', *Banca Nazionale del Lavoro Quarterly Review*, (83), December, 3–57.

Sylos Labini, P. (1979a), 'Industrial Pricing in the United Kingdom', *Cambridge Journal of Economics*, 3, 153–63.

Sylos Labini, P. (1979b), 'Prices and Income Distribution in Manufacturing Industry', *Journal of Post Keynesian Economics*, 2 (1), Fall, 3–25.

Sylos Labini, P. (1984a), *The Forces of Economic Growth and Decline*, Cambridge, Mass.: MIT Press.

Sylos Labini, P. (1984b), 'New Aspects of the Cyclical Development of the Economy', *Banca Nazionale del Lavoro Quarterly Review*, (148), March, 15–31.

Sylos Labini, P. (1989), 'Oligopoly: Static and Dynamic Analysis', *Rivista di Politica Economica*, 79 (9), September, 57–78.

Sylos Labini, P. (1990a), 'Capitalism, Socialism and Democracy and Large-scale Firms', University of Rome (mimeo).

Sylos Labini, P. (1990b), 'Technical Progress, Unemployment, and Economic Dynamics', *Structural Change and Economic Dynamics*, 1 (1), 41–55.

Thomsen, C.T. (1984), 'Dangers in Discounting', *Management Accounting*, LXV, 37–9.

Tinbergen, J. (1935), 'Annual Survey: Suggestions on Quantitative Business Cycle Theory', *Econometrica*, 3 (3), July, 268–70.

Tobin, J. (1969), 'A General Equilibrium Approach to Monetary Theory', *Journal of Money, Credit and Banking*, 1 (1), February, 15–29.

Toporowski, J. (1986), 'Introduction', in Kalecki (1986), 1–18.

Tsokhas, K. (1986), *Beyond Dependence: Companies, Labour Processes and Australian Mining*, Melbourne: Oxford University Press.

Ulph, A. (1987), 'Recent Advances in Oligopoly Theory from a Game Theory Perspective', *Journal of Economic Surveys*, 1 (2), 149–172.

Vercelli, A. (1989), 'Uncertainty, Technological Flexibility and Long-term Fluctuations', in M. Di Matteo, R.M. Goodwin and A. Vercelli (eds), *Technological and Social Factors in Long Term Fluctuations*, Berlin: Springer-Verlag, 130–44.

Verspagen, B. (1992), *Uneven Growth Between Interdependent Economies: An Evolutionary View on Technology Gaps, Trade and Growth*, PhD dissertation No. 92–10, Faculty of Economics and Business Administration, University of Limburg, Maastricht: Universitaire Pers Maastricht.

Vickers, D. (1987), *Money Capital in the Theory of the Firm*, Cambridge: Cambridge University Press.

Walsh, M. (1991a), 'Deregulation and the Moral Hazard', *Sydney Morning Herald*, 7 February, 11.

Walsh, M. (1991b), 'After the Collapse of Communism, it's the Shrinking of Socialism', *Sydney Morning Herald*, 19 September, 11.

Walsh, M. (1993), 'Jack McEwen's Black Legacy is Still With Us', *Sydney Morning Herald*, 15 April, 29.

Wood, A. (1975), *A Theory of Profits*, Cambridge: Cambridge University Press.

Wood, G.A., Lewis, P.E.T. and Petridis, R. (1991), 'Has Investment in Australia's Manufacturing Sector Become More Export Oriented?', *Australian Economic Review*, (94), Second Quarter, April-June, 13–19.

Wray, L.R. (1992), 'Commercial Banks, the Central Bank, and Endogenous Money', *Journal of Post Keynesian Economics*, **14** (3), Spring, 297–310.

Yin, R.K. (1989), *Case Study Research: Design and Methods*, Newbury Park, Cal.: Sage Publications.

Zarnowitz, V. (1973), *Orders, Production, and Investments: Cyclical and Structural Analysis*, New York: National Bureau of Economic Research.

Zarnowitz, V. (1985), 'Recent Work on Business Cycles in Historical Perspective: a Review of Theories and Evidence', *Journal of Economic Literature*, **XXIII**, June, 523–80.

Index

New Directions in Modern Economics

Post-Keynesian Monetary Economics
New Approaches to Financial Modelling
Edited by Philip Arestis

Keynes's Principle of Effective Demand
Edward J. Amadeo

New Directions in Post-Keynesian Economics
Edited by John Pheby

Theory and Policy in Political Economy
Essays in Pricing, Distribution and Growth
Edited by Philip Arestis and Yiannis Kitromilides

Keynes's Third Alternative?
The Neo-Ricardian Keynesians and the Post Keynesians
Amitava Krishna Dutt and Edward J. Amadeo

Wages and Profits in the Capitalist Economy
The Impact of Monopolistic Power on Macroeconomic Performance
in the USA and UK
Andrew Henley

Prices, Profits and Financial Structures
A Post-Keynesian Approach to Competition
Gokhan Capoglu

International Perspectives on Profitability and Accumulation
Edited by Fred Moseley and Edward N. Wolff

Mr Keynes and the Post Keynesians
Principles of Macroeconomics for a Monetary Production Economy
Fernando J. Cardim de Carvalho

The Economic Surplus in Advanced Economies
Edited by John B. Davis

Foundations of Post-Keynesian Economic Analysis
Marc Lavoie

The Post-Keynesian Approach to Economics
An Alternative Analysis of Economic Theory and Policy
Philip Arestis

Income Distribution in a Corporate Economy
Russell Rimmer

The Economics of the Profit Rate
Competition, Crises and Historical Tendencies in Capitalism
Gérard Duménil and Dominique Lévy

Corporatism and Economic Performance
A Comparative Analysis of Market Economies
Andrew Henley and Euclid Tsakalotos

Competition, Technology and Money
Classical and Post-Keynesian Perspectives
Edited by Mark A. Glick

Investment Cycles in Capitalist Economies
A Kaleckian Behavioural Contribution
Jerry Courvisanos